Hiking Pinnacles National Park

Hiking Pinnacles National Park

A Guide to the Park's Greatest Hiking Adventures

Linda B. Mullally and David S. Mullally

FALCONGUIDES

GUILFORD, CONNECTICUT
HELENA, MONTANA

An imprint of Rowman & Littlefield
Falcon, FalconGuides, and Outfit Your Mind are registered trademarks of Rowman & Littlefield.

Distributed by NATIONAL BOOK NETWORK

Copyright © 2015 by Rowman & Littlefield

Photos by David S. Mullally

Maps: Alena Joy Pearce © Rowman & Littlefield

British Library Cataloguing-in-Publication Information Available

Library of Congress Cataloging-in-Publication Data
Mullally, Linda B.
  Hiking Pinnacles National Park : a guide to the park's greatest hiking adventures / Linda and David Mullally.
     pages cm
  Includes index.
  ISBN 978-1-4930-0009-8 (pbk. : alk. paper) – ISBN 978-1-4930-1487-3 (e-book) 1. Hiking—California—Pinnacles National Park–Guidebooks. 2. Trails—California—Pinnacles National Park—Guidebooks. 3. Pinnacles National Park (Calif.)—Guidebooks. I. Mullally, David S. II. Title.
  GV199.42.C22P5656 2015
  796.5109794—dc23

                                                                                    2014047115

The paper used in this publication meets the minimum requirements of American National Standard for Information Sciences—Permanence of Paper for Printed Library Materials, ANSI/NISO Z39.48-1992.

Contents

The Hikes

Map Overview

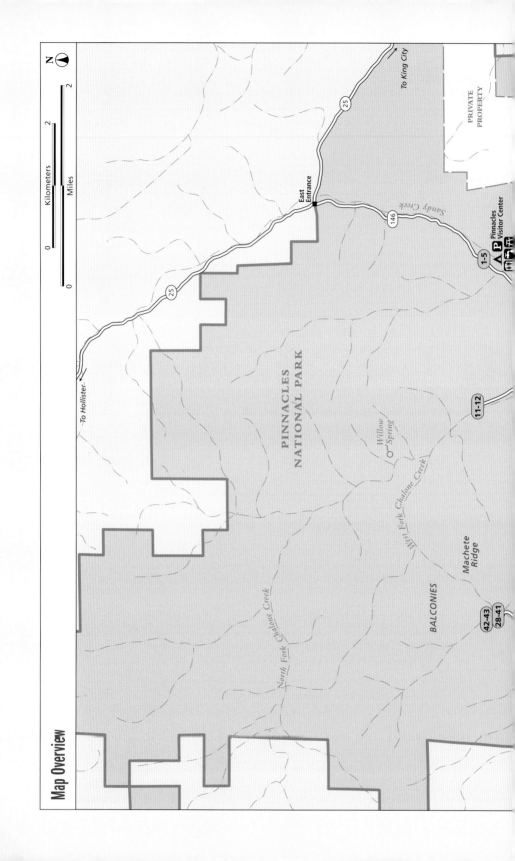

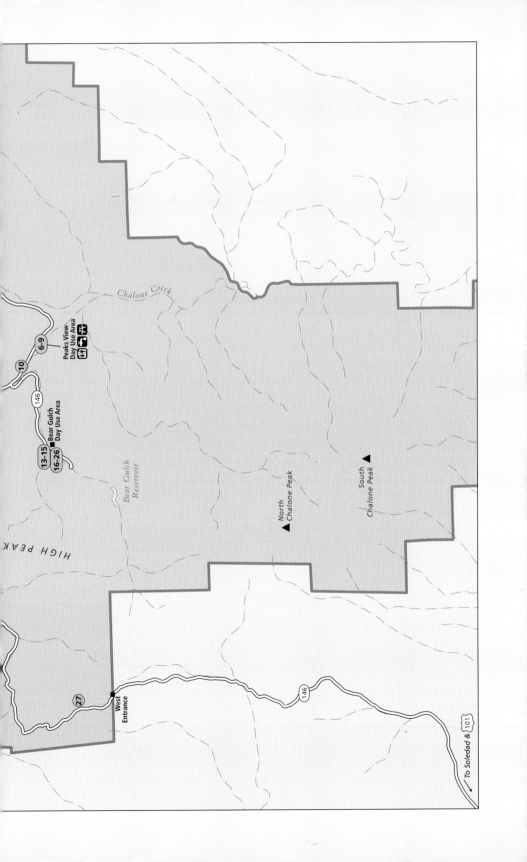

Acknowledgments

It was a privilege to be asked to write this book and be part of Pinnacles' debut as a national park. David and I stepped into the park's new Visitor Contact Station on the one-year anniversary of Pinnacles National Park, January 10, 2013. We were greeted by Beatrice Lujan, who was continuing her sixteen-year career in Pinnacles as part of the visitor-use assistance staff.

Every member of Pinnacles National Park's family of staff and volunteers with whom we interacted over the course of the six months we spent exploring the park was enthusiastic about their role in polishing this new gem in the crown of national parks. Several of the staff had worked at other national parks in the system, from iconic parks like California's Yosemite and Utah's Zion to remote ones like Bering Land Bridge National Preserve in Alaska's subarctic region. Seasonal park ranger Lupe Zaragosa had dreamed of becoming Pinnacles' visual information specialist. Nichole Andler, chief of Interpretation and public information officer had enjoyed twenty years in "nine gorgeously distinct parks" before putting her efforts into enhancing the public's park experience in Pinnacles.

David and I are grateful for the cooperation and assistance we received from the park staff and volunteers. The hiking part was easy, but framing the park's beautiful ecological story and fascinating geological journey while doing justice to the cultural history would not have been possible without the staff's knowledge and passion.

A special thanks to Nichole Andler, chief of Interpretation, for taking the time to respond to my many e-mails and phone calls. Park superintendent Karen Beppler-Dorn made time to meet with us and connect us with the various rangers and staff members who could give us the most informed answers to our questions about the park's history, geology, fauna, and flora. Thank you to Denise Louie, chief of Cultural and Resource Management for her input as well as wildlife biologists, Paul Johnson, and Gavin Emmons, and park botanist Brent Johnson for their expertise. Russell W. Graymer, geologist with the U.S. Geological Survey, helped me paint a bigger picture of the Pinnacles geological journey. Timothy Babalis, the park historian, provided valuable feedback. James Bouknight, the park's fence and trail supervisor, gladly took time to share his knowledge about present and future trail plans. Interpretive park ranger Michelle Armijo made some of our weekend evenings in the outdoor amphitheater educational and relaxing.

Law enforcement rangers like Jason Gigliotti were always gracious, and their presence was a reminder that when a park sees traffic of thousands of visitors, law enforcement plays an important role in monitoring human behavior to keep our public lands a safe and pleasurable experience for all.

The friendliness of the interns from the Student Conservation Association and the American Conservation Experience and their willingness to be of assistance also impressed us.

Although this guide focuses on "hiking" in Pinnacles National Park, the Pinnacles and the rock climbing community share a rich history, and we thank Bruce Hildenbrand, president of Friends of Pinnacles, for his responsiveness to my queries.

We want to express our gratitude to Alec Arago, district director in Congressman Sam Farr's office for sharing some of the political background in creating Pinnacles National Park and Adam Russell, Congressman Farr's press secretary, for his diligence and responsiveness.

We developed a special and intimate relationship with the park during those several weeklong camping trips in Pinnacles National Park. We were there to witness the landscape reveal its many magnificent facets in the glow of sunrise, in the shadow of moonrise, under the glitter of a starlit night, through the mystery of fog and the subduing mood of rain. Our R-Pod was our base camp on wheels, and the park became home. It was a special and unforgettable adventure we are pleased to share in the forty-three hikes described in this book.

2016 will be the 100th anniversary of the National Park System. To echo the sentiment expressed in Ken Burns's 2009 PBS series, Pinnacles is one more affirmation that national parks are still "America's Best Idea."

Introduction

The Pinnacles is a rare, ecologically pristine swath of California landscape because of its long-standing protected status (since 1908 as a national monument), geological origins, and off-the-beaten-track access. The park straddles two counties, San Benito and Monterey, in the southern portion of the Gabilan Mountain Range eco-region, which is part of California's Central Coast Range. The park sits 80 miles south of San Francisco Bay and 40 miles inland from the Pacific Ocean and the Monterey Peninsula, a world-renowned tourist destination.

US 101 is the primary road gateway from the north and the south to the East and West Entrances of Pinnacles National Park. The closest airports with commercial airline service and rental car agencies south of San Francisco International Airport are San Jose International Airport and Monterey Regional Airport. The closest Amtrak train station is in Salinas (800-872-7245; www.amtrak.com).

Pinnacles National Park's 27,000 acres, 16,000 of which are Wilderness, are not just rock spires, boulder-stacked tunnels, and talus caves. Elevations range from 790 feet along seasonal Chalone Creek to 3,304 feet atop panoramic North Chalone Peak.

The park attracts hikers, rock climbers, and bird watchers. Campers enjoy the developed campground at the East Entrance. Whether you relish the thrill of hiking up to the High Peaks and spotting condors soar, tramping up the chaparral hills to the historic fire tower for a panoramic view, or exploring the park's phenomenal talus caves, or you just crave the solitude of the North and South Wilderness Trails, Pinnacles National Park will astonish you. Pinnacles frees the imagination as visitors bask in the park's pioneer and geological history. The 30 miles of developed trails do not make Pinnacles the biggest or flashiest park, but there's a reason the crusade to protect it began so long ago. The more time you spend in Pinnacles, the more you realize that the seduction goes beyond its more obvious geologic wow factor! From vertiginous to bucolic, Pinnacles displays a range of unique faces and changing moods with every season. Like painting a new masterpiece, Mother Nature adds the brushstrokes, highlighting magenta buckwheat against a dormant fall and winter background. Winter rains shine the cliffs and fill the reservoir as still pools of water in the gulches turn to cascades and waterfalls. In spring shady canopies sprout above your head, and carpets of green with a brilliant patchwork of wildflowers spread beneath your feet. What a treat to hike on a drizzly winter day when veils of fog turn the volcanic spires, domes, and cones into a mystical rock garden. The cycle of desert to garden and brown to green that sustains the park's biodiversity never ceases to inspire and captivate the observer.

On any day, whether the sky is crisp and blue or dotted with marshmallow clouds, the light gives the park's meadows, canyons, and rocky sentinels a magical quality as the sun journeys from one horizon to the other. Stargazing is dazzling in Pinnacles, and moonlit nights are enchanting. Any of the forty-three hikes described in this book will introduce you to a unique aspect of the Pinnacles realm.

ROCK CLIMBING

Hikers share Pinnacles National Park with rock climbers.

Pinnacles has a rock climbing history that goes back to the 1930s. Routes range from easy topropes to multipitch climbs. The prevailing ethic for over eighty years has been to establish routes from the ground up on lead. Power drills are prohibited, and there are advisories posted regarding seasonal route closures during the breeding season for raptors. Prairie falcons nest in particularly high concentrations in the cavities of cliff walls, and an amazing diversity of twelve nesting raptor species have been documented at Pinnacles National Park. The Friends of Pinnacles was established in 1989 and works with park staff on all issues regarding climbing including access, education, trail building/restoration, and rebolting. Friends of Pinnacles also works with National Park Service staff on the Climbing Management Plan.

Transportation

Pinnacles National Park is divided into a west side and an east side by its most prominent geological feature: the volcanic rampart running north and south that is known as the Pinnacles. There are two distinct entrances to Pinnacles National Park, and *no road* crosses the park connecting the West and East Entrances. Although the map shows a section of CA 146 on each side of the park, it is *not* a through road. The only way to access the park from west to east or east to west by road—and the shortest route around—is to drive south from either entrance via King City on surface roads between US 101 and CA 25.

Strong hikers can travel from west to east or vice versa on a variety of route combinations for out-and-back, lollipop, or loop-type day hikes. The most direct options range from moderate on Old Pinnacles Trail through the Balconies Cave or along the Balconies Cliffs to strenuously challenging over the Pinnacles on the High Peaks Trail. Several hiking route options to traverse from one side to the other are described in this book.

The west-side entrance is accessed from US 101 in Soledad. The West Entrance has the new West Pinnacles Visitor Contact Station, a day-use area with picnic tables, grills, water, restrooms, and three trailheads at the Chaparral parking lot.

The East Entrance is accessed off CA 25 from Hollister and has the most visitor traffic and services. There are eight primary trailheads with parking on the east side.

The main Pinnacles Visitor Center at the East Entrance

The East Entrance at the main Pinnacles Visitor Center has a picnic area with tables, grills, water, restrooms, a camp store, a campground for tent and recreational vehicles (some electric outlets), water, showers, a dump station, and an outdoor amphitheater for ranger programs.

The East Entrance has an additional day-use area—the Bear Gulch Day Use Area with the seasonal Bear Gulch Nature Center, which is also the main hiker and climber staging area on the east side.

The only transportation within the park on the west side is your vehicle. On the east side there is a seasonal free shuttle that ferries visitors from the visitor center at the East Entrance to Bear Gulch Day Use Area. The shuttle typically runs at 30-minute intervals during peak visitor season on weekends from President's Day weekend in February to Memorial Day weekend at the end of May. The shuttle may run on other holiday weekends or special events during the year. For up-to-date shuttle information see Twitter Feed @PinnaclesNPS or Pinnacles' Facebook page. Check the park website at www.nps.gov/pinn or call (831) 389-4485 for updates and alerts.

Communication

Except for an unreliable and sporadic signal with AT&T service in the High Peaks, there is no cell service in the park. There is a pay phone that operates with a calling card or credit card outside the Pinnacles Visitor Center and campground store at the East Entrance. Your best bet in the event of an emergency is the park headquarters in Bear Gulch.

History

Native Americans thrived in California for thousands of years prior to the arrival of Europeans. Costanoan (Spanish for "people of the coast") and Ohlone are the generic names given to the various tribes who lived along the Central California coast south of San Francisco Bay to Monterey Bay. Although the pre-European cultural history in Pinnacles National Park is still being studied and discovered, artifacts found within the park, mission records, and oral history confirm Native American presence in the Pinnacles area when the Spanish arrived.

Acorns and wildflower seeds were staples of California Indian tribe diets. Rabbits, deer, elk, and antelope provided other food sources. Cooperative efforts between Pinnacles National Park staff and Chalon and Mutsun tribal members, descendants of the native people whom Europeans first encountered in the area more than two centuries ago, work toward a better understanding of Native American history and the connection to their ancestral home.

Spanish Missionaries

Back when California was an extension of Spain's empire, twenty-one religious missions were established between 1769 and 1823. The missions stretching north from San Diego to Sonoma were intended to be within one day's walk or horseback ride apart.

The Soledad mission built in 1791 and the San Juan Bautista mission were closest to Pinnacles. Many of California's native peoples, including the Chalon and Mutsun of the Pinnacles region, were forced into abandoning their way of life and culture to become Christianized and the labor force for the missionaries. By the mid-1800s European disease and brutal treatment by their conquerors had decimated California's indigenous population.

Pinnacles Pioneers

Removal and death of most of the native people in the region by 1810 left the Pinnacles area void of permanent human settlements until the arrival of Euro-American pioneers in 1865. In the absence of human activity for a half century, the land reverted to wilderness, possibly for the first time in thousands of years.

By the 1880s the unusual rock outcrop (Pinnacles) then called the "Palisades" reappeared on the radar as a local destination for picnicking, camping, and cave exploring. In the early 1890s accounts of this enigmatic region in newspaper articles attracted the curiosity of adventuresome spirits. Schuyler Hain, a homesteader to Bear Valley from Michigan, began actively promoting the Pinnacles with tours to the area and through the caves.

The Path to National Park and the Journey Forward

When a cousin of Hain's brought one of his professors from Stanford University on a tour, the professor's enthusiasm and awe of the scenery spurred Hain on to advocate the formal preservation of the Pinnacles area.

In 1904 Hain's dedication paid off when Stanford president David Starr Jordan contacted Gifford Pinchot, first chief forester of the United States, and convinced President Theodore Roosevelt that Pinnacles was worthy of special protection. With the assistance of local congressman James C. Needham, Pinnacles was initially protected as a Forest Reserve in 1906.

In 1908 the Antiquities Act gave President Roosevelt the power to designate just over 2,000 acres of the scenic centerpiece as Pinnacles National Monument. The monument remained under nominal Forest Service management until 1910 and under the General Land Office (predecessor of the BLM) until 1916. The monument had no staff and was rarely visited by government officials; it did not have a drivable road from Hollister until 1914. If Pinnacles National Monument had a patchy start, the path to national park would remain elusive for almost another 100 years.

The National Park Service (NPS) was established in 1916, and Pinnacles National Monument came under the authority of the NPS that year. Initially the NPS was not particularly enthusiastic about managing this remote monument. Fortunately a fresh report gave new perspective, which resulted in a small expansion of the monument by President Warren G. Harding, the hiring of the first resident custodian, and the construction of rudimentary trails. Another proclamation by Calvin Coolidge enlarged the monument in 1924 to almost 3,000 acres and added campsites with water. More lands were consolidated into Pinnacles National Monument, a ranger's cabin was built, and improvements to the trails got underway. The inclusion and protection of the Balconies area and Machete Ridge on the west side starting in the 1920s was in large part a result of the park management's awareness of the value of cliffs for falcon nesting. These areas were labeled "falcon sanctuaries" as part of early efforts to protect and manage for the natural resources of the park. By 1929 President Herbert Hoover had added almost 2,000 additional acres of land donated by San Benito County.

The tunnel to the High Peaks was constructed as part of the 1930s trail expansion program. In 1933 the park's infrastructure and network of trails got a real boost with a Civilian Conservation Corps crew of 200 volunteers. Among the improvements was a better road up Bear Gulch, tourist cabins, a visitor center (now the seasonally open nature center in Bear Gulch), and the dam at the Bear Gulch Reservoir. The original Chalone Peak fire lookout was built in 1935 and rebuilt in 1952 following a blaze the previous year. With the exception of the nature center, most of the small original wood cabins with local-stone foundations in Bear Gulch now serve as administrative offices for the national park headquarters.

In 2000, under President Clinton, the 17,000-acre monument was expanded to nearly 27,000 acres. Nearly 8,000 acres of adjacent BLM lands were added to the monument that year. In 2006, 2,000 acres of private ranch land at the East Entrance, including historic homesteads, were acquired and consolidated into the monument. In addition to broadening the monument's ecosystem and adding another cultural dimension, the once privately owned campground became part of the monument.

By the time the monument was redesignated as the fifty-ninth national park, Pinnacles' boundaries now embraced almost 27,000 acres, 16,000 acres of which are designated Wilderness. The Pinnacles Wilderness was renamed the Hain Wilderness in honor of Schuyler Hain, who spearheaded the original campaign to protect the Pinnacles. Wilderness designation ensures more solitude and the privilege to time travel into our natural past and experience the land as it was and can be when mankind's presence is removed or minimized.

If Hain was the original advocate to establish the monument, the San Benito County business community takes some credit for putting Pinnacles on the national park track. Sometime around 2000 they got the ear of US congressman Sam Farr at a San Juan Bautista Rotary Club meeting. Although a bill was drafted within a year, it took another tenacious ten years for it to get legislative traction. By late 2012 a park was born out of political partnerships fueled by dogged determination, and Congress approved the park bill. In Congressman Farr's words: "National Parks offer us more than a chance to escape to nature. They are an essential part of our shared American heritage. The experience of exploring a national park connects us to the generations of people who traveled there before us and to those who will visit that special place long after we have left."

On January 10, 2013, President Barack Obama signed the park bill into law, redesignating Pinnacles from national monument to national park.

Contrary to what you might expect, a change in status did not come with a dowry to help with the already needed infrastructure improvements or the necessary staffing upgrades for the new tasks at hand. The park came online when the political tone was already loudly about budget squeezes, and public lands were gasping for air. The economic crash of 2008 threatened to choke off what little funding was finally coming down the pipe for projects approved years earlier. Coincidentally the onset of the Great Recession inspired the American Recovery and Reinvestment Act (ARRA), making possible the longtime plans to replace the rudimentary ranger booth at the West Entrance out of Soledad with a new visitor contact station. A small but fresh and functional, LEED-certified building with new bathrooms, engaging interpretive signs, and state-of-the-art audio/visual/tactile aids for sight- and hearing-impaired visitors was unveiled in 2012.

By 2014 Pinnacles National Park's new status put it in the local, national, and international spotlight, attracting 30 percent more visitors. Ken Burns's PBS TV miniseries *The National Parks: America's Best Idea* a few years earlier had certainly helped spark a renewed interest and appreciation for our national parks.

Fortuitously the West Pinnacles Visitor Contact Station, in the foreground of the craggy palisades, was a timely and fitting first impression for new visitors to the youngest national park in the system.

At the East Entrance from Hollister, a rustic ranch-style wooden structure, now park property with the campground, houses the main Pinnacles Visitor Center and entrance fee pay station as well as the campground check-in counter and camp store, both managed by a National Park Service concessioner.

As a result of the pressures from regional growth in recent years, increased popularity of the park with publicized national park status, expansion of the park's territory, and other evolving ecological and logistic factors, a new General Management Plan was undertaken to consider options for balancing recreation, interpretation and education, and resource protection. The alternative adopted by the plan focuses on bringing "people and nature" closer together. The short- and long-term goals are manpower, budget, and funding dependent. The park's mission continues to focus on protection, research, and education while enhancing the visitor experience in Pinnacles National Park. The park welcomes over 200,000 visitors annually, with the peak traffic during March, April, and May. Parking, day-use areas, campgrounds, visitor centers, intra-park shuttle service, expansion of the 30-mile hiking trail network, more access to the wilderness experience, and interpretive programs are among the long list of visitor-centered topics addressed in the new General Management Plan.

In the shorter term, visitors can expect the construction of two new trails to begin in 2016. A 2.25-mile trail will connect the West Pinnacles Visitor Contact Station with the Chaparral Day Use Area parking and associated trailheads. Currently there is only a paved road and no exclusively pedestrian access linking the contact station with the trailheads. The other trail is the construction of a 0.5-mile ADA-compliant loop that will start and end at the west-side visitor contact station.

MONUMENT VS. PARK

National monuments are designated by presidential proclamation and national parks require Acts of Congress.

Long-term projects being explored will involve new educational and park orientation amenities centered around the historic homestead land at the East Entrance as well as campground improvements and possible limited wilderness camping opportunities.

Geology

The timeline to present-day Pinnacles National Park spans millions of years of dynamic geology before humans made their imprint on the landscape. The unique "pinnacles," for which the park is named, are a tale of subducting and grinding tectonic plates, volcanic fields, earthquakes, and erosion. Rhyolitic breccia, composed of lava sand, ash, and angular chunks of rock, is what the High Peaks and other rock formations in Pinnacles National Park are made of.

Going back about 30 million years ago, the spreading ridge-transform boundary between the Farallon and Pacific plates reached the subduction zone along the western margin of North America. Where the two plate margins came together, a new plate margin between the Pacific and North American plates was formed.

By about 23 million years ago, the new Pacific-North American transform plate margin had grown to stretch from about where Santa Barbara is now to about where San Diego is now. To the east, as the new transform plate boundary grew, heat from below partially melted the crust and formed several volcanic fields, including Pinnacles/Neenach. The exact mechanism that allowed the heat to rise up is not agreed upon among geologists.

Between 20 and 12 million years ago (the exact timing is not agreed upon among geologists), the Pacific-North American transform plate boundary shifted eastward to form the San Andreas Fault and other faults. The San Andreas Fault rift zone runs from California's Mendocino Coast to the Gulf of Mexico. The San Andreas Fault split the Pinnacles/Neenach volcanics, and the strike-slip motion on the San Andreas Fault over millions of years has moved the two halves of the volcanic stack roughly 200 miles apart.

As the west half of the split stack (the Pinnacles Volcanics) moved northward, the layers were also tilted, faulted, and to a large extent eroded. The Pinnacles Volcanics you see today are mainly a sliver caught between the Pinnacles Fault and the Chalone Creek Fault, where they were preserved from uplift and erosion. West of the Pinnacles Fault, only tiny scraps of Pinnacles Volcanics remain, while east of the Chalone Creek Fault, any Pinnacles Volcanics are buried under thousands of feet of younger sedimentary rocks. The Chalone Creek Fault parallel to the park's east-side drainage is still active and believed to be the original fissure to the San Andreas Fault, which now slices the land 4 miles east of the park.

Examining the angular chunks of rock encased in hardened volcanic material

Starting about 2 million years ago, the intersecting surfaces of the layers and sets of cracks that had formed as the rocks were faulted and tilted guided the erosion, while wind, water, heat, cold, ice, and tectonic shakes helped sculpt the landscape of towers, crags, monoliths, palisades, and canyons that continue to fascinate visitors to Pinnacles National Park. Heaps of gigantic boulders jammed in crevices and steep gorges became the ceilings to the awesome talus caves. Pinnacles has some of the most accessible talus caves in the National Park System.

Uplifts and faults continue today. Pinnacles moves northward about 1 inch per year relative to the land on the other side of the San Andreas Fault. The uplift is much slower, but marked by how the streams are cutting narrow canyons through the uplifting rocks. Fault lines and rock fractures also allow for water to percolate to the surface and create trickles called "springs" that nourish riparian pockets.

Subtle but tangible evidence of dynamic geology along the San Andreas Fault can be seen when you travel to Pinnacles National Park's East Entrance from Hollister on CA 25, where small sections of the road's painted white line are offset where the fissure traverses the road.

Wine connoisseurs will appreciate the fact that the minimally acidic volcanic soil in the Pinnacles region is a boon for the growing number of local vintners and fans of the grape elixir.

Weather

To summarize Pinnacles National Park's climate by saying it's a Mediterranean climate of hot, dry summers with cold, moist winters is a bit of an oversimplification. Although it is relatively close to the tempering influence of the Pacific Ocean, the Santa Lucia Mountains create a meteorological barrier between the park and the coast. The temperature (Fahrenheit) variation between the coast (40 miles as the condor flies) can be as much as 50 degrees, especially in the summer when days can rise to 100 degrees in the park and remain in the 50s under a cloak of fog on the coast. Nighttime temperatures in the winter easily drop into the low 30s and on occasion into the 20s in the park, while the coast remains more temperate, rarely dipping to freezing. The Santa Lucia Mountains capture most of the winter rainfall from Pacific storms, leaving the park with an annual average of about 16 inches. It is not uncommon for the higher elevations to get a dusting of white powder between December and March when an "Arctic Express" chills the state.

Close up there are microclimates within the park. Exposed slopes can be unbearably hot for summer hiking, but pleasant in the leafy canyons and in the moist cool of the caves. Springtime northwest winds on the ridges and peaks can make you wish you had an extra layer, while hikers in the creekbed canyons are stripping down to T-shirts. Although mornings can start out cold, once the sun hits the park, a warm-day forecast for Hollister or Soledad can quickly turn to "hot" by a 10-degree differential

Pinnacles National Park blooms with springtime California poppies following winter rains.

SAFETY FIRST

- Wear layers to transition from cold to hot or from breezy to windy on the ridges.
- Choose footwear for ankle support and traction.
- Carry a hat and lather up with sunscreen for sun protection.
- Always carry water to stay hydrated and snacks for energy.
- Caves require a good flashlight or headlight (smartphones and penlights won't cut it through the dark craggy caves) and steady footing.

in Pinnacles National Park. Check the forecast for Hollister on the east side and Soledad for the west side. Check www.nps.gov/pinn and click on Plan Your Visit for current park "Alerts" on weather and other crucial seasonal information.

California climate cycles between wet and dry with flood and drought years. Pinnacles National Park suffers the brunt of these historical extremes. At the time this book was researched in 2014, California was experiencing severe drought. We hiked in temperatures hovering above 80 degrees in January. There wasn't a new drop of water to quench the thirst of seasonal creeks, trees, grasses, and wildlife. Finally minimal rainfall gave the land and wildlife relief in March and April. Like magic, over a couple of weeks we watched a parched, dusty landscape turn green with a splash of wildflower color. Even if only momentarily, water draped sheer rock walls and creeks surprised us with a trickle that grew into cascades in some gulches. All of it is a testament to the resilience of the land.

Flora

The primarily dual-season Mediterranean climate characterized by relatively cool, wet winters and hot, dry summers nurtures the more drought-resistant vegetation mix of California chaparral. Eighty percent of the plant community within Pinnacles National Park is chaparral, which is characterized by plants with small waxy leaves for retaining moisture, deep taproots, and summer dormancy cycles. Small spiny-needle chamise dominates the chaparral shrub- and brushlands mixed with manzanita and buck brush.

From March to May rolling green grassy hills of winter and spring become the incubators for splashes of orange poppies, purple bush lupine, pink shooting stars, yellow monkey flower, crimson Indian warriors, and a myriad of delicate wildflowers before green turns to summer gold and autumn brown.

Gray pines and blue oaks (deciduous) dot the arid summer slopes. But coast live oaks (evergreen), cottonwoods, and sycamores burgeon and huddle in the park's riparian hideaways. The buckeye's growth cycle has adapted well by flourishing in the late winter to early spring months and shedding its leaves to go dormant in the dry summer months. The deciduous valley oak, largest oak in America, graces the

Lichen and moss are part of nature's palette along the trail.

banks along stretches of the Chalone Creek watershed. In sharp contrast the park's precious few lush leafy canyons, moist mossy gorges, and spring-fed riparian islands in gravel creekbeds form a necklace of natural habitats that sets off the majestic volcanic centerpiece. Almost 300 types of lichen, natural indicators of air quality, have been identified within Pinnacles National Park.

Extremes of hot summers (with highs over 100 degrees Fahrenheit in the daytime), cold winters (as low as teens and 20s in the nighttime), and longtime protection as a federal public land have acted as natural buffers, preserving the park's high ratio of native plants and animals. But the yellow star thistle, part of the sunflower family, is one of the most invasive and tenacious nonnative invaders. This plant alters native ecosystems by snuffing out native plants and displacing the wildlife that feed on native plants. Its spiny prick is quite hostile to human skin. It is known as the "plant that ate California." The seeds love to travel as stowaways on your shoes, socks, and gear. Help prevent the spread of this intruder and others by cleaning off your apparel before entering the park.

Major portions of the park's grasslands were completely infested with yellow star thistle, and through consistent effort over the past six years, using various techniques from hand pulling, hoeing, mowing, grazing, prescribed burning, and limited herbicide use, the area is recovering.

Fauna

From stealth mammalian predators and majestic raptors to rare amphibians and tiny insects, Pinnacles National Park provides a wide range of habitat for many species and is a model for a healthy ecosystem. On land, mammals like mountain lions, bobcats, coyotes, gray foxes, raccoons, badgers, jackrabbits, and small rodents make the park home. Black-tailed deer and wild turkeys are common. Reptiles include eight lizards and thirteen snakes. Rattlesnake sightings are rare. Among the eight species of amphibians that survive near seasonal ponds and dribbles of stream water, two are listed as threatened species under the Endangered Species Act: the California

Wild turkeys strut past the viewing scopes near the visitor center.

An acorn woodpecker stashes supplies for winter.

red-legged frog and the California tiger salamander. An interpretive panel at the Bear Gulch Reservoir describes the efforts to reverse the decline of red-legged frogs.

The only native fish is the small stickleback.

Imagine 70 species of butterflies, 500 species of moths, 40 species of dragonflies, and 400 types of bees taking their place in the park's ecosystem.

Fall is the breeding season for tarantulas, when they are most visible aboveground as males prowl day and night in search of a mate. Tarantulas are fascinating and harmless unless provoked, but their bite is painful.

In the air, over 170 species of birds have been documented. In the spring and summer, birds flock to the riparian oases, while woodpeckers can be heard tapping the pines and oaks.

The raptors are a special treat. Falcons, hawks, eagles, and owls nest and roost in the crags of cliffs. Turkey vultures—carrion eaters and cousins of their larger and more rare winged relative, the California condor—circle the heights tippy-tipping their wings. Listen for the barn owl's calls piercing the night air.

Of the many winged inhabitants (from the most delicate to the most imposing) that benefit from the unique conditions in the park's thriving ecosystem, bats, prairie falcons, and condors deserve special mention.

Fourteen of twenty-four species of California bats are found in Pinnacles. The Bear Gulch Caves' lower and upper configuration and temperature range provides the Townsend's big-eared bat, listed as a "sensitive species" in California, an ideal wintering ground while providing a safe maternity ward to pup and raise youngsters in the warmer months. The Bear Gulch colony is known as "the largest maternity colony between San Francisco and Mexico." In order to protect the bats from being disturbed during these two critical cyclical periods of life, the talus caves are monitored for periodic seasonal closures. The schedule is updated and posted on the park's website (www.nps.gov/pinn).

Prairie falcons are obligate cliff-cavity nesters, and their historical nesting contributed significantly to the inclusion and protection of the Balconies and Machete Ridge areas as part of the park on the west side in the early twentieth century. Prairie falcons breed in higher concentrations at Pinnacles than in any other NPS unit.

After an absence of eighty years the California condor, largest flying bird in North America, has returned to Pinnacles National Park, which is one of three condor release sites in California (two in Central California and one in Southern California). Several human-related factors have been attributed to the near demise of the California condor. By the end of the 1980s, the reality that the number of soaring California condors was spiraling down toward extinction spawned a plan for an experimental breeding program. Breeding condors in captivity gave hope to reintroducing condors in the wild. Pinnacles National Park has been part of the condor recovery program since 2003. The park currently monitors over twenty condors, which are tagged and

Condors are frequently spotted in the High Peaks.

CONDOR FAST FACTS

Condor refers to two species of "New World" vultures, the Andean condor of South America and the California condor of North America. These carrion feeders are essential cleaners in the ecosystem. Both are the largest flying land birds in the Western Hemisphere. Condors are scavengers, and the toxic lead fragments from lead bullets left in the carcasses of coyotes and other hunted wildlife continue to be a serious threat to the struggling condor flocks. Condors can soar up to 4,000 feet and 70 miles per hour. Their wingspan can stretch up to 9.5 feet.

tracked by radio transmitters. A camouflaged camera, the "Condor Cam," posted at a bait site "scale" disguised as a perch, allows park biologists to assess the health of the birds as well as observe some of their natural behavior through the still photos. The park partners with the Ventana Wildlife Society to ensure the survival of the endangered condors in Central California. You can celebrate their return, watching them glide silently on the High Peaks' warm updrafts and sometimes perched on a rocky spire warming their outstretched wings.

Visitors to the park have the joy and privilege of witnessing how a fluke of nature and circumstances have preserved the park as a model and microcosm of biodiversity.

Wilderness

More than half the land (16,000 of the 27,000 acres) within Pinnacles National Park's boundaries is protected as "Wilderness" per the Wilderness Act of 1964. Unlike many parks where the Wilderness boundaries mostly begin in the backcountry, in Pinnacles sections of some of the most popular and well-traveled trails—like the High Peaks or Juniper Canyon Trails—are protected under Wilderness Act criteria, which bans roads, power lines, and other civilized or mechanized intrusions that would make man's imprint permanent and trespass in the home of plants and animals.

Wilderness is also synonymous with solitude, and soul space seekers can find such retreats within Pinnacles National Park.

Park Fees

Single Visit:

Vehicle or motorcycle (valid for 5 days)	$10
Walk-in or bicycle (valid for 7 days)	$5

Annual Pass:

Pinnacles Annual Pass	$20
Interagency Annual Pass	$80

Lifetime Passes:

Interagency Senior Pass (62 and over)	$10
Interagency Access Pass (disabled)	free

Pets

Pets are allowed in Pinnacles Campground only if attended. Pets are not allowed on the trails. Dogs on leash are only allowed in the campground, picnic areas, and parking lots and on the paved roads. National park policy is to "preserve and protect the park's natural conditions, scenic beauty and wildlife." The presence of dogs on the trails threatens to disturb habitat and harass wildlife that need their energy and resources for survival. The park discourages visitors from leaving pets in a car in the park, where the temperature can rise above 100 degrees. Even outdoor temperatures of 75 degrees or more can be deadly to a pet in a car. Cracking windows never allows enough cool air circulation under those conditions. For information on dog-friendly public lands in Monterey and San Benito Counties, see the "Regional Information and Recreation" chapters.

Camping

West Entrance: No camping is available.

East Entrance: Pinnacles Campground at the entrance has 149 sites including 99 tent sites. Each tent site in each loop has a picnic table, fire ring, water, and restrooms. Thirty-nine RV sites have 30 amp electricity (water and dump station nearby), picnic tables, and fire rings. Fourteen group sites can accommodate up to five cars and twenty people; each site has one to three picnic tables and a fire ring. Restrooms and water are nearby.

The campground has showers near the visitor center and several garbage and recycling containers. There is an outdoor amphitheater for ranger-led campfire

programs. The outdoors swimming pool is not heated and open seasonally from 10 a.m. to 6 p.m.

The campground is very busy during the warming spring peak-season months, when the park transforms into a wildflower bouquet following winter rains. Be sure to plan ahead if you wish to camp on weekends in the spring. For reservations call (877) 444-6777 or visit www.recreation.gov. The campground store telephone number is (831) 389-4538.

At this time there is no backcountry camping permitted in the park.

BEST TIMES TO VISIT PINNACLES NATIONAL PARK

The bloom of wildflowers and the palette of green make spring the "high season" in the park. For a more peaceful experience, avoid April weekends and spring-break weeks when parking lots fill up early and popular trails are more crowded. Shoulder seasons are a quieter time for absorbing the uniqueness of the park, and autumn may well be the park's best-kept secret, with late blooming flowers along roads and trails. Some park staff call autumn in Pinnacles the "second spring."

How to Use This Guide

This guide describes forty-three hikes starting from six designated parking lots or developed day-use areas in Pinnacles National Park. Twenty-six hikes originate on the east side, close to the town of Hollister off CA 25, where the main Pinnacles Visitor Center and the Pinnacles Campground are located at the East Entrance. Seventeen hikes originate from the west side, close to Soledad off US 101, where the new West Pinnacles Visitor Contact Station is located at the West Entrance.

It is important to note that CA 146 off CA 25 into the park at the East Entrance is not a through road to the West Entrance, nor are there any other vehicular through roads in the park. Although there are no vehicular roads or shuttles of any kind connecting the east and west sides of Pinnacles National Park, this guide does describe trails and combinations of various lengths and difficulty levels for hikers who wish to experience both sides of the park as part of a round-trip day hike, a round-trip from the west side with camping reservations for an overnight(s) in Pinnacles Campground, or a one-way hike with a private shuttle.

The two sections, both east and west, begin with an overview of the access, terrain, and services as well as park hours for access and exit at the respective entrances. At the end of each section, the "Regional Information and Recreation" chapter provides useful information about places to sleep, eat, and shop for provisions as well as a list of nearby public lands, noteworthy parks and open space areas, including dog-friendly hiking trails, and activities, points of cultural or historical interest, and local information resources.

In addition to the thirteen most popular day hikes (nine on the east side and four on the west side) described in the Pinnacles National Park literature, we explored the 30-plus miles of developed trails, combining routes for an additional thirty hikes that challenge hikers of all fitness levels, satisfy the solitude seekers, and enhance and broaden visitors' experience with exposure to Pinnacles National Park's biodiversity.

The hike summary at the beginning of each hike chapter is an overview of the highlights along the way. Below the summary is a quick reference list of information to help you narrow down the options and determine which hike is most appropriate for you and your party's needs. The information begins with the **Start** point or location of the trailhead.

Distance is the length of the hike in miles and whether it's an out and back, loop, or lollipop. Distances were measured and verified using a GPS. On some trails there are discrepancies between our GPS data and the park's map (generally slight). These instances were discussed with park staff, and this guide uses the GPS data.

The **Hiking time** is approximate, based on a 2-mile-per-hour walking pace on flat and level terrain with some buffer for photo and snack stops. Your personal and your companion(s)' fitness level, especially if you are hiking with children, will determine your pace on the uphills.

The **Difficulty** rating (easy, moderate, or strenuous) takes into account length of hike as well as steepness of trail.

Trail surface prepares you for rocks and slippery surfaces. The **Trailhead elevation** and **Highest point** give you an idea of elevation changes along the trail. **Best seasons** helps you choose a hike for maximum temperature comfort or seasonal highlights like wildflowers.

The **Maps** listed include the big-picture USGS maps for your trail as well as national park maps with more details of the area.

The **Nearest town** helps orient you for access to the park and services.

The **Trail contact** is helpful for advance information.

Trail tips contains information about amenities at the trailhead and advisories specific to each hike, including hikes especially suited to an overnight in the East Pinnacles campground from West Pinnacles trailheads. Note that any hike traversing from east to west or vice versa can be made into a "shuttle" hike if you choose to have someone pick you up and drive you back around to your vehicle at the trailhead. Make sure you check the park entrance hours at the West Entrance to know when the gate closes to inbound vehicular traffic.

Finding the trailhead contains the specific driving directions from the nearest main town and main highway to the parking area closest to your trailhead.

The Hike is a detailed description of the route. Although this book is not a field guide, this section includes prominent geological and historical landmarks, ecological highlights, and personal impressions of the landscape along the way. Since the trails were hiked at various times of year, the descriptions may reflect sights and impressions specific to a particular season or time of day (rainy winter morning, sunny spring afternoon, or balmy early summer evening) but not necessarily exclusive to that season or time of day.

Miles and Directions is a succinct thumbnail sketch of the route by mileage to underscore turns or identify changes in trail names or directions as well as highlight notable points of interest or other landmarks for orientation.

Each hike map helps visually identify access roads, towns, and the highlighted hike route with directional arrows pointing the way. Water, significant services, landmarks, and geographical features are also shown using symbols from the map legend, which is listed under Contents.

Park fees, the pet policy, camping, and the park's shuttle service are addressed in the Introduction, where you will also find sections on the park's history, geology, fauna, and flora.

Trail Finder

Hikes Most Likely to See Condors

10. Fire Wayside Parking Area to High Peaks
14. Condor Gulch Trail to High Peaks
23. Bear Gulch Day Use Area to High Peaks
24. Bear Gulch Day Use Area to Chaparral Day Use Area via High Peaks Trail
26. Bear Gulch Day Use Area to North Wilderness via High Peaks
29. Juniper Canyon Trail to High Peaks
31. Juniper Canyon Trail to Bear Gulch Day Use Area via High Peaks

Best Cave Hikes

11. Old Pinnacles Trail to Balconies Cave
17. Bear Gulch Day Use Area to Lower Cave
18. Bear Gulch Day Use Area to Lower and Upper Caves
25. Bear Gulch Day Use Area to Bear Gulch Caves and Balconies Cave
33. Juniper Canyon Trail to Bear Gulch Caves
40. Balconies Trail to Balconies Cliffs via Balconies Cave

Best Hikes for Shade

6. Peaks View Day Use Area to Bear Gulch Day Use Area
9. Peaks View Day Use Area to Old Pinnacles Trailhead
16. Bear Gulch Trail
17. Bear Gulch Day Use Area to Lower Cave
18. Bear Gulch Day Use Area to Lower and Upper Caves

Best Hikes with Children

1. Visitor Center to Bacon Ranch
13. Condor Gulch Trail to Overlook
16. Bear Gulch Trail
17. Bear Gulch Day Use Area to Lower Cave
18. Bear Gulch Day Use Area to Lower and Upper Caves
19. Bear Gulch Day Use Area to Rim Trail via Reservoir
20. Bear Gulch Day Use Area to Reservoir via Rim Trail
27. Visitor Contact Station to Vista Point
39. Balconies Trail to Machete Ridge

Best Hikes for Solitude

3. Visitor Center to South Wilderness
12. Old Pinnacles Trail to Balconies Cave via North Wilderness Trail
21. Bear Gulch Day Use Area to Chalone Peaks

27. Visitor Contact Station to Vista Point
35. Juniper Canyon Trail to Chalone Peaks
36. Juniper Canyon Trail to South Wilderness
42. North Wilderness Trail to Twin Knolls
43. North Wilderness Trail to Balconies Cliffs via Old Pinnacles Trail

Short Hikes (less than 5 miles)
1. Visitor Center to Bacon Ranch
2. Visitor Center to Butterfield Homestead
4. Visitor Center to Peaks View Day Use Area
6. Peaks View Day Use Area to Bear Gulch Day Use Area
8. Peaks View Day Use Area to Chalone Creek Overlook
9. Peaks View Day Use Area to Old Pinnacles Trailhead
13. Condor Gulch Trail to Overlook
16. Bear Gulch Trail
17. Bear Gulch Day Use Area to Lower Cave
18. Bear Gulch Day Use Area to Lower and Upper Caves
19. Bear Gulch Day Use Area to Rim Trail via Reservoir
20. Bear Gulch Day Use Area to Reservoir via Rim Trail
22. Bear Gulch Day Use Area to Scout Peak
27. Visitor Contact Station to Vista Point
28. Juniper Canyon Trail to Scout Peak
29. Juniper Canyon Trail to High Peaks
39. Balconies Trail to Machete Ridge
40. Balconies Trail to Balconies Cliffs via Balconies Cave
42. North Wilderness Trail to Twin Knolls

Medium Hikes (5–10 miles)
3. Visitor Center to South Wilderness
5. Visitor Center to Bear Gulch Day Use Area
7. Peaks View Day Use Area to Condor Gulch
10. Fire Wayside Parking Area to High Peaks
11. Old Pinnacles Trail to Balconies Cave
14. Condor Gulch Trail to High Peaks
15. Condor Gulch Trail to Chaparral Day Use Area
23. Bear Gulch Day Use Area to High Peaks
24. Bear Gulch Day Use Area to Chaparral Day Use Area via High Peaks Trail
25. Bear Gulch Day Use Area to Bear Gulch Caves and Balconies Cave
30. Juniper Canyon Trail to Bear Gulch Day Use Area
31. Juniper Canyon Trail to Bear Gulch Day Use Area via High Peaks
32. Juniper Canyon Trail to Reservoir and Moses Spring
33. Juniper Canyon Trail to Bear Gulch Caves

34. Juniper Canyon Trail to Bear Gulch Day Use Area via Bench Trail
37. Juniper Canyon Trail to Balconies Cave via Bench Trail
41. Balconies Trail to Old Pinnacles Trailhead
43. North Wilderness Trail to Balconies Cliffs via Old Pinnacles Trail

Long Hikes (more than 10 miles)
12. Old Pinnacles Trail to Balconies Cave via North Wilderness Trail
21. Bear Gulch Day Use Area to Chalone Peaks
26. Bear Gulch Day Use Area to North Wilderness via High Peaks
35. Juniper Canyon Trail to Chalone Peaks
36. Juniper Canyon Trail to South Wilderness
38. Juniper Canyon Trail to North Wilderness via Visitor Center

CLIMBING AND HIKING
ADVISORY AREA

Raptor advisories are in effect. This is the beginning of a sensitive area. Please do not hike or climb beyond this sign. Your cooperation is valued to assist us in protecting these magnificent birds of prey.

Disturbance of wildlife is a citable offense (36 CFR 2.2(a)(2)).

Questions? See a climbing advisory or contact a Ranger.

Please do not hike or climb beyond this sign. Climbs on the south side of the trail (Toogs to Flimsy Flume) and the trail itself remain open for your use.

Thank you for helping to protect park resources.

Balconies

△
North

Flimsy
Flume

Machete

✻ You are here

Map Legend

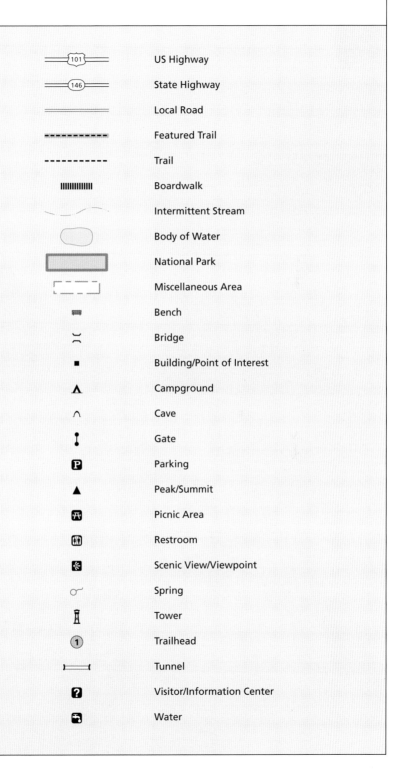

- US Highway (101)
- State Highway (146)
- Local Road
- Featured Trail
- Trail
- Boardwalk
- Intermittent Stream
- Body of Water
- National Park
- Miscellaneous Area
- Bench
- Bridge
- Building/Point of Interest
- Campground
- Cave
- Gate
- Parking
- Peak/Summit
- Picnic Area
- Restroom
- Scenic View/Viewpoint
- Spring
- Tower
- Trailhead (1)
- Tunnel
- Visitor/Information Center
- Water

East Pinnacles–Hollister Gateway

The park is open 24 hours a day, and the Pinnacles Visitor Center is open from 9:30 a.m. to 5 p.m. daily for entrance fees, maps, and information. Self-pay envelopes are available outside of the visitor center after hours. The visitor center is at the entrance to the campground and shares the wooden ranch-style building with the camp store and campground check-in counter. The small visitor center space has a few exhibits alongside the bookstore and park-related retail items. There is a pay phone on the outside wall of the building that takes calling cards but no coins. Parking and a day-use area with picnic tables, grills, restrooms, and seasonally open swimming pool are located behind the visitor center.

There are twenty-six hikes described from the east side of park that sample eight trailheads from which to explore distinct and overlapping ecosystems as well as natural and cultural history. Peaks, meadows, gulches, talus caves, a reservoir, and wilderness woodlands await to stoke your curiosity and rejuvenate your spirit.

Bear Gulch Day Use Area, 3 miles up the road into the park, has the seasonally open Bear Gulch Nature Center, the national monument's original visitor center, in one of the historic buildings crafted with local rock by the Civilian Conservation Corps (CCC) in the 1930s. The small nature center houses cultural and natural history exhibits, an earthquake seismograph, and a topographic relief map. Maps and information are also available. The day-use area has parking for several trailheads and picnic tables with grills, drinking water, and restrooms. Park headquarters and related administrative offices and some employee residences are also at the Bear Gulch Day Use Area.

1 Visitor Center to Bacon Ranch

This historic property is part of Pinnacles National Park's newest land acquisitions and is the park's future interpretive program in progress. This is a convenient, flat, skip-and-a-hop type of hike from the visitor center or campground. It is ideal for a leg stretch or end of day stroll with young children or folks with limited stamina, or for visitors who like to round off the park's geologic wonders with a dose of nostalgia for early California ranching life.

Start: From the picnic area parking lot behind Pinnacles Visitor Center
Distance: 0.5-mile lollipop
Hiking time: 30 minutes
Difficulty: Easy
Trail surface: Dirt
Trailhead elevation: 1,070 feet
Highest point: 1,092 feet
Best seasons: Spring for wildflowers, late fall and winter for cooler temperatures. Although summer and early fall can be very hot, this hike is short enough to beat the heat on summer mornings and evenings.

Maps: USGS North Chalone Peak; Pinnacles National Park map; Tom Harrison map of Pinnacles National Park
Nearest town: Hollister
Trail contact: Pinnacles National Park, 5000 CA 146, Paicines, CA 95043-9770; (831) 389-4485 or (831) 389-4427; www.nps.gov/pinn
Trail tips: This trail is open to the public but was too new to be on the park map or have a marked trailhead at the time of publication. It makes for an especially lovely stroll in the late afternoon light.

Finding the trailhead: From US 101 at San Juan Bautista/Hollister exit 345 (approximately 17 miles north of Salinas and 10 miles south of Gilroy), take exit 345 and drive 7.5 miles to the Hollister turnoff on the right. Drive 3.5 miles and turn right onto CA 25. Drive 28 miles on CA 25 to the Pinnacles National Park entrance. Turn right into the park and drive 2 miles to the visitor center to pay the entrance fee and pick up a map and information. The visitor center is on your left just before the T intersection for the campground on the right and the picnic area parking lot on the left. Turn left for the picnic area parking lot behind the visitor center. The unmarked trail begins at the gate signed Authorized Vehicles Only. GPS: N36 29.66' / W121 08.71'.

From US 101 at King City, take exit 282B/Broadway Street and turn right onto Broadway Street. Drive 1 mile on Broadway Street to the T intersection with First Street. Turn left onto First Street and drive 14 miles to the T intersection with CA 25. (First Street becomes Bitterwater Road at the sign for East Pinnacles.) Turn left onto CA 25 to Pinnacles and drive 14 miles to the CA 146 intersection. Turn left into Pinnacles National Park and follow directions above to the trailhead.

The Hike

At the time of publication, this trail was unmarked. From the gate with the Authorized Vehicles Only sign, you walk on the dirt service/ranch road through the picnic area and through the opening in a wooden split rail fence. Sandy Creek is on the right and the main park road is on the left until you walk across the wooden bridge over Sandy

Visitor Center to Bacon Ranch

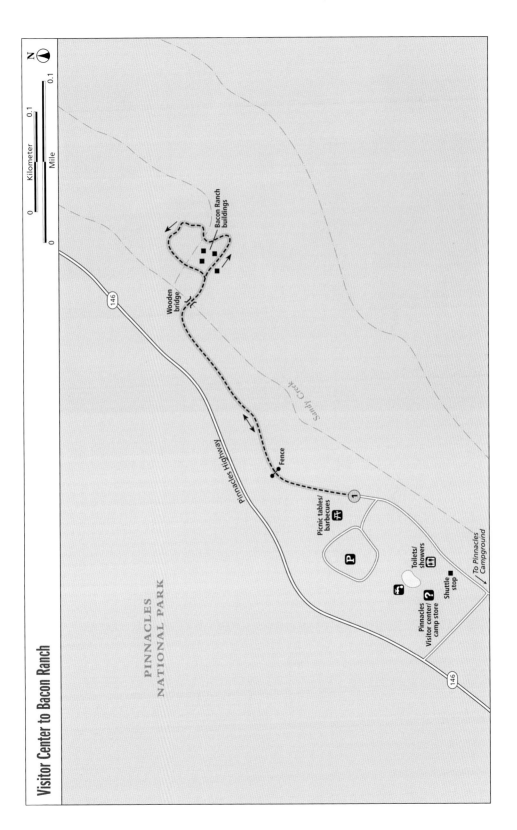

Outbuilding and barn at the historic Bacon Ranch

Creek. The creek is then on your left and the Bacon Ranch house and outbuildings are straight ahead. Wander around the ranch buildings in a counterclockwise loop. The house is on your left, and the paddock and barn are on your right. Notice the picnic table under the oak tree inviting you to a picnic, and let yourself be transported to days gone by on this early California spread. Rejoin the main ranch road to close the loop. The ranch road continues to the right for just under 2 miles to CA 25. Turn left to walk across the bridge and go back to the trailhead the way you came.

Miles and Directions

0.0 Start at the metal gate signed Authorized Vehicles Only in the picnic area parking lot.

0.1 Come to a wooden split rail fence and solar panels (scheduled to be removed) on the left. Walk through the opening in the fence.

0.2 Cross the wooden bridge over Sandy Creek and come to the Bacon Ranch house and buildings. Begin your loop around the buildings in a counterclockwise direction.

0.3 Close the loop back on the ranch road at the bridge. Cross the bridge and go back to the trailhead the way you came.

0.5 Arrive back at the trailhead.

2 Visitor Center to Butterfield Homestead

This hike puts a whole other face on Pinnacles National Park. Rather than formidable volcanic fortresses and phenomenal talus caves, this hike, which is suitable for families with very young children or for any less-than-hardy hiker, is a pleasant stroll past a historic ranch house and through another homestead, crossing meadows bordered by rolling hills with majestic oaks. Whether you hike in the lush green of spring or the warmth of the golden fall, the landscape transports you back to an earlier California setting. A short spur on the way back treats hikers to a surprise peek of the High Peaks. You may be the lucky hiker who spots a bobcat.

Start: From the picnic area parking lot behind Pinnacles Visitor Center
Distance: 3.8 miles out and back (4.4 miles with optional spur)
Hiking time: 2 hours
Difficulty: Easy on level terrain
Trail surface: Dirt
Trailhead elevation: 1,070 feet
Highest point: 1,193 feet
Best seasons: Spring for wildflowers (fans of the California state flower will be in poppy heaven in the spring), late fall and winter for cooler temperatures. (Although summer and early fall can be very hot in the open, this is a pleasant year-round hike in the early morning and evening.)

Maps: USGS North Chalone Peak; Pinnacles National Park map; Tom Harrison map of Pinnacles National Park
Nearest town: Hollister
Trail contact: Pinnacles National Park, 5000 CA 146, Paicines, CA 95043-9770; (831) 389-4485 or (831) 389-4427; www.nps.gov/pinn
Trail tips: There is no water or restroom facility on the trail past the visitor center. Restrooms are in the building behind the visitor center. The picnic area has tables, grills, animal-proof metal food-storage boxes, and trash and recycling receptacles. There is a camp store in the visitor center building for the adjacent campground. Dogs are not allowed on these roads, but bicycles are permitted.

Finding the trailhead: From US 101 at San Juan Bautista/Hollister exit 345 (approximately 17 miles north of Salinas and 10 miles south of Gilroy), take exit 345 and drive 7.5 miles to the Hollister turnoff on the right. Drive 3.5 miles and turn right onto CA 25. Drive 28 miles on CA 25 to the Pinnacles National Park entrance. Turn right into the park and drive 2 miles to the visitor center to pay the entrance fee and pick up a map and information. The visitor center is on your left just before the T intersection for the campground on the right and the picnic area parking lot on the left. Turn left for the picnic area parking lot behind the visitor center. The unmarked trail begins at the gate signed Authorized Vehicles Only. GPS: N36 29.66' / W121 08.71'.

From US 101 at King City, take exit 282B/Broadway Street and turn right onto Broadway Street. Drive 1 mile on Broadway Street to the T intersection with First Street. Turn left onto First Street and drive 14 miles to the T intersection with CA 25. (First Street becomes Bitterwater Road at the sign for East Pinnacles.) Turn left onto CA 25 to Pinnacles and drive 14 miles to the CA 146 intersection. Turn left into Pinnacles National Park and follow directions above to the trailhead.

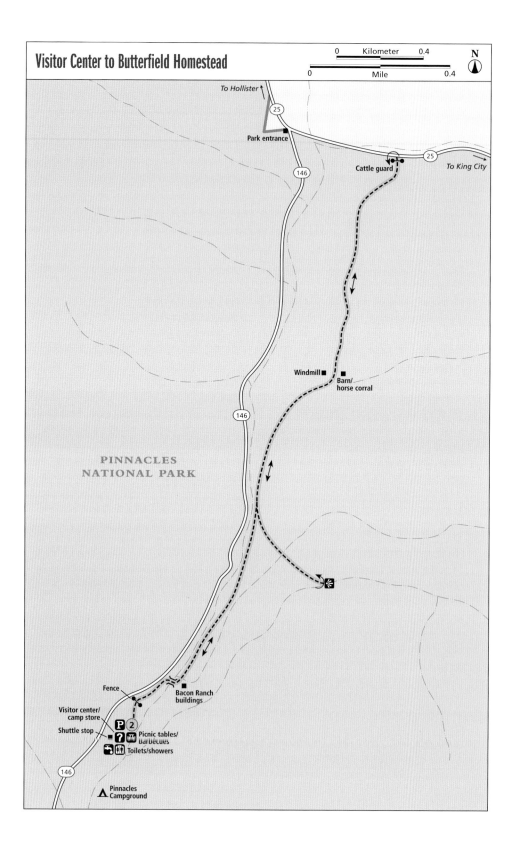

Visitor Center to Butterfield Homestead

Kilometer
0   0.4

Mile
0   0.4

N

To Hollister

25

Park entrance

146

Cattle guard

25

To King City

Windmill

Barn/
horse corral

146

PINNACLES
NATIONAL PARK

146

Bacon Ranch
buildings

Fence

Visitor center/
camp store

Shuttle stop

P 2

Picnic tables/
barbecues

Toilets/showers

Pinnacles
Campground

The Hike

At the time of publication of this book, this trail was open to the public but unmarked and did not appear on the park map. The homestead parcel was added to the park in 2006 and is part of future improvements per the General Management Plan.

The service/ranch road goes through the picnic area with Sandy Creek on the right and the park road on the left. You walk through the opening in a split rail wooden fence with solar panels on the left (note that there are plans to remove these panels) before crossing a bridge over Sandy Creek to the Bacon Ranch and the buildings surrounding the old ranch house. At this point the dirt ranch road becomes your trail heading northeast toward CA 25, passing an old corral and several cattle gates along the way. Please close all gates behind you.

From here the trail takes you across meadows bordered by rolling hills and dotted with majestic oaks. Sandy Creek is on the left of the ranch road, and the paved park road (CA 146) parallels the creek on the north bank of Sandy Creek.

At 0.7 mile you pass a trail junction where another spur ranch road heads right toward private property. For now continue walking straight, but on the way back, if time permits, this is the spur you can walk up for about 0.3 mile on park land to catch an unexpected distant view of the High Peaks, looking back toward the west, before going back to the trailhead the way you came. Please respect private property; beyond this point the High Peaks disappear from view anyway.

Park pack animals corralled at Butterfield Homestead

As you continue up the main ranch road, it curves away from the creek toward a couple of barns and a horse corral on the right and an Aermotor windmill on the left. This is the Butterfield homestead. From the windmill site, open meadows stretch on either side of this idyllic sweeping ranch road all the way to the cattle guard and gate at CA 25, which is the park boundary and your turnaround point. (GPS: N36 31.00'/ W121 07.87'. Elevation 1,193 feet.) Pick a spot for a picnic and enjoy the open views.

Miles and Directions

0.0 Start at the gate signed Authorized Vehicles Only in the picnic area parking lot behind the visitor center.

0.1 Come to solar panels on the left and a wooden split rail fence. Walk through the opening in the fence.

0.2 Come to a wooden bridge across Sandy Creek. Walk across the bridge and past the Bacon Ranch house and outbuildings.

0.7 Come to a road junction. This is where you have the option of walking up the spur for about 0.3 mile on the way back. For now continue walking straight on the ranch road past a cattle gate with a pedestrian gate on the right. Observe the signs that say, "Keep gate closed."

1.3 Come to a horse corral and barn on the right. The Aermotor windmill is on the left.

1.9 Come to the cattle guard and gate at CA 25 and your turnaround point. Go back in the direction you came from. If time and energy allow, take the spur at 0.7 mile.

3.8 Arrive back at the trailhead for a direct out and back.

4.4 Arrive back at the trailhead if you walked the 0.3 mile up the spur for a peek of the High Peaks.

3 Visitor Center to South Wilderness

The trailhead at the entrance to the campground's paved road is nothing to get excited about, but it gets better quickly. First you are rewarded with two condor-spotting telescopes on an ADA-accessible concrete pad within 200 feet of the trailhead. After the first 0.5 mile across the campground—paralleling or walking on the paved campground road—the hike is on a pleasant, lightly used dirt trail lacing a pine woodland and meadow portal to the solitude of the South Wilderness, then tracing the seasonal Chalone Creek at the foot of chaparral-covered hills.

Start: From the corner of the campground entrance at the Bench trailhead
Distance: 7.0 miles out and back
Hiking time: 3.5 hours
Difficulty: Moderate
Trail surface: Dirt, pavement, and gravel
Trailhead elevation: 1,063 feet
Highest point: 1,063 feet
Best seasons: Spring for wildflowers, late fall and winter for cooler temperatures (summer and early fall can be very hot)

Maps: USGS North Chalone Peak; Pinnacles National Park map; Tom Harrison map of Pinnacles National Park
Nearest town: Hollister
Trail contact: Pinnacles National Park, 5000 CA 146, Paicines, CA 95043-9770; (831) 389-4485 or (831) 389-4427; www.nps.gov/pinn
Trail tips: There is a camp store in the visitor center building for the adjacent campground. Water, restrooms, and a picnic area with grills, food-storage containers, and recycling and trash containers are behind the visitor center.

Finding the trailhead: From US 101 at San Juan Bautista/Hollister exit 345 (approximately 17 miles north of Salinas and 10 miles south of Gilroy), take exit 345 and drive 7.5 miles to the Hollister turnoff on the right. Drive 3.5 miles and turn right onto CA 25. Drive 28 miles on CA 25 to the Pinnacles National Park entrance. Turn right into the park and drive 2 miles to the visitor center to pay the entrance fee and pick up a map and information. The visitor center is on your left. Turn left at the campground entrance and park in the picnic area parking lot behind the visitor center. Walk back toward the visitor center and campground entrance. The Bench trailhead is across from the visitor center at the campground entrance. GPS: N36 29.59' / W121 08.78'.

From US 101 at King City, take exit 282B/Broadway Street and turn right onto Broadway Street. Drive 1 mile on Broadway Street to the T intersection with First Street. Turn left onto First Street and drive 14 miles to the T intersection with CA 25. (First Street becomes Bitterwater Road at the sign for East Pinnacles.) Turn left onto CA 25 to Pinnacles and drive 14 miles to the CA 146 intersection. Turn left into Pinnacles National Park and follow directions above to the trailhead.

The Hike

At the start, this may seem like an odd hike since it follows the paved campground road for the first 0.5 mile, but it should not be dismissed for several reasons. The parking is easy and ample behind the visitor center. It is the closest trailhead to the visitor

Trail passes through meadow and pine and oak woodland.

center and therefore the quickest way to get moving after the drive. Since parts of it are ADA friendly and wheelchair accessible, you may get the best view of condors in flight without much exertion. The Condor interpretive panels are just 200 feet from the trailhead, with two telescopes pointed toward the southern ridge where condors frequently catch thermals.

The hike into the South Wilderness is mostly flat with minimal elevation change and becomes more interesting and nourishing after the first 0.5 mile, where it transitions to dirt and you walk through the gate at the wild pig fence. The interpretive panel gives a detailed explanation of why it is important to keep these nonnative mammals outside of park boundaries and how their rooting behavior causes erosion. For the next mile the creek on your left infuses new life to the area, even during the lowest flow season in drier years. At 0.9 mile an interpretative panel about air quality stations in the park describes yet another feature that makes Pinnacles National Park significant ecologically. One of the air quality stations is directly across the paved road as you lift your eyes from the information board. The stations are part of a study to measure air pollution and its effects on the ecosystem.

Just ahead, the trail intersects a dirt service/fire road in an oak and pine meadow. As beautiful as the green and rainbow colors of spring grass and wildflowers are, the

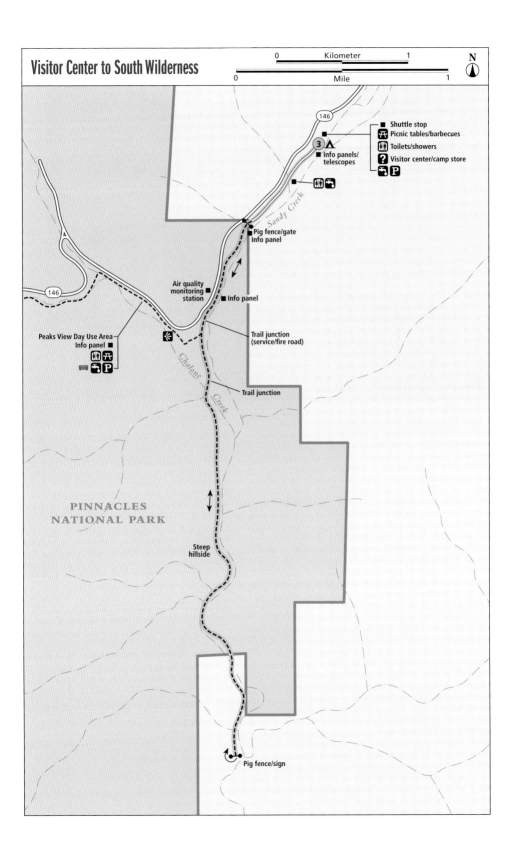

Visitor Center to South Wilderness

0 Kilometer 1

0 Mile 1

N

146

3

Info panels/
telescopes

■ Shuttle stop
Picnic tables/barbecues
Toilets/showers
Visitor center/camp store

Sandy Creek

Pig fence/gate
Info panel

Air quality
monitoring
station ■ Info panel

Peaks View Day Use Area
Info panel ■

Trail junction
(service/fire road)

Chalone Creek

Trail junction

PINNACLES
NATIONAL PARK

Steep
hillside

Pig fence/sign

146

maroon of the drought-resistant scrub against the pale cream blooms of buckwheat in the muted late autumn and winter light is also a surprisingly beautiful palette.

Turn left onto the service road and notice the High Peaks on the horizon on your right through the foliage as you walk past the trail junction for the Bear Gulch Day Use Area and Old Pinnacles Trail on the right. Continue straight on the service road. At 1.3 miles the service road forks, then bears left at the No Entry sign. Bear right along the narrower South Wilderness Trail. The trail continues in the meadow interrupted by sycamore, pine, and oak woodland until it reaches the banks of seasonal Chalone Creek. This is the only tricky section of the trail, with an unmarked junction and a spur trail to the left. Bear right and cross the creek. The creek will stay on your left until you reach the pig fence and the "end of South Wilderness Trail" sign.

At about 2.3 miles the trail narrows and skirts the bank on a steep hillside above the creek before meandering back into what feels like the creek's floodplain corralled between the chaparral-covered hills. The end of the South Wilderness Trail and pig fence is about 1.2 miles ahead.

If you have looked at the USGS map, you might confuse an old trail to South Chalone Peak with the track of the pig fence that continues beyond the end of the South Wilderness Trail. You may get misled into thinking that the couple of feet of clearing along the fence is a trail to South Chalone Peak, about 3 miles farther. This is *not* a trail. Furthermore, the barbed-wire pig fence would be less than "hand-friendly" when the terrain gets so steep that you instinctively reach for the fence to stop from slipping backward. Contrary to what you may think, South Chalone Peak is smothered in too much tall chaparral to reward you with fabulous views.

Soak up the quiet and solitude of the South Wilderness Trail while enjoying a snack at the fence line before going back to the trailhead the way you came.

Miles and Directions

0.0 Start at the Bench trailhead across from the visitor center at the entrance to the campground and walk 200 feet to the Condor interpretive panels and telescopes to help you spot soaring condors. Continue walking to the corner and trail sign for South Wilderness Junction 0.9, Bear Gulch Area 2.6, High Peaks Junction 2.2, Balconies Area 4.4. Watch for Bench Trail markers on the right. The trail parallels the campground's paved road to the right.

0.3 Come to the campground restrooms (flush toilets and sinks).

0.5 The trail transitions from pavement to dirt at the Hiker trail sign. Sandy Creek is on your left.

0.6 Arrive at the Wild Pig interpretive panel and fence with a gate. Walk through the gate and latch it carefully. There is an information panel just ahead.

0.9 Come to an information panel describing air quality checkpoints. An air quality monitoring station is visible across the road.

1.1 The trail intersects a dirt service/fire road. Turn left onto the service road.

1.15 Come to a trail junction with a sign for South Wilderness Trail (straight), Bear Gulch Area 1.7 (right); Old Pinnacles Trail 1.1 (right). Continue walking straight on the service road.

1.3 Come to a fork in the road at the No Entry sign on the service road on the left. Bear right on the South Wilderness Trail.

1.5 Come to an unmarked trail junction with a spur to the left. Bear right and cross the seasonal Chalone Creek. The creek will remain on your left to the end of the South Wilderness Trail.

2.3 The trail narrows and skirts the bank on a steep hillside above the creek.

3.5 Arrive at the end of the South Wilderness Trail at the pig fence. (GPS: N36 27.16'/ W121 09.23'. Elevation: 877 feet.) Have a snack and go back to the trailhead the way you came.

7.0 Arrive back at the trailhead.

4 Visitor Center to Peaks View Day Use Area

If you can get past this hike's lackluster section along the campground road, you will be rewarded with two condor-spotting telescopes on an ADA accessible concrete pad within 250 feet of the trailhead. From the 0.5 mile mark to Peaks View Day Use Area, it's a relaxing stroll along a creek and through pine woodland, ending with a postcard view of the High Peaks' volcanic palisade.

Start: From the corner of the campground entrance at the Bench trailhead
Distance: 3.0 miles out and back
Hiking time: 1.5 hours
Difficulty: Easy
Trail surface: Pavement and dirt
Trailhead elevation: 1,063 feet
Highest point: 1,063 feet
Best seasons: Spring for wildflowers, late fall and winter for cooler temperatures (summer and early fall can be very hot)

Maps: USGS North Chalone Peak; Pinnacles National Park map; Tom Harrison map of Pinnacles National Park
Nearest town: Hollister
Trail contact: Pinnacles National Park, 5000 CA 146, Paicines, CA 95043-9770; (831) 389-4485 or (831) 389-4427; www.nps.gov/pinn
Trail tips: There is a camp store in the visitor center building for the adjacent campground. Water, restrooms, and a picnic area with grills, food-storage containers, and recycling and trash containers are behind the visitor center.

Finding the trailhead: From US 101 at San Juan Bautista/Hollister exit 345 (approximately 17 miles north of Salinas and 10 miles south of Gilroy), take exit 345 and drive 7.5 miles to the Hollister turnoff on the right. Drive 3.5 miles and turn right onto CA 25. Drive 28 miles on CA 25 to the Pinnacles National Park entrance. Turn right into the park and drive 2 miles to the visitor center to pay the entrance fee and pick up a map and information. The visitor center is on your left. Turn left at the campground entrance and park in the picnic area parking lot behind the visitor center. Walk back toward the visitor center and campground entrance. The Bench trailhead is across from the visitor center at the campground entrance. GPS: N36 29.59' / W121 08.78'.

From US 101 at King City, take exit 282B/Broadway Street and turn right onto Broadway Street. Drive 1 mile on Broadway Street to the T intersection with First Street. Turn left onto First Street and drive 14 miles to the T intersection with CA 25. (First Street becomes Bitterwater Road at the sign for East Pinnacles.) Turn left onto CA 25 to Pinnacles and drive 14 miles to the CA 146 intersection. Turn left into Pinnacles National Park and follow directions above to the trailhead.

The Hike

At the start, this may seem like an odd hike since it follows the paved campground road for the first 0.5 mile, but it should not be dismissed for several reasons. The parking is easy and ample behind the visitor center. It is one of the closest trailheads to the visitor center and therefore the quickest way to get moving after the drive. Since

Close the gate as you pass through the "wild pig fence" on the Bench Trail.

parts of it are ADA friendly and wheelchair accessible, you may get the best view of condors in flight without much exertion. The Condor interpretive panels are just 200 feet from the trailhead, with two telescopes pointed toward the southern ridge where condors frequently catch thermals. Bench Trail is an easy, flat hike suitable for hikers of all ages, and parents with toddlers who like to be carried will appreciate the absence of radical elevation change.

The trail becomes more interesting and nourishing after the first 0.5 mile, where it transitions to dirt and you walk through the gate at the wild pig fence. The interpretive sign gives a detailed explanation of why it is important to keep these non-native mammals outside of park boundaries and how their rooting behavior causes erosion. For the next mile the creek on your left infuses new life to the area, even during the lowest flow season in drier years. At 0.9 mile an interpretive panel about air quality stations in the park describes yet another feature that makes Pinnacles

Visitor Center to Peaks View Day Use Area

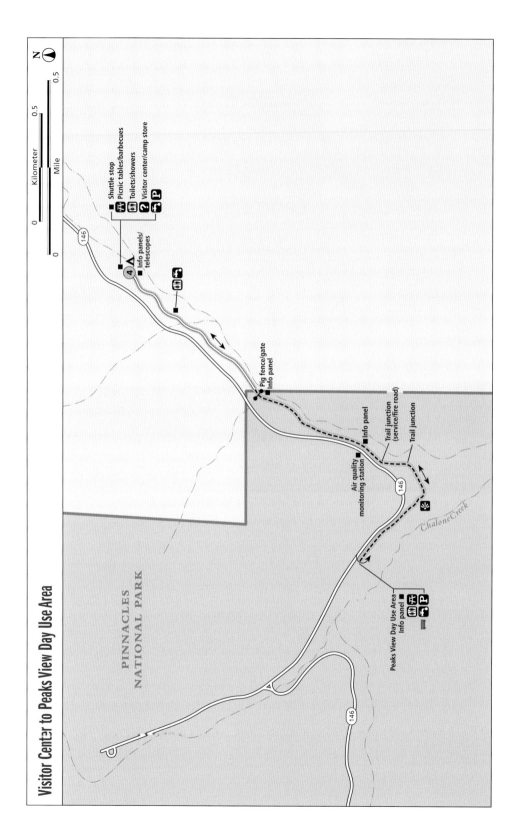

Shuttle stop
Picnic tables/barbecues
Toilets/showers
Visitor center/camp store

Info panels/
telescopes

Pig fence/gate
Info panel

Air quality
monitoring station

Info panel

Trail junction
(service/fire road)

Trail junction

PINNACLES
NATIONAL PARK

Chalone Creek

Peaks View Day Use Area
Info panel

N

Kilometer

Mile

National Park significant ecologically. One of the air quality stations is directly across the paved road as you lift your eyes from the information board. The stations are part of a study to measure air pollution and its effects on the ecosystem.

Just ahead on the trail, you cross a dirt service/fire road in an oak and pine meadow. As beautiful as the green and rainbow colors of spring grass and wildflowers are, the maroon of the drought-resistant scrub against the pale cream blooms of buckwheat in the muted late autumn and winter light is also a surprisingly beautiful palette.

The sandy trail rises at 1.3 miles, revealing the first view of the Pinnacles' peaks across the wash. The trail continues above the wash and traces a path paralleling the park road. You arrive at Peaks View Day Use Area and the Condor Crags information panel at 1.5 miles. The strategically placed bench invites hikers to sit and absorb the views. This is your destination and an idyllic spot for a picnic or snack and a good dose of fluids. Go back to the trailhead the way you came.

Miles and Directions

0.0 Start at the Bench trailhead across from the visitor center at the entrance to the campground and walk 200 feet to the Condor interpretive panel and telescopes to help you spot soaring condors. Continue walking to the corner and trail sign for South Wilderness Junction 0.9, Bear Gulch Area 2.6, High Peaks Junction 2.2, Balconies Area 4.4. Watch for Bench Trail markers on the right. The trail parallels the campground's paved road to the right.

0.3 Come to the campground bathrooms (flush toilets and sinks).

0.5 The trail transitions from pavement to dirt at the Hiker trail sign. Sandy Creek is on your left.

0.6 Arrive at the Wild Pig interpretive panel and fence with a gate. Walk through the gate and latch it carefully. There is an information board just ahead.

0.9 Come to an information panel describing air quality checkpoints. An air quality monitoring station is across the road.

1.1 The trail intersects with a dirt service/fire road. Turn left onto the service road. Shortly arrive at a trail junction with a sign for South Wilderness Trail (straight); Bear Gulch Area 1.7 (right); Old Pinnacles Trail 1.1 (right). Turn right to continue walking on Bench Trail.

1.3 The trail rises gently, revealing a view of the Pinnacles' peaks across the wash.

1.5 Arrive at the Peaks View Day Use Area. (GPS: N36 28.97'/ W121 09.72'. Elevation 974 feet.) Walk across the parking lot entrance to the Condor Crags interpretive panel and bench. This is a perfect spot for admiring this unique ancient geological formation where condors nest and roost once again. Go back to the trailhead the way you came.

3.0 Arrive back at the trailhead.

5 Visitor Center to Bear Gulch Day Use Area

If you can get past the lackluster beginning of this hike along the campground road, you will be rewarded with two condor-spotting telescopes on an ADA-accessible concrete pad within 200 feet of the trailhead, a lovely meadow and pine woodland with a postcard view of the High Peaks' volcanic palisade, and this hike's "pièce de résistance"—Bear Gulch Trail along a seasonally tumbling Bear Gulch Creek.

Start: From the corner of the campground entrance at the Bench trailhead
Distance: 5.7 miles out and back
Hiking time: 3 hours
Difficulty: Moderate
Trail surface: Pavement and dirt
Trailhead elevation: 1,063 feet
Highest point: 1,275 feet
Best seasons: Spring for wildflowers, winter and spring for water in the creek, and late fall and winter for cooler temperatures (summer and early fall can be very hot)
Maps: USGS North Chalone Peak; Pinnacles National Park map; Tom Harrison map of Pinnacles National Park

Nearest town: Hollister
Trail contact: Pinnacles National Park, 5000 CA 146, Paicines, CA 95043-9770; (831) 389-4485 or (831) 389-4427; www.nps.gov/pinn
Trail tips: There is a camp store in the visitor center building for the adjacent campground. Water, restrooms, and a picnic area with grills, food-storage containers, and recycling and trash containers are behind the visitor center. The Bear Gulch Day Use Area has water, restrooms, and a picnic area.

Finding the trailhead: From US 101 at San Juan Bautista/Hollister exit 345 (approximately 17 miles north of Salinas and 10 miles south of Gilroy), take exit 345 and drive 7.5 miles to the Hollister turnoff on the right. Drive 3.5 miles and turn right onto CA 25. Drive 28 miles on CA 25 to the Pinnacles National Park entrance. Turn right into the park and drive 2 miles to the visitor center to pay the entrance fee and pick up a map and information. The visitor center is on your left. Turn left at the campground entrance and park in the picnic area parking lot behind the visitor center. Walk back toward the visitor center and campground entrance. The Bench trailhead is across from the visitor center at the campground entrance. GPS: N36 29.59' / W121 08.78'.

From US 101 at King City, take exit 282B/Broadway Street and turn right onto Broadway Street. Drive 1 mile on Broadway Street to the T intersection with First Street. Turn left onto First Street and drive 14 miles to the T intersection with CA 25. (First Street becomes Bitterwater Road at the sign for East Pinnacles.) Turn left onto CA 25 to Pinnacles and drive 14 miles to the CA 146 intersection. Turn left into Pinnacles National Park and follow directions above to the trailhead.

The Hike

At the start, this may seem like an odd hike since it follows the paved campground road for the first 0.5 mile, but it should not be dismissed for several reasons. The parking is easy and ample behind the visitor center. It is one of the closest trailheads to the

Bear Gulch Creek cascades following a rainstorm

visitor center and therefore the quickest way to get moving after the drive. Since the first 0.5 mile is ADA friendly and wheelchair accessible, you may get the best view of condors in flight without much exertion. The Condor interpretive panels are just 200 feet from the trailhead, with two telescopes pointed toward the southern ridge where condors frequently catch thermals.

The hike becomes more interesting and nourishing at 0.5 mile, where the pavement transitions to dirt and you walk through the gate at the wild pig fence. The interpretive panel gives a detailed explanation of why it is important to keep these nonnative mammals outside of park boundaries and how their rooting behavior causes erosion. For the next mile the creek on your left infuses new life to the area, even during the lowest flow season in drier years. At 0.9 mile an interpretative panel about air quality stations in the park describes yet another feature that makes Pinnacles National Park significant ecologically. One of the air quality stations is directly across the paved road as you lift your eyes from the information board. The stations are part of a study to measure air pollution and its effects on the ecosystem.

Just ahead on the trail, you cross a dirt service road in an oak and pine meadow. As beautiful as the green and rainbow colors of spring grass and wildflowers are, the maroon of the drought-resistant scrub against the pale cream blooms of buckwheat in the muted late autumn and winter light is also a surprisingly beautiful palette.

The sandy trail rises at 1.3 miles, revealing the first view of the Pinnacles' peaks across the wash. The trail continues above the wash and traces a path paralleling the park road. You arrive at Peaks View Day Use Area and the Condor Crags information panel at 1.5 miles. The strategically placed bench invites hikers to sit and absorb the views before continuing on Bench Trail to where it veers left and crosses a double wooden footbridge across seasonal Chalone Creek toward Bear Gulch. With a bit of luck in the spring, the wide, rocky wash of Chalone Creek may treat you to ribbons of bright orange poppies paralleling the banks. The unmarked spur trail at this junction on the east side of the creek continues straight to an overflow parking area of about ten spaces.

Just across the two wooden footbridges you come to a trail junction where the unmarked Bench Trail goes right, paralleling Chalone Creek on the west side, and unmarked Bear Gulch Trail begins. A trail sign for Bear Gulch Day Use Area is on the right side of the trail. Bear left on this trail and hike up the wider mouth of the gulch, where Bear Gulch Creek flows into Chalone Creek. Bear Gulch Creek is on your left as you start walking uphill. Six wooden footbridges lace the creek over the last and sweetest mile-long section of this hike. In the winter and early spring, the water cascading over boulders and spilling into waterfalls between volcanic rock outcrops is truly enchanting.

Once you reach the driveway of the private park employee residence, the trail levels across the last two footbridges just 0.2 mile from Bear Gulch Day Use Area. There are a few picnic tables on both sides of the road and a larger picnic area with grills just up the trail west of the parking area and bathrooms. Note that the Bear Gulch Nature Center is typically open on weekends during peak season from March to May,

Visitor Center to Bear Gulch Day Use Area

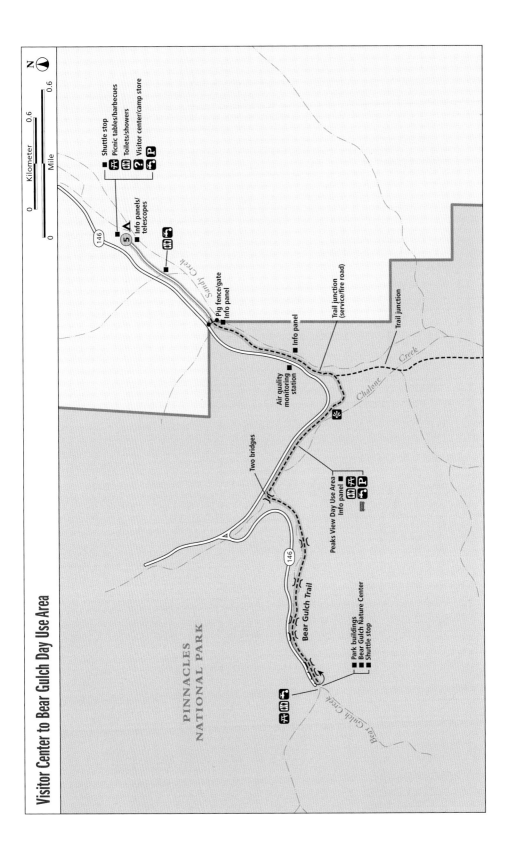

PINNACLES NATIONAL PARK

146

Bear Gulch Trail

Two bridges

Sandy Creek

Chalone Creek

Bear Gulch Creek

Park buildings
Bear Gulch Nature Center
Shuttle stop

Peaks View Use Area
Info panel

Air quality monitoring station

Pig fence/gate
Info panel

Info panel

Trail junction (service/fire road)

Trail junction

Info panels/telescopes

146

5

N

Kilometer 0 0.6
Mile 0 0.6

■ Shuttle stop
⛱ Picnic tables/barbecues
🚻 Toilets/showers
❓ Visitor center/camp store
P

and there are some very interesting exhibits. The free park shuttle runs between the visitor center and Bear Gulch Day Use Area during that peak season.

Go back to the trailhead the way you came. If you are hiking this trail between March and May, check the shuttle schedule, as this may be an option for the return if you or hikers in your party are less enthusiastic about hiking back.

Miles and Directions

0.0 Start at the Bench trailhead across from the visitor center at the entrance to the campground and walk 200 feet to the Condor interpretive panels and telescopes to help you spot soaring condors. Continue walking to the corner and trail sign for South Wilderness Junction .9, Bear Gulch Area 2.6, High Peaks Junction 2.2, Balconies Area 4.4. Watch for Bench Trail markers on the right. The trail parallels the campground's paved road to the right.

0.3 Come to the campground bathrooms (flush toilets and sinks).

0.5 The trail transitions from pavement to dirt at the Hiker trail sign. The creek is on your left.

0.6 Arrive at the Wild Pig interpretive panel and fence with a gate. Walk through the gate and latch it carefully. The information board is just ahead.

0.9 Come to an information panel describing air quality checkpoints. An air quality monitoring station is visible across the road.

1.1 The trail intersects a dirt service road. Turn left onto the service road. Shortly arrive at a trail junction with a sign for South Wilderness Trail (straight); Bear Gulch Area 1.7 (right); Old Pinnacles Trail 1.1 (right). Turn right to continue walking on Bench Trail.

1.3 The trail rises gently, revealing a view of the Pinnacles' peaks across the wash.

1.5 Arrive at the Peaks View Day Use Area. Walk across the parking lot entrance to the Condor Crags interpretive panel and bench. This is a perfect spot for taking a break and admiring this unique ancient geological formation where condors nest and roost once again.

1.8 Come to a trail junction for Bear Gulch Day Use Area and an unmarked spur to a parking area. Turn left and walk across the double wooden footbridges. Immediately come to the unmarked trail junction for Bear Gulch Trail and a trail sign for Bear Gulch Day Use Area. Bench Trail continues right. Bear left and walk up Bear Gulch Trail toward the day-use area.

2.05 Walk across the wooden footbridge. You will cross three more bridges in the next 0.5 mile.

2.65 Walk across the driveway at the employee residence.

2.7 Walk across two more wooden footbridges in quick succession. Park buildings are on the left.

2.85 Arrive at Bear Gulch Day Use Area. GPS: N36 28.90'/ W121 10.86'. Elevation 1,275 feet.

5.7 Arrive back at the trailhead.

6 Peaks View Day Use Area to Bear Gulch Day Use Area

This is a nice snapshot of the lush Bear Gulch area via the sweetest mile of trail in the park. There's something enchanting about hiking up this narrow gulch laced with six wooden footbridges across seasonal Bear Gulch Creek, which is lined with buckeye, sycamore, and oaks. Ferns, cattails, and clump grass–like sedges, cascades, and a waterfall are some of the seasonal centerpieces.

Start: From Peaks View Day Use Area
Distance: 2.7 miles out and back
Hiking time: 1.5 hours
Difficulty: Moderate
Trail surface: Dirt
Trailhead elevation: 974 feet
Highest point: 1,275 feet
Best seasons: Spring for wildflowers, late fall and winter for cooler temperatures (summer and early fall can be very hot)
Maps: USGS North Chalone Peak; Pinnacles National Park map; Tom Harrison map of Pinnacles National Park

Nearest town: Hollister
Trail contact: Pinnacles National Park, 5000 CA 146, Paicines, CA 95043-9770; (831) 389-4485 or (831) 389-4427; www.nps.gov/pinn
Trail tips: Water, a portable toilet, picnic tables, and recycling and trash containers are at Peaks View Day Use Area. Bear Gulch Day Use Area has flush toilets and all of the above amenities. Watch for poison oak along some stretches of the trail.

Finding the trailhead: From US 101 at San Juan Bautista/Hollister exit 345 (approximately 17 miles north of Salinas and 10 miles south of Gilroy), take exit 345 and drive 7.5 miles to the Hollister turnoff on the right. Drive 3.5 miles and turn right onto CA 25. Drive 28 miles on CA 25 to the Pinnacles National Park entrance. Turn right into the park and drive 2 miles to the Visitor Center to pay the entrance fee and pick up a map and information. The visitor center is on your left. Return to the main park road and drive 1.3 more miles to the Peaks View Day Use parking lot. GPS: N36 28.97' / W121 09.72'.

From US 101 at King City, take exit 282B/Broadway Street and turn right onto Broadway Street. Drive 1 mile on Broadway Street to the T intersection with First Street. Turn left onto First Street and drive 14 miles to the T intersection with CA 25. (First Street becomes Bitterwater Road at the sign for East Pinnacles.) Turn left onto CA 25 to Pinnacles and drive 14 miles to the CA 146 intersection. Turn left into Pinnacles National Park and follow directions above to the trailhead.

The Hike

Peaks View Day Use Area welcomes you with a strategically located bench to absorb the view of the High Peaks on the horizon and an educational panel about the relationship between condors and the Pinnacles. This is a perfect spot for admiring the unique ancient geological formation where condors nest and roost once again.

The Bench Trail is named for the way it traces the banks of the seasonal Chalone Creek, and not for the "bench" at Peaks View. Start by heading north with the creek

Seasonal waterfall along Bear Gulch Trail

on your left. Just 0.3 mile up the trail you come to a trail junction. An unmarked spur trail continues straight to an overflow parking area; the unmarked Bench Trail goes left and crosses a double wooden footbridge over Chalone Creek toward Bear Gulch. Just across the two wooden footbridges you come to a trail junction where the unmarked Bench Trail goes right, paralleling Chalone Creek on the west side, and the unmarked Bear Gulch Trail begins straight ahead. Bear left up the wider mouth of the gulch, where seasonal Bear Gulch Creek flows into Chalone Creek. Bear Gulch Creek is on your left as you start up the trail, but six wooden footbridges take you back and forth across the creek over the last and sweetest mile-long section of this hike.

The gulch is laced with buckeye, sycamore, oak, and cottonwood trees. Even in drier periods the creekbed at the bottom of the gulch retains enough moisture to nourish the thriving ferns and clump grass–like sedges at the bottom of the gulch. The trail meanders, climbing gradually for the first 0.5 mile up to the first couple of bridges. The next 0.2 mile between bridges #2 and #3 is significantly steeper, and if you are lucky enough to hike this trail after a winter rainstorm, you'll see how the terrain enhances the creek's cascades and rewards hikers with a rushing water-fall through the boulder channel higher up. Just short of bridge #3 the trail finally

Peaks View Day Use Area to Bear Gulch Day Use Area

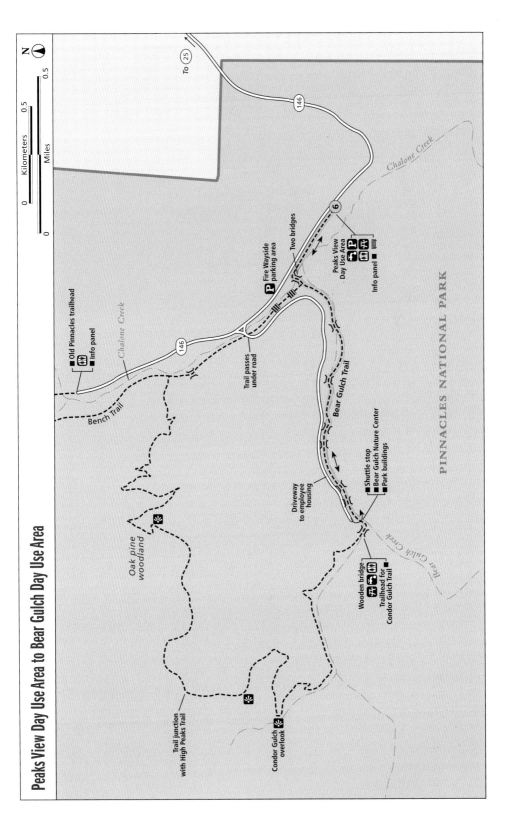

Kilometers
Miles

N

To 25

146

Chalone Creek

PINNACLES NATIONAL PARK

Old Pinnacles trailhead
Info panel

Bench Trail

Chalone Creek

Fire Wayside parking area

Two bridges

Peaks View Day Use Area

Info panel

Trail passes under road

6

Bear Gulch Trail

Driveway to employee housing

Shuttle stop
Bear Gulch Nature Center
Park buildings

Oak pine woodland

Bear Gulch Creek

Wooden bridge
Trailhead for Condor Gulch Trail

Trail junction with High Peaks Trail

Condor Gulch overlook

plateaus, ending your cardio workout for a while. The trail crosses bridge #4 and the employee residence driveway before leveling off at the last two footbridge crossings. At 1.35 miles Bear Gulch Creek is on your left and you come to the end of Bear Gulch Trail at the head of the Bear Gulch Day Use Area parking lot. The Bear Gulch Nature Center is on your left. If the seasonal nature center is open, make sure you stop to enjoy the exhibits.

There are a few picnic tables on both sides of the road and a restroom and drinking fountain across the road. There is a larger developed picnic area with grills and water about 200 feet to the left of the restrooms over the wooden footbridge. Follow the sign for the picnic area. Enjoy a leisurely picnic before going back to the trailhead the way you came.

Miles and Directions

0.0 Start at Peaks View Day Use Area and walk north on Bench Trail.

0.3 Come to a trail junction for Bear Gulch Day Use Area and an unmarked spur to a parking area. Turn left and walk across the double wooden footbridges. Shortly come to the unmarked trail junction for Bear Gulch Trail and a trail sign for Bear Gulch Day Use Area. Bench Trail continues right. Bear left and walk up Bear Gulch Trail toward the day-use area.

0.55 Walk across the wooden footbridge. You will cross three more bridges in the next 0.5 mile.

1.15 Walk across the driveway at the employee residence.

1.2 Walk across two more wooden footbridges in quick succession. Park buildings are on the left.

1.35 Arrive at Bear Gulch Day Use Area. GPS: N36 28.90'/ W121 10.86'. Elevation: 1,275 feet.

2.7 Arrive back at the trailhead.

7 Peaks View Day Use Area to Condor Gulch

This hike begins with a distant view of the volcanic High Peaks and treats you to lovely, leafy Bear Gulch's six wooden footbridges across seasonal Bear Gulch Creek. The close-up views of the High Peaks' stark and astounding beauty lure you up Condor Gulch's exposed switchbacks to a panoramic crest before you make a long, rugged descent interrupted by a bucolic patch of oak- and pine-studded swales and meadows.

Start: From Peaks View Day Use Area
Distance: 6.05-mile lollipop
Hiking time: 3.5 hours
Difficulty: Strenuous
Trail surface: Dirt and rock
Trailhead elevation: 974 feet
Highest point: 2,329 feet
Best seasons: Spring for wildflowers, late fall and winter for cooler temperatures (summer and early fall can be very hot)
Maps: USGS North Chalone Peak; Pinnacles National Park map; Tom Harrison map of Pinnacles National Park

Nearest town: Hollister
Trail contact: Pinnacles National Park, 5000 CA 146, Paicines, CA 95043-9770; (831) 389-4485 or (831) 389-4427; www.nps.gov/pinn
Trail tips: There is water in the Peaks View Use Area and in the Bear Gulch Day Use Area along with restrooms (portable toilet at Peaks View), picnic tables, and trash and recycling containers. Note that no water is available after you start on the Condor Gulch Trail for the next 5 miles until you return to the trailhead at Peaks View.

Finding the trailhead: From US 101 at San Juan Bautista/Hollister exit 345 (approximately 17 miles north of Salinas and 10 miles south of Gilroy), take exit 345 and drive 7.5 miles to the Hollister turnoff on the right. Drive 3.5 miles and turn right onto CA 25. Drive 28 miles on CA 25 to the Pinnacles National Park entrance. Turn right into the park and drive 2 miles to the Visitor Center to pay the entrance fee and pick up a map and information. The visitor center is on your left. Return to the main park road and drive 1.3 more miles to the Peaks View Day Use parking lot. GPS: N36 28.97' / W121 09.72'.

From US 101 at King City, take exit 282B/Broadway Street and turn right onto Broadway Street. Drive 1 mile on Broadway Street to the T intersection with First Street. Turn left onto First Street and drive 14 miles to the T intersection with CA 25. (First Street becomes Bitterwater Road at the sign for East Pinnacles.) Turn left onto CA 25 to Pinnacles and drive 14 miles to the CA 146 intersection. Turn left into Pinnacles National Park and follow directions above to the trailhead.

The Hike

Peaks View Day Use Area welcomes you with a strategically located bench to absorb the view of the High Peaks on the horizon and an educational panel about the relationship between condors and the Pinnacles. This is a perfect spot for admiring the unique ancient geological formation where condors nest and roost once again.

The Bench Trail is named for the way it traces the banks of the seasonal Chalone Creek, and not for the "bench" at Peaks View. Start by heading north with the creek

on your left. Just 0.3 mile up the trail you come to a trail junction. An unmarked spur trail continues straight to an overflow parking area; the unmarked Bench Trail goes left and crosses a double wooden footbridge over Chalone Creek toward Bear Gulch. Just across the two wooden footbridges you come to a trail junction where the unmarked Bench Trail goes right, paralleling Chalone Creek on the west side, and the unmarked Bear Gulch Trail begins straight ahead. Bear left up the wider mouth of the gulch, where seasonal Bear Gulch Creek flows into Chalone Creek. Bear Gulch Creek is on your left as you start up the trail, but six wooden footbridges take you back and forth across the creek over the last and sweetest mile-long section of this hike.

The gulch is laced with buckeye, sycamore, oak, and cottonwood trees. Even in drier periods the creekbed at the bottom of the gulch retains enough moisture to nourish the thriving ferns and clump grass–like sedges at the bottom of the gulch. The trail meanders, climbing gradually for the first 0.5 mile up to the first couple of bridges. The next 0.2 mile between bridges #2 and #3 is significantly steeper, and if you are lucky enough to hike this trail after a winter rainstorm, you'll see how the terrain enhances the creek's cascades and rewards hikers with a rushing waterfall through the boulder channel higher up. Just short of bridge #3 the trail finally plateaus, ending your cardio workout for a while. The trail crosses bridge #4 and the employee residence driveway before leveling off at the last two footbridge crossings. At 1.35 miles Bear Gulch Creek is on your left and you come to the end of Bear Gulch Trail at the head of the Bear Gulch Day Use Area parking lot. The Bear Gulch Nature Center is on your left. If the seasonal nature center is open, make sure you stop to enjoy the exhibits.

There are a few picnic tables on both sides of the road and a restroom and drinking fountain across the road to the left of a bench, wooden footbridge, and the Condor Gulch trailhead. Continue up Condor Gulch, which wastes no time getting your heart pumping again with a relentless uphill. The next mile and four switchbacks of huffing and puffing are rewarded with a postcard view of the peaks at the Condor Gulch Overlook on the left. This is the perfect stopover for a snack and water break before continuing up the gulch.

You lose the peaks for a short time where views turn eastward toward the legendary San Andreas Fault rift zone. At 2.9 miles you're hit with a 360-degree view with another postcard shot of the High Peaks as you turn west. The trail heads north, and at 3.1 miles Condor Gulch Trail ends at the junction with the High Peaks Trail. Bear right and begin your descent along the exposed saddle on High Peaks Trail to Bench Trail. At about 3.8 miles you come to a panoramic viewpoint north and eastward. The trail veers left and begins a steady downhill in the chaparral canyon and over swales of oak-studded meadows and rolling hills before long switchbacks begin to trace chaparral and gray pine–studded slopes.

Rocks sculpted by Bear Gulch Creek

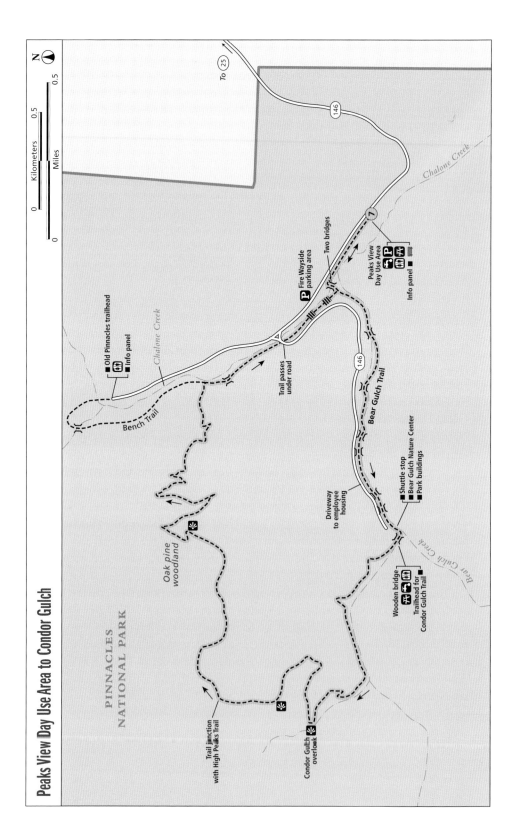

Peaks View Day Use Area to Condor Gulch

PINNACLES NATIONAL PARK

Oak pine woodland

Trail Junction with High Peaks Trail

Condor Gulch overlook

Trail passes under road

Bench Trail

Old Pinnacles trailhead
Info panel

Chalone Creek

Fire Wayside parking area

Two bridges

Peaks View Day Use Area

Info panel

Driveway to employee housing

Bear Gulch Trail

Shuttle stop
Bear Gulch Nature Center
Park buildings

Wooden bridge
Trailhead for Condor Gulch Trail

Bear Gulch Creek

Chalone Creek

To 25

146

146

7

N

Kilometers   0   0.5

Miles   0   0.5

At 5.1 miles High Peaks Trail ends at the junction for the unmarked Bench Trail above Chalone Creek. Turn right onto Bench Trail and walk across a seasonal creek on a wooden footbridge. At 5.4 miles you'll walk under the road overpass. There are two boardwalks along an eroded section of Chalone Creek's bank before you reach the close of your lollipop at 5.7 miles. Turn left at the trail junction, cross the double wooden footbridge over Chalone Creek, and go back to the trailhead the way you came.

Miles and Directions

0.0 Start at Peaks View Day Use Area and walk north on Bench Trail.

0.3 Come to a trail junction for Bear Gulch Day Use Area and an unmarked spur to a parking area. Turn left and walk across the double wooden footbridges. Shortly come to the unmarked trail junction for Bear Gulch Trail and a trail sign for Bear Gulch Day Use Area. Bench Trail continues right. Bear left and head up Bear Gulch Trail toward the day-use area. This is where your lollipop will close when you return from the right.

0.55 Walk across the wooden footbridge. You will cross three more bridges in the next 0.5 mile.

1.15 Walk across the driveway at the employee residence.

1.2 Walk across two more wooden footbridges in quick succession. Park buildings are on the left.

1.35 Arrive at Bear Gulch Day Use Area. Walk across the road to the bench and wooden footbridge.

1.4 Come to the Condor Gulch trailhead.

2.4 Come to the Condor Gulch Overlook.

2.9 Soak up a 360-degree view as you approach the High Peaks.

3.1 The Condor Gulch Trail ends at the junction with the High Peaks Trail. Bear right and continue walking on High Peaks Trail toward Bench Trail.

3.8 Come to a panoramic viewpoint. The trail veers left and downhill.

5.1 Come to a T-junction for the unmarked Bench Trail. High Peaks Trail ends here. Turn right, then shortly walk across the seasonal creek on the wooden footbridge.

5.4 Walk under the park road overpass. In 0.2 mile walk on two closely spaced boardwalks along an eroded section of Chalone Creek.

5.7 Come to a trail junction with the unmarked Bear Gulch Trail. This is the close of your lollipop. Go back across the double wooden footbridge. Shortly come to an unmarked spur trail on the left. Bear right and go back to the trailhead the way you came.

6.05 Arrive back at the trailhead.

8 Peaks View Day Use Area to Chalone Creek Overlook

This out and back begins and ends with views at either end of a steady cardio climb. The hike begins with the High Peaks silhouetted against the western horizon across seasonal Chalone Creek. The trail follows the creekbed on the east and west banks before the mile-long huff on a mostly exposed slope. A prominent rock outcrop on your left is your unmarked overlook destination above Chalone Creek, looking across the stadium of mountain ranges eastward. If your timing is right, you might even have the privilege of seeing the dry, rocky Chalone Creek's banks morph into a spring stream of golden California poppies.

Start: From Peaks View Day Use Area
Distance: 4.5 miles out and back
Hiking time: 2.5 hours
Difficulty: Moderate with a steady uphill
Trail surface: Coarse sand, dirt, and gravel
Trailhead elevation: 974 feet
Highest point: 1,898 feet
Best seasons: Spring for wildflowers, late fall and winter for cooler temperatures (summer and early fall can be very hot)
Maps: USGS North Chalone Peak; Pinnacles National Park map; Tom Harrison map of Pinnacles National Park

Nearest town: Hollister
Trail contact: Pinnacles National Park, 5000 CA 146, Paicines, CA 95043-9770; (831) 389-4485 or (831) 389-4427; www.nps.gov/pinn
Trail tips: There are picnic tables, a portable toilet, a drinking fountain, and trash and recycling containers in the Peaks View Day Use Area. The last mile is a long, arduous climb on an exposed slope.

Finding the trailhead: From US 101 at San Juan Bautista/Hollister exit 345 (approximately 17 miles north of Salinas and 10 miles south of Gilroy), take exit 345 and drive 7.5 miles to the Hollister turnoff on the right. Drive 3.5 miles and turn right onto CA 25. Drive 28 miles on CA 25 to the Pinnacles National Park entrance. Turn right into the park and drive 2 miles to the Visitor Center to pay the entrance fee and pick up a map and information. The visitor center is on your left. Return to the main park road and drive 1.3 more miles to the Peaks View Day Use parking lot. GPS: N36 28.97' / W121 09.72'.

From US 101 at King City, take exit 282B/Broadway Street and turn right onto Broadway Street. Drive 1 mile on Broadway Street to the T intersection with First Street. Turn left onto First Street and drive 14 miles to the T intersection with CA 25. (First Street becomes Bitterwater Road at the sign for East Pinnacles.) Turn left onto CA 25 to Pinnacles and drive 14 miles to the CA 146 intersection. Turn left into Pinnacles National Park and follow directions above to the trailhead.

The Hike

Peaks View Day Use Area welcomes you with a strategically located bench to absorb the view of the High Peaks on the horizon and an educational panel about the relationship between condors and the Pinnacles. This is a perfect spot for admiring the

Peaks View Day Use Area to Chalone Creek Overlook

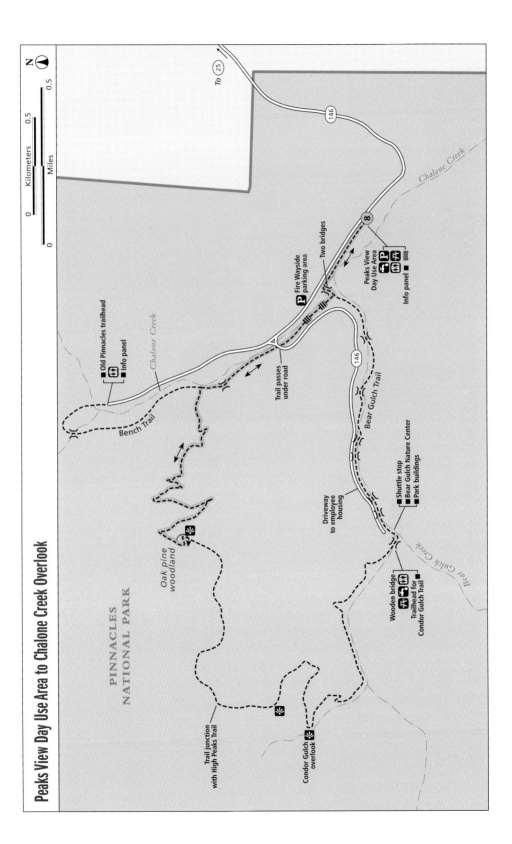

PINNACLES NATIONAL PARK

Oak pine woodland

Trail junction with High Peaks Trail

Condor Gulch overlook

Bench Trail

■ Old Pinnacles trailhead
■ Info panel

Chalone Creek

Trail passes under road

Fire Wayside parking area

Two bridges

Peaks View Day Use Area

■ Info panel

Driveway to employee housing

146

Bear Gulch Trail

■ Shuttle stop
■ Bear Gulch Nature Center
■ Park buildings

Wooden bridge

■ Trailhead for Condor Gulch Trail

Bear Gulch Creek

Chalone Creek

146

To 25

N

Kilometers
0   0.5

Miles
0   0.5

Enjoying the view at the Chalone Creek Overlook

unique ancient geological formation where condors nest and roost once again before setting out to a higher viewpoint.

The hike follows Bench Trail, which is named for the way it traces the banks of the seasonal Chalone Creek and was cut into the slope on the west side of the creek, and not for the "bench" at Peaks View. The trail heads north with the creek on your left. Just 0.3 mile up the trail you come to a trail junction. An unmarked spur trail continues straight to an overflow parking area; the unmarked Bench Trail goes left and crosses a double wooden footbridge over Chalone Creek toward Bear Gulch and the Old Pinnacles Trail. Just across the two wooden footbridges you come to a trail junction where the unmarked Bench Trail goes right, paralleling Chalone Creek on the west side. Shortly thereafter you walk across two boardwalks on a short eroded stretch of the trail before walking under the road overpass and across a wooden footbridge just over 0.75 mile from the trailhead.

At 0.95 mile you come to the trail junction for High Peaks. Turn left toward the High Peaks. The trail starts off with a short, steep, steady uphill that is tempered by numerous switchbacks for the next mile. Except for a small patch of oaks with budding leaves in the late spring into summer 0.5 mile up the hill, this trail is very exposed. The tradeoff is the expansive views.

At 2.0 miles you pass a Sphinx-like rock formation on the left, and finally the trail relents and the landscape softens unexpectedly, morphing from arid chaparral to a pine and oak woodland in a grassy vale. In an average spring following winter rains, the meadows will be carpeted in green and dotted with pale purple shooting stars.

At 2.25 miles you reach the natural rock outcrop viewpoint on the left above Chalone Creek with views eastward and northward across a stadium of mountain ranges (GPS: N36 29.48'/ W121 10.86'). Enjoy a picnic stop before going back down the way you came.

Miles and Directions

0.0 Start at Peaks View Day Use Area and walk north on the Bench Trail, which parallels the creekbed and park road.

0.3 Come to a trail junction for Bear Gulch Day Use Area and Old Pinnacles Trail going left and an unmarked spur to an overflow parking area straight ahead. Turn left and walk across the double wooden footbridges. Shortly come to the trail junction for Bear Gulch Trail straight and Old Pinnacles Trail right. Turn right to continue on Bench Trail toward Old Pinnacles Trail.

0.4 Walk on two closely spaced boardwalks along the eroded bank of the creek.

0.65 Bench Trail continues under a road overpass.

0.85 Walk across the wooden footbridge.

0.95 Come to the trail junction for High Peaks Trail and turn left.

2.15 Come to a pine and oak woodland.

2.25 Come to your viewpoint destination on the left. Enjoy a picnic with a view before going back to the trailhead the way you came.

4.5 Arrive back at the trailhead at Peaks View Day Use Area.

⑨ Peaks View Day Use Area to Old Pinnacles Trailhead

This is an easy route for visitors with limited time or energy looking to begin a hike with a peek at the High Peaks on the western horizon before enjoying a bit of solitude on a shady, mostly flat trail. The trail parallels the seasonal but generally dry, wide Chalone Creek on the west side until you cross a wooden footbridge to the east bank for the last 0.2 mile to the Old Pinnacles trailhead. If winter and spring have been reasonably generous with rainfall, the rocky Chalone creekbed can be a spectacle of deep blue bush lupine and brilliant golden-orange California poppies. This hike has the option of being made even easier and shorter with a vehicle parked in the Old Pinnacles trailhead parking lot for a shuttle back to Peaks View Day Use Area.

Start: From Peaks View Day Use Area.
Distance: 3.3 miles out and back (possible 1.65-mile shuttle)
Hiking time: 2 hours
Difficulty: Easy
Trail surface: Coarse sand, gravel, and dirt
Trailhead elevation: 974 feet
Highest point: 1,059 feet
Best seasons: Spring for wildflowers, late fall and winter for cooler temperatures (summer and early fall can be very hot)
Maps: USGS North Chalone Peak; Pinnacles National Park map; Tom Harrison map of Pinnacles National Park
Nearest town: Hollister
Trail contact: Pinnacles National Park, 5000 CA 146, Paicines, CA 95043-9770; (831) 389-4485 or (831) 389-4427; www.nps.gov/pinn
Trail tips: There are picnic tables, a drinking fountain, a portable toilet, and trash and recycling receptacles in the Peaks View Day Use Area. There is a portable toilet and a trash and recycling receptacle but no water or picnic tables at the Old Pinnacles trailhead parking lot. If you wish to make this hike into a loop, you can walk back to the trailhead at Peaks View Day Use Area along the paved road. There is no pedestrian path, but the park traffic on this dead-end segment of road to the Old Pinnacles trailhead is light. Chalone Creek is on your right going back if you walk on the paved road.

Finding the trailhead: From US 101 at San Juan Bautista/Hollister exit 345 (approximately 17 miles north of Salinas and 10 miles south of Gilroy), take exit 345 and drive 7.5 miles to the Hollister turnoff on the right. Drive 3.5 miles and turn right onto CA 25. Drive 28 miles on CA 25 to the Pinnacles National Park entrance. Turn right into the park and drive 2 miles to the Visitor Center to pay the entrance fee and pick up a map and information. The visitor center is on your left. Return to the main park road and drive 1.3 more miles to the Peaks View Day Use parking lot. GPS: N36 28.97' / W121 09.72'.

From US 101 at King City, take exit 282B/Broadway Street and turn right onto Broadway Street. Drive 1 mile on Broadway Street to the T intersection with First Street. Turn left onto First Street and drive 14 miles to the T intersection with CA 25. (First Street becomes Bitterwater Road at the sign for East Pinnacles.) Turn left onto CA 25 to Pinnacles and drive 14 miles to the CA 146 intersection. Turn left into Pinnacles National Park and follow directions above to the trailhead.

Peaks View Day Use Area to Old Pinnacles Trailhead

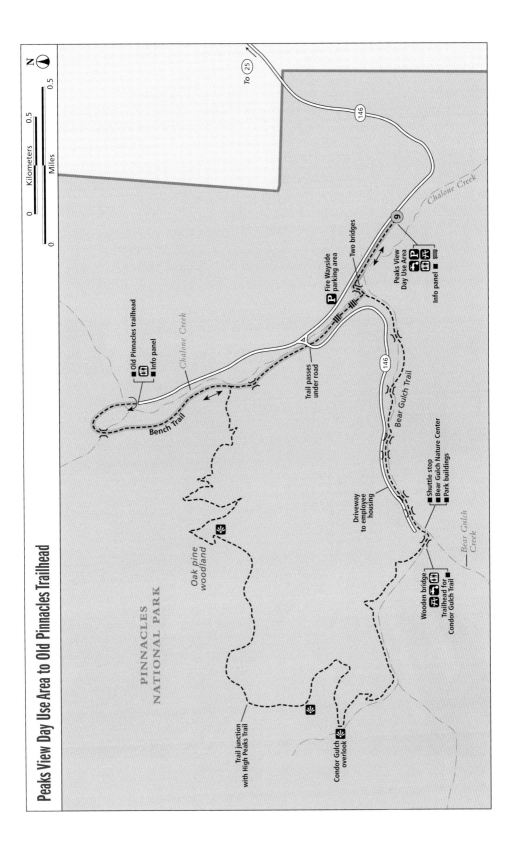

PINNACLES
NATIONAL PARK

Oak pine
woodland

Bench Trail

Chalone Creek

■ Old Pinnacles trailhead
🚻 Info panel

Trail passes
under road

P Fire Wayside
parking area

Two bridges

9

Chalone Creek

P Peaks View
Day Use Area
■ Info panel

146

To 25

146

Bear Gulch Trail

Driveway
to employee
housing

■ Shuttle stop
■ Bear Gulch Nature Center
■ Park buildings

Wooden bridge
■ Trailhead for
Condor Gulch Trail

Bear Gulch
Creek

Trail junction
with High Peaks Trail

Condor Gulch
overlook

N

Kilometers
0   0.5

Miles
0   0.5

The Hike

Peaks View Day Use Area welcomes you with a strategically located bench to absorb the view of the High Peaks on the horizon and an educational panel about the relationship between condors and the Pinnacles. This is a perfect spot for admiring the unique ancient geological formation where condors nest and roost once again before starting your hike.

The Bench Trail is named for the way the trail was cut to trace the banks of the seasonal Chalone Creek and its wide and typically dry creekbed, and not for the "bench" at Peaks View. From the entrance to Peak's View Day Use Area, head north on Bench Trail with the creek on your left.

Just 0.3 mile up the trail you come to a trail junction. An unmarked spur trail continues straight to an overflow parking area; the unmarked Bench Trail goes left and crosses a double wooden footbridge over Chalone Creek toward Bear Gulch and

One of two boardwalks on the Bench Trail above Chalone Creek

the Old Pinnacles Trail. Just across the two wooden footbridges you come to a trail junction where the unmarked Bench Trail turns right, paralleling Chalone Creek on the west side. Shortly thereafter you walk across two boardwalks on a short eroded stretch of the trail before walking under the road overpass and across a wooden footbridge at 0.85 mile.

At 0.95 mile you walk past the trail junction for High Peaks on the left. Continue walking on the Bench Trail for another 0.5 mile and cross a wooden footbridge back to the east side of Chalone Creek. Come to a trail junction with Old Pinnacles Trail. Bench Trail ends at this junction. Before you bear right to Old Pinnacles trailhead, notice an information board straight ahead, approximately 75 feet from the trail junction. This is an information panel about the Chalone Creek Restoration. Take a minute to detour to the panel before continuing to the Old Pinnacles trailhead.

The last 0.2 mile from the trail junction to the Old Pinnacles trailhead leaves the bank of the creekbed for a coarse sand path through arid chaparral vegetation. At 1.65 miles the trail ends at the Old Pinnacles trailhead parking lot. (GPS: N36 29.70'/ W121 10.38'. Elevation: 1,059 feet.) Although there is no water here, nor were there picnic tables at the time of publication, there is the convenience of a portable toilet. There are several large rocks perfect for sitting and taking time for a water and snack break before going back to the trailhead the way you came.

Miles and Directions

0.0   Start at Peaks View Day Use Area and walk north on Bench Trail.

0.3   Come to a trail junction for Bear Gulch Day Use Area and Old Pinnacles Trail going left and an unmarked spur to an overflow parking area straight ahead. Turn left and walk across the double wooden footbridges. Shortly come to the trail junction for Bear Gulch Trail straight and Old Pinnacles Trail right. Turn right to continue on Bench Trail toward Old Pinnacles Trail. Chalone Creek is on the right.

0.4   Walk on two closely spaced boardwalks along the eroded bank of the creek.

0.65 The trail continues under a road overpass.

0.85 Walk across the wooden footbridge.

0.95 Come to the trail junction for High Peaks Trail on the left. Continue walking north on Bench Trail.

1.45 Walk across the wooden footbridge to the east bank of Chalone Creek and the trail junction. Bench Trail ends at this junction with Old Pinnacles Trail. Bear right and walk to Old Pinnacles trailhead.

1.65 Arrive at Old Pinnacles trailhead and the parking lot. Go back the way you came.

3.3   Arrive back at the trailhead in Peaks View Day Use Area.

10 Fire Wayside Parking Area to High Peaks

This strenuous hike touches two of Pinnacles contrasting worlds—panoramic, lofty view trails from starkly beautiful volcanic spires and towers and the poetic beauty of the lush Bear Gulch and its six wooden footbridges across the seasonal Bear Gulch Creek. Adventuresome hikers will appreciate the exhilaratingly challenging, up-and-down, narrow stretch of chiseled rock steps across the High Peaks and welcome the enchanting downhill finale along seasonal Bear Gulch Creek's riparian habitat.

Start: From the Fire Wayside parking area 0.3 mile past Peaks View Day Use Area
Distance: 7.25-mile lollipop
Hiking time: 5 hours
Difficulty: Strenuous
Trail surface: Dirt and rock
Trailhead elevation: 989 feet
Highest point: 2,598 feet
Best seasons: Spring for wildflowers, late fall and winter for cooler temperatures (summer and early fall can be very hot)

Maps: USGS North Chalone Peak; Pinnacles National Park map; Tom Harrison map of Pinnacles National Park
Nearest town: Hollister
Trail contact: Pinnacles National Park, 5000 CA 146, Paicines, CA 95043-9770; (831) 389-4485 or (831) 389-4427; www.nps.gov/pinn
Trail tips: There is no water at this trailhead or anywhere along the way to the viewpoint. The closest water and restroom is the drinking fountain and portable toilet in the Peaks View Day Use Area 0.3 mile back.

Finding the trailhead: From US 101 at San Juan Bautista/Hollister exit 345 (approximately 17 miles north of Salinas and 10 miles south of Gilroy), take exit 345 and drive 7.5 miles to the Hollister turnoff on the right. Drive 3.5 miles and turn right onto CA 25. Drive 28 miles on CA 25 to the Pinnacles National Park entrance. Turn right into the park and drive 2 miles to the visitor center to pay the entrance fee and pick up a map and information. The visitor center is on your left. Return to the main park road and drive 1.6 more miles to the unmarked Fire Wayside parking lot 0.3 mile past Peaks View Day Use Area. The ten-space parking lot is on the right-hand side of the road, and the trailhead is across the road at the Fire in the Chaparral information board. GPS: N36 29.13' / W121 10.03'.

From US 101 at King City, take exit 282B/Broadway Street and turn right onto Broadway Street. Drive 1 mile on Broadway Street to the T intersection with First Street. Turn left onto First Street and drive 14 miles to the T intersection with CA 25. (First Street becomes Bitterwater Road at the sign for East Pinnacles.) Turn left onto CA 25 to Pinnacles and drive 14 miles to the CA 146 intersection. Turn left into Pinnacles National Park and follow directions above to the trailhead.

The Hike

Beginning in a quiet corner of the park less than 2 miles past the visitor center and campground, you start your hike with a short walk to the double wooden footbridges where the unmarked Bench Trail crosses the seasonal Chalone Creek. At the trail junction for Bear Gulch Day Use Area, turn right to continue along the Bench Trail, paralleling the west bank of Chalone Creek. Don't expect to find any "bench" seats along the trail. The trail's name simply describes its location on the banks, or "bench," above the creek. Shortly thereafter you walk across two boardwalks on a short eroded stretch of the trail before walking under the road overpass and across a wooden footbridge about half a mile from the trailhead.

At 0.7 mile you come to the trail junction for High Peaks. Turn left toward the High Peaks. This is where the hate/love relationship between you and this hike begins as you begin an arduous, exposed, 2-mile climb tempered by switchbacks and rewarded by expansive views. At 1.5 miles you'll catch a little shade and breeze and walk past a Sphinx-like rock on the left. Finally the trail relents and the landscape softens unexpectedly, morphing from arid chaparral to a pine and oak woodland in a grassy vale. You come to a natural viewpoint on the left looking east toward Bear Gulch below and north toward a stadium of mountain ranges. The view of a razorback ridge reminds you that the park's volcanic past is ever present. Just a short walk ahead you'll catch a glimpse of the fire tower on North Chalone Peak to the left and a hint of the High Peaks. At 2.5 miles the views open to the southwest for a better view of the fire tower, the Pinnacles, and across to the Condor Gulch Trail before your trail veers north around a knoll and back to a saddle. The High Peaks and fire tower are to your left and a wall of vertical volcanic ridges are on the right as you approach the trail junction for the unmarked Condor Gulch Trail going left to Bear Gulch Day Use Area. Continue walking straight up on High Peaks Trail, which transitions from dirt to more of an uneven terraced rock trail. At 3.0 miles the Balconies Cliffs, where prairie falcons nest, come into view across the canyon on the left, and The Citadel rock formation crowns the foreground.

You pass two climber access trails on the right and a stunning view of the Balconies Cliffs as the trail threads along a corridor of volcanic towers to the west side's soaring views and sheer rock walls.

At 3.3 miles you come to the trail junction for Tunnel Trail going right. Continue walking straight on High Peaks Trail. In the morning after a spring rain, sunlight hitting the moss-covered boulders highlights the green with an almost radioactive glow as you come to the first of several sets of steep and narrow stone-chiseled staircases and footholds with metal pipe handrails along rock faces. The raw engineering of this stretch of trail is a feat of skill and sheer determination. The trail will crest at a wider slab within 0.5 mile. This is a great place to spot condors, enjoy a snack, and breathe in the awesome views before continuing down toward the saddle that straddles the East and West Pinnacles. At 4.0 miles you come to the wooden bench beneath Scout Peak and the trail junction for Juniper Canyon going down to the west side on the right. Continue on High Peaks Trail past the bench and bear left. There is a small stone building with two vault toilets just past the bench and to the right. There is no water at Scout Peak.

As you begin the descent back along the east side's volcanic flank, you may get a brief glimpse of a long patch of water in the distance. That's the reservoir off the Rim

Trail crosses Chalone Creek on two wooden footbridges.

Trail farther down off High Peaks Trail. The arched rock tunnel carved by the 1930s Civilian Conservation Corps is the next highlight as you make the gradual sweep back down to Bear Gulch, passing an anvil-shaped rock and a climber access on the right before reaching the Rim Trail junction at 5.5 miles. Bear left at the junction and continue walking down High Peaks Trail toward Bear Gulch Day Use Area, passing a climber access on the right and the climber access to the top of Tourist Trap on the left just before the junction for Moses Spring Trail on the right at 5.8 miles. High Peaks Trail ends at this junction. Bear left and continue walking downhill to the Moses Spring trailhead. Cross the road through the picnic area and walk across a wooden footbridge. There is a restroom on the left and a drinking fountain on the right. The picnic tables in this parking area are a good place to refuel with a snack and water before crossing the road at the crosswalk to pick up your trail on the left at the sign for Peaks View Day Use Area. If the seasonally open Bear Gulch Nature Center across the road is open, don't miss a chance to visit before heading down the trail along Bear Gulch Creek toward Peak's View.

Fire Wayside Parking Area to High Peaks

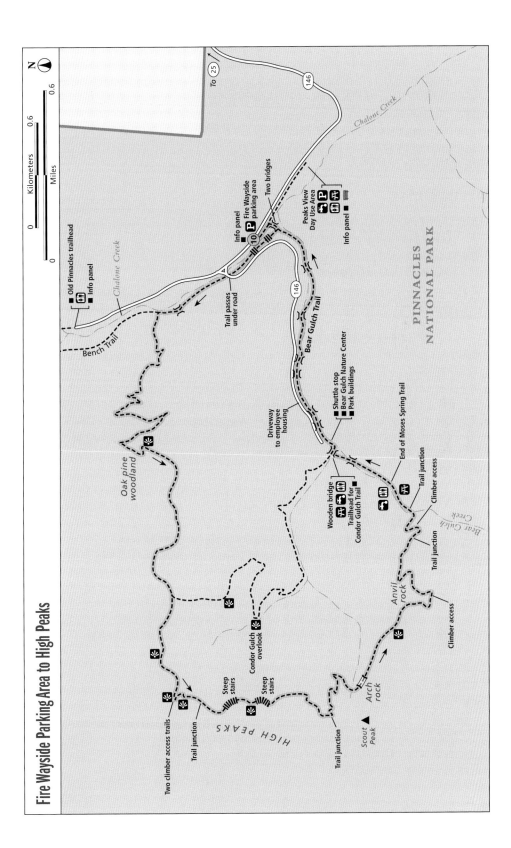

This last mile of trail is one of the sweetest sections of your hike as you cross six wooden footbridges over seasonal Bear Gulch Creek. Even in drier conditions without cascades draping the boulders or a waterfall, the gulch is cool, shady, and alive with ferns and clump grass–like sedges.

At 7.15 miles you come to the trail junction for the unmarked Bench Trail. This closes your lollipop. Continue straight across the double wooden footbridges to go back to the trailhead at the overflow parking lot the way you came.

Miles and Directions

0.0 Start at the unmarked trailhead and information panel and Fire interpretation panel across from the overflow parking lot. Turn left.

0.05 Come to the trail junction and turn right to cross the seasonal Chalone Creek on the double wooden footbridges.

0.1 Come to the trail junction for Bear Gulch Day Use Area and the unmarked Bench Trail. Turn right toward Old Pinnacles Trail on the unmarked Bench Trail. Your lollipop will close here when you come down Bear Gulch. Immediately walk over two closely spaced boardwalks along the eroded bank of the creek.

0.6 Walk across the wooden footbridge, then come to the trail junction for High Peaks Trail and turn left.

2.7 Come to the trail junction for unmarked Condor Gulch on the left. Continue walking straight up to High Peaks. The trail will crest and open north across to Balconies Cliffs.

3.2 Come to two climber access trails on the right, then emerge on the west side of a narrow corridor of sculpted rock formations to the junction for Tunnel Trail. Continue walking on High Peaks Trail and up narrow stone steps to the crest.

3.7 Start down the steep stone steps to the saddle beneath Scout Peak and trail junction for Juniper Canyon. Bear left and walk downhill on the east side of the Pinnacles.

4.5 Walk through the rock tunnel. View of North Chalone Peak fire tower will come into view to the south just ahead.

5.0 Come to the anvil-shaped rock on the left and a climber access on the right.

5.5 Come to the trail junction for Rim Trail. Bear left down to Bear Gulch Day Use Area, passing a climber access on the right. Continue walking downhill past Tourist Trap climber access on the left and continue walking downhill past the trail junction for Moses Spring Trail.

5.9 Come to the Moses Spring trailhead. Walk across the road and follow the hiker trail across the wooden footbridge to Bear Gulch Day Use Area. Walk across the road in the crosswalk and turn left to the trailhead and sign for Peaks View Day Use Area with seasonal Bear Gulch on your left.

6.25 Walk across two wooden footbridges in quick succession.

6.35 Walk across the driveway at the employee residence.

6.5 Walk across a wooden footbridge. You will cross three more bridges in the next 0.5 mile.

7.15 Come to the trail junction for the unmarked Bench Trail. Bear Gulch Trail ends here. This is the close of your lollipop. Continue straight across the double wooden footbridge and go back to the trailhead the way you came.

7.25 Arrive back at the trailhead.

11 Old Pinnacles Trail to Balconies Cave

This is the easiest route to the Balconies Cave from the park's east side as it is a mostly level trail with a moderate climb on the return lollipop along Balconies Cliff. The trail begins in the open, paralleling the wide Chalone Creek before veering into a shadier corridor with multiple seasonal West Fork Chalone Creek crossings. The short but dramatic passage through the talus cave requires a flashlight, careful footwork, and some limberness.

Start: From Old Pinnacles trailhead
Distance: 5.2-mile lollipop
Hiking time: 3 hours
Difficulty: Moderate
Trail surface: Coarse sand, gravel, and rock in the cave
Trailhead elevation: 1,059 feet
Highest point: 1,470 feet
Best seasons: Spring for wildflowers, late fall and winter for cooler temperatures (summer and early fall can be very hot); cool in the cave
Maps: USGS North Chalone Peak; Pinnacles National Park map; Tom Harrison map of Pinnacles National Park
Nearest town: Hollister

Trail contact: Pinnacles National Park, 5000 CA 146, Paicines, CA 95043-9770; (831) 389-4485 or (831) 389-4427; www.nps.gov/pinn
Trail tips: There is no water at this trailhead. You will find a portable toilet and trash receptacle in the parking lot. Be aware that the Balconies Cave can be closed after heavy rains in the winter and spring season, so it is best to check with the ranger station about the status of the cave before setting out. The cave section of the trail is more difficult when the rocks are wet. Be prepared to get your feet wet or carry sandals for the 7 West Fork Chalone Creek crossings if you are hiking during a normal to heavy rainfall year in the winter or spring.

Finding the trailhead: From US 101 at San Juan Bautista/Hollister exit 345 (approximately 17 miles north of Salinas and 10 miles south of Gilroy), take exit 345 and drive 7.5 miles to the Hollister turnoff on the right. Drive 3.5 miles and turn right onto CA 25. Drive 28 miles on CA 25 to the Pinnacles National Park entrance. Turn right into the park and drive 2 miles to the visitor center to pay the entrance fee and pick up a map and information. The visitor center is on your left. Return to the main park road and follow the signs for the Old Pinnacles trailhead. Drive 2 miles and turn right just before the bridge at the sign for Old Pinnacles. Drive 0.5 mile to the trailhead parking lot at the end of the road. GPS: N36 29.70' / W121 10.38'.

From US 101 at King City take exit 282B/Broadway Street and turn right onto Broadway Street. Drive 1 mile on Broadway Street to the T intersection with First Street. Turn left onto First Street and drive 14 miles to the T intersection with CA 25. (First Street becomes Bitterwater Road at the sign for East Pinnacles.) Turn left onto CA 25 to Pinnacles and drive 14 miles to the CA 146 intersection. Turn left into Pinnacles National Park and follow directions above to the trailhead.

The Hike

The trailhead is in the Old Pinnacles Trail parking lot at the end of the road. From here the gravel and coarse sand trail follows the wide and seasonal Chalone Creek on the left. The trail veers right toward the Balconies Cave at the junction for High Peaks Trail and Bench Trail going left. Just ahead on the left side of the trail is an information panel about the Chalone Creek Restoration.

At about 0.5 mile you cross a narrower section of the creekbed on a wooden footbridge. The next junction is just 0.2 mile ahead on the right for the North Wilderness Trail. Bear left and continue walking on the Old Pinnacles Trail toward Balconies Cave. This junction is also where the West Fork Chalone Creek and North Fork Chalone Creek on your right meet to pour into Chalone Creek. In drier winters like the drought of 2014, you may see ribbons of water, but don't expect a vigorous flow to fill that wide creekbed.

From here you cross the seasonal West Fork Chalone Creek seven times as it zigzags across this shady, leafy corridor before you come to the trail junction for the Balconies Cliffs Trail on your right. Bear left to continue to the Balconies Cave entrance just ahead. The trail narrows and becomes more primitive as you navigate rock steps and slither your way between and over boulders into the talus cave-like tunnel. Some of the giant boulders that create this tunnel-like passage look like they are levitating above you. Turn your flashlight or headlight on and proceed slowly and cautiously through the short but dark maze, keeping your eye on the painted white arrows. The exit is a climb out of the cave to the light.

When you exit the cave, you are now technically on the west side of the park. You quickly come to the trail junction for Balconies Cliffs Trail on the right, which is your route back over the caves and above the canyon back to the east side of the park.

The trail switches back and forth, passing the Tilting Terrace climber access trail on the left and another climber access ahead up stone steps on the left.

At 2.7 miles the trail levels, and views open toward looming Machete Ridge in the foreground and the High Peaks in the background to the right. As the name indicates, the Balconies Cliffs Trail traces the base of the Balconies Cliffs, giving hikers a unique vantage point to admire the canyon walls where prairie falcons and other raptors nest.

A little farther ahead you may see wooden railroad tie steps up a slope on the left. They look inviting, but the sign indicates that this area is closed to hikers and climbers because of raptor habitat.

The trail gradually drops back down to the canyon floor at the junction for the Balconies Cave. This is where you close the lollipop. Turn left to go back to the Old Pinnacles trailhead the way you came.

Old Pinnacles Trail to Balconies Cave

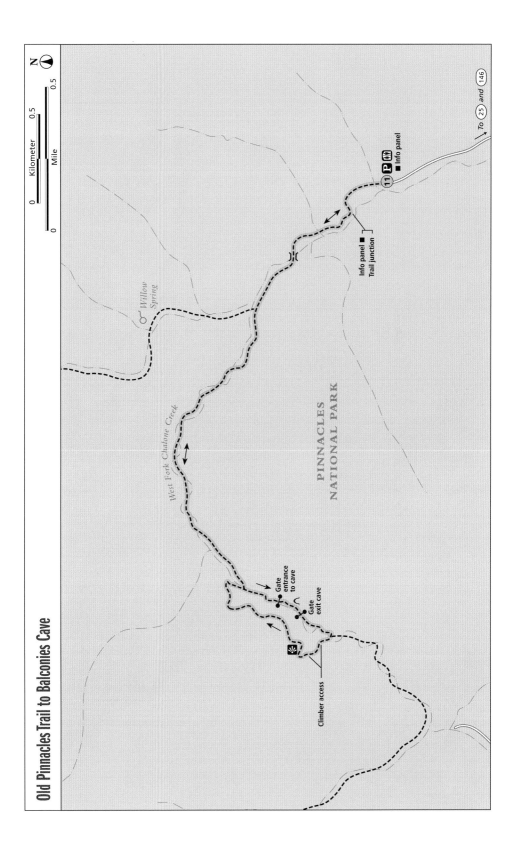

Miles and Directions

0.0 Start at the Old Pinnacles trailhead. Chalone Creek is on the left. The trail junction for High Peaks Trail and Bench Trail is just ahead on the left. Turn right at the trail junction and continue walking toward Balconies Cave via the Old Pinnacles Trail. The Chalone Creek Restoration information board is just ahead on the left.

0.5 Walk across the wooden footbridge and bear left at the trail junction for North Wilderness Trail to continue walking on the Old Pinnacles Trail to Balconies Cave.

1.0 Step across the seasonal West Fork Chalone Creek. You will cross the creek five more times in the next 0.7 mile.

2.0 Step across the creek once more and come to the trail junction for the Balconies Cliffs Trail on the right. Continue walking straight toward the Balconies Cave entrance.

2.2 Come to the gate entrance to Balconies Cave. You exit Balconies Cave in 0.1 mile, then cross West Fork Chalone Creek again.

2.4 Come to the trail junction for the Balconies Cliffs Trail and turn right.

2.5 Arrive at the climber access trail for Tilting Terrace on the left, then come to stone steps on the left and another climber access.

2.7 Viewpoint toward Machete Ridge to the left and High Peaks to the right in the background.

3.2 Come to the trail junction for Balconies Cave to the right. This is the close of your lollipop. Turn left onto Old Pinnacles Trail and go back to the trailhead the way you came.

5.2 Arrive back at the trailhead.

Gated entrance to Balconies Cave—flashlight needed

12 Old Pinnacles Trail to Balconies Cave via North Wilderness Trail

This is a longer and less traveled route to the phenomenal tunnel of stacked giant boulders that forms the Balconies Cave. The mostly level but more primitive trail on the park's east side takes you along and in the North Fork Chalone creekbed in the North Wilderness of Pinnacles National Park before climbing up to a scenic ridge on the west side. Your lollipop route continues through the Balconies Cave to emerge back on the east side. The hike combines the solitude of the North Wilderness with the excitement of the talus cave passage. This hike requires a flashlight or a headlight for the cave.

Start: From Old Pinnacles trailhead
Distance: 10.7-mile lollipop
Hiking time: 5.5 hours
Difficulty: Strenuous
Trail surface: Coarse sand, gravel, and rock in the cave
Trailhead elevation: 1,059 feet
Highest point: 2,116 feet
Best seasons: Spring for wildflowers, late fall and winter for cooler temperatures (summer and early fall can be very hot); cool in the cave
Maps: USGS North Chalone Peak; Pinnacles National Park map; Tom Harrison map of Pinnacles National Park
Nearest town: Hollister
Trail contact: Pinnacles National Park, 5000 CA 146, Paicines, CA 95043-9770; (831) 389-4485 or (831) 389-4427; www.nps.gov/pinn

Trail tips: The North Wilderness Trail is a more primitive trail and requires that you keep an eye out for the cairns guiding you as you crisscross the North Fork Chalone creekbed for the first 4 miles. You need a flashlight or headlight for the cave. Check with the ranger station to confirm that the Balconies Cave is open, as it may be closed in the winter and spring following a heavy rain. If you find that the Balconies Cave is closed when you get there or if you wish to do this hike but are uncomfortable in a cave, you can bypass the cave by hiking back to the trailhead along the Balconies Cliff Trail, which adds 0.4 mile to this hike.

Finding the trailhead: From US 101 at San Juan Bautista/Hollister exit 345 (approximately 17 miles north of Salinas and 10 miles south of Gilroy), take exit 345 and drive 7.5 miles to the Hollister turnoff on the right. Drive 3.5 miles and turn right onto CA 25. Drive 28 miles on CA 25 to the Pinnacles National Park entrance. Turn right into the park and drive 2 miles to the visitor center to pay the entrance fee and pick up a map and information. The visitor center is on your left. Return to the main park road and follow the signs for the Old Pinnacles trailhead. Drive 2 miles and turn right just before the bridge at the sign for Old Pinnacles. Drive 0.5 mile to the trailhead parking lot at the end of the road. GPS: N36 29.70' / W121 10.38'.

From US 101 at King City take exit 282B/Broadway Street and turn right onto Broadway Street. Drive 1 mile on Broadway Street to the T intersection with First Street. Turn left onto First Street and drive 14 miles to the T intersection with CA 25. (First Street becomes Bitterwater Road at the sign for East Pinnacles.) Turn left onto CA 25 to Pinnacles and drive 14 miles to the CA 146 intersection. Turn left into Pinnacles National Park and follow directions above to the trailhead.

The Hike

The trailhead is in the Old Pinnacles Trail parking lot at the end of the road. From here the gravel and coarse sand trail follows the wide and seasonal Chalone Creek on the left. The trail veers right toward the Balconies Cave at the junction for High Peaks Trail and Bench Trail going left. Just ahead on the left side of the trail is an information panel about the Chalone Creek Restoration.

At about 0.5 mile you cross a narrower section of the creekbed on a wooden footbridge. The next junction is just 0.2 mile ahead on the right for the North Wilderness Trail. Turn right onto this trail. In the spring you may have the privilege of seeing nature's workshop with the wide variety of bees busy pollinating wildflowers along the trail. You will be lacing across the north and south banks of the seasonal North Fork Chalone Creek for the next 4 miles, sometimes walking in the wide and typically dry creekbed. The vegetation varies from mostly chaparral-covered hillsides, but Willow Spring, between 0.9 mile and 1.2 miles, feeds a stretch of riparian oasis. Following a moderately wet winter and spring, this trail blooms with violet bush lupine and brilliant orange California poppies, the state flower.

A couple of miles up the creek, the trail veers away from the main channel and enters a pine and oak woodland that turns into a burgeoning meadow after a nourishing wet winter. The trail is primitive, especially in the creekbed, but it is well worn, with cairns visibly stacked at potentially tricky locations.

At 4.3 miles the trail crosses back to the north bank toward a rock outcrop, and after a few more zigzags in the creekbed, you come to the final crossing of North Fork Chalone Creek. Pick up the trail on the other side and begin your climb to the ridge. The initial climb is stiff but brief, and the next mile of trail is mostly a gradual ascent out of a grassy. tree-lined ravine interrupted by a few more steep sprints until you reach the ridge. Here views open up to the west side from the northern end of the volcanic Pinnacles. This ravine is a veritable pink shooting star alley in the late spring after an average winter rainfall.

The trail marker at 5.1 miles will reassure you that you are still on the North Wilderness Trail. Less than 0.5 mile of hoofing and huffing and the trail emerges closer to the ridge at another marker for the North Wilderness Trail, which directs you to a sharp left. Shortly after the turn the views open southward to the High Peaks and the North Chalone Peak fire tower just short of the ridgeline's summit-uplifting viewpoint.

At 6.0 miles you come to another stunning viewpoint. Walk about 50 feet left off the trail in the chamise clearing and imagine a moonrise over the pinnacles. The pinnacles and the fire tower on North Chalone Peak stay in view all the way down to the trailhead, only occasionally disappearing behind a curtain of tall chamise. Some vantage points in the late afternoon light make it feel like you could reach out and touch the High Peaks. Savor this last 0.5 mile of leveling terrain where the breeze tickling the pines on the nearby ridges is the only background sound as you approach the Chaparral Picnic Area. The North Wilderness Trail ends at 7.5 miles in the Chaparral

Start of the North Wilderness Trail into a more primitive landscape

Picnic Area, an ideal place for a picnic. There are restrooms, a water fountain, and trash and recycling receptacles in this day-use area.

At 7.6 miles, still in the picnic area, turn left at the trailhead on your left toward Balconies Cave. Follow the wooden rail fence corridor. Just ahead you cross a wooden footbridge over seasonal West Fork Chalone Creek and come to a trail junction for Juniper Canyon Trail to the right and the interpretive sign for Juniper Canyon. Continue walking straight toward Balconies Cave. At 7.9 miles walk across another wooden footbridge over West Fork Chalone Creek. Just across the footbridge is a junction for a climber access trail to Elephant Rock and The Citadel. Bear left to continue to Balconies Cave. A gargantuan boulder arch is your portal into the canyon to the cave. You will walk across West Fork Chalone Creek on three more wooden footbridges before you reach the junction for the Balconies Cliffs Trail on the left. Bear right and continue to the cave entrance through a rock wall portal leading to the open metal gate (unless it is closed and locked because of flooding). You will need your flashlight or a headlamp to walk through to the other side of the cave. Note that coming into the cave from the west side and exiting on the east side requires you climb down to get through the talus cave-like boulder tunnel. The cave route is short but involves some crawling, sideways slithering, and hand-over-hand up and down. The colossal maze is nothing short of awesome.

You exit back in the canyon and continue on the trail to a junction where the Balconies Cliffs Trail merges into the unmarked Old Pinnacles Trail from the left. Bear right following signs for Pinnacles Campground 3.7 and Pinnacles Visitor Center 4.1. Although it is not marked as such, you are now on the Old Pinnacles Trail. The trail crosses West Fork Chalone Creek several times until you come to the junction with

Old Pinnacles Trail to Balconies Cave via North Wilderness Trail

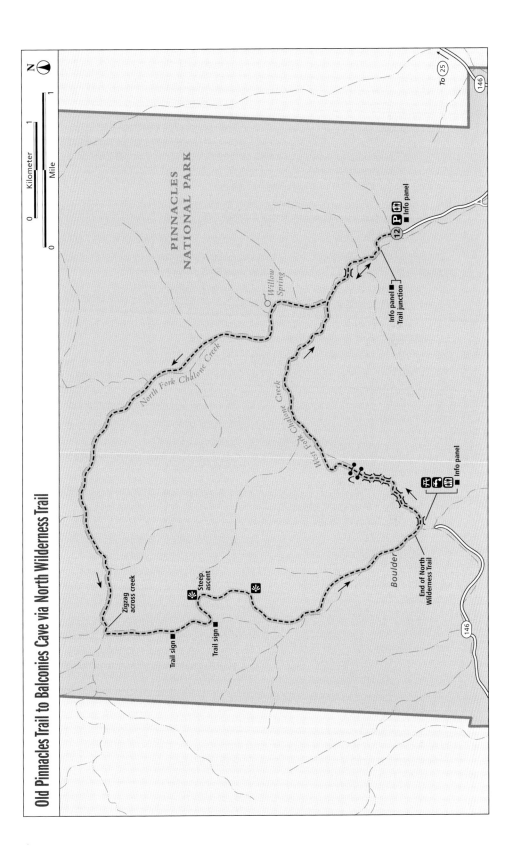

the North Wilderness Trail on your left at 10.0 miles. This is the close of your lollipop. From this junction continue walking straight back to the trailhead the way you came.

Miles and Directions

0.0   Start at the Old Pinnacles trailhead. Chalone Creek is on the left. The trail junction for High Peaks Trail and Bench Trail is just ahead on the left. Turn right at the trail junction and continue walking toward Balconies Cave via the Old Pinnacles Trail. The Chalone Creek Restoration information panel is just ahead on the left.

0.5   Walk across the wooden footbridge and turn right on the North Wilderness Trail. Prepare to lace the banks of seasonal North Fork Chalone Creek. Keep an eye out for the cairns.

0.9   Cross the outflow of Willow Spring, then shortly cross three trickling veins of Willow Spring.

4.3   Cross North Fork Chalone Creek to the north bank past a large rock outcrop and continue zigzagging in the creekbed. The cairns guide your path.

4.5   Cross North Fork Chalone Creek. Shortly come to the final North Fork Chalone Creek crossing and begin the climb up the swale to the ridge.

5.1   Come to a trail marker confirming you are on the North Wilderness Trail. In 0.3 mile arrive at another trail marker for the North Wilderness Trail. Turn left.

5.6   Come to a 360-degree viewpoint at the summit of the ridgeline. The High Peaks and the North Chalone Peak fire tower are prominent to the south, and the eastern views open across the Gabilan Range.

6.0   Come to another viewpoint and walk 50 feet left off the trail in the chamise clearing for a stunning view of the High Peaks. Begin the descent off the ridge.

7.3   Walk across an unnamed seasonal creek at the boulder.

7.5   Come to the end of North Wilderness Trail in the Chaparral Picnic Area, then turn left at the trailhead for Balconies Cave.

7.7   Walk across West Fork Chalone Creek on a wooden footbridge and come to a trail junction on the right and a map board and interpretive sign on the left for Balconies Cave and Juniper Canyon. Bear left toward Balconies Cave.

7.9   Come to West Fork Chalone Creek and walk across the footbridge. Shortly cross another footbridge to the trail junction and a sign on the right for the climber access trail to Elephant Rock and The Citadel. Bear left and walk under the gargantuan boulder arch toward Balconies Cave. You will cross two more footbridges in quick succession over West Fork Chalone Creek.

8.3   Come to Machete Ridge and a climber access on the right and a footbridge across West Fork Chalone Creek. Walk across the footbridge to the trail junction for Balconies Cliffs Trail and Balconies Cave. Turn right to Balconies Cave and immediately walk across the creek to enter Balconies Cave through the gate. Turn on your flashlight or headlamp to continue into the cave. You exit Balconies Cave through the gate in 0.1 mile.

8.7   Come to the trail junction for Balconies Cliffs Trail to the left. Bear right on unmarked Old Pinnacles Trail and walk across West Fork Chalone Creek. You will cross the creek six more times in the next mile.

10.0 Come to the trail junction with North Wilderness Trail on the left. This is the close of your lollipop. Continue walking back to the trailhead the way you came.

10.7 Arrive back at the trailhead.

13 Condor Gulch Trail to Overlook

This trail is exposed, with a mile-long uphill huff and puff that rewards with views and a seasonal creek that drapes over the rocks at the overlook. The hike makes for a pleasant picnic destination on late spring afternoons.

Start: From Condor Gulch trailhead
Distance: 2.0 miles out and back
Hiking time: 1 hour
Difficulty: Moderate
Trail surface: Dirt
Trailhead elevation: 1,279 feet
Highest point: 1,812 feet
Best seasons: Spring for wildflowers, late fall and winter for cooler temperatures (summer and early fall can be very hot)
Maps: USGS North Chalone Peak; Pinnacles National Park map; Tom Harrison map of Pinnacles National Park

Nearest town: Hollister
Trail contact: Pinnacles National Park, 5000 CA 146, Paicines, CA 95043-9770; (831) 389-4485 or (831) 389-4427; www.nps.gov/pinn
Trail tips: There is water, restrooms, picnic tables, and trash and recycling containers left of the trailhead in the Bear Gulch Day Use Area. The Bear Gulch Nature Center is open seasonally. Although summers are hot, this hike is a pleasant destination for a picnic at dusk or spotting a full moonrise.

Finding the trailhead: From US 101 at San Juan Bautista/Hollister exit 345 (approximately 17 miles north of Salinas and 10 miles south of Gilroy), take exit 345 and drive 7.5 miles to the Hollister turnoff on the right. Drive 3.5 miles and turn right onto CA 25. Drive 28 miles on CA 25 to the Pinnacles National Park entrance. Turn right into the park and drive 2 miles to the visitor center to pay the entrance fee and pick up a map and information. The visitor center is on your left. Return to the main park road and drive 3 more miles to the Bear Gulch Day Use Area parking lot. Walk across the road in the crosswalk to the bench and the Condor Gulch trailhead. GPS: N36 28.88' / W121 10.89'.

From US 101 at King City, take exit 282B/Broadway Street and turn right onto Broadway Street. Drive 1 mile on Broadway Street to the T intersection with First Street. Turn left onto First Street and drive 14 miles to the T intersection with CA 25. (First Street becomes Bitterwater Road at the sign for East Pinnacles.) Turn left onto CA 25 to Pinnacles and drive 14 miles to the CA 146 intersection. Turn left into Pinnacles National Park and follow directions above to the trailhead.

The Hike

Bear Gulch Day Use Area is somewhat of an oasis of seasonal creeks and leafy canopies amid the stark volcanic palisades and chaparral-covered mountain ranges. Condor Gulch Overlook, at the head of the gulch above the Bear Gulch area, offers a scenic vantage point from which to admire the contrast between the backdrop of volcanic walls and spires and the mountainous chaparral foreground, with Bear Gulch's lusher transition zone bridging the two realms.

Condor Gulch Trail to Overlook

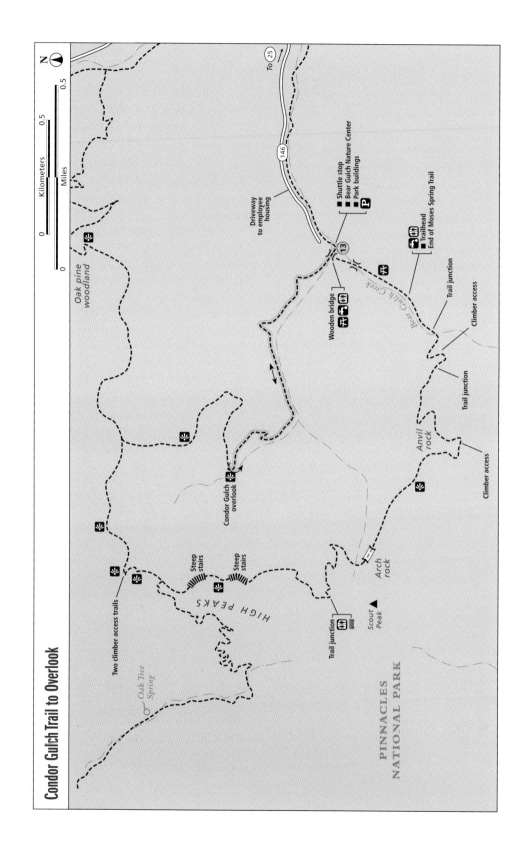

Oak pine woodland

Two climber access trails

Oak Tree Spring

HIGH PEAKS

Steep stairs

Steep stairs

Condor Gulch overlook

Trail junction

Scout Peak

Arch rock

Anvil rock

Climber access

Trail junction

Trail junction

Climber access

Bear Gulch Creek

Trailhead
End of Moses Spring Trail

PINNACLES NATIONAL PARK

Wooden bridge

Driveway to employee housing

Shuttle stop
Bear Gulch Nature Center
Park buildings

13

146

To 25

N

Kilometers

0   0.5

Miles

0   0.5

View down Condor Gulch from the overlook

This short hike wastes no time getting your heart pumping with a relentless uphill made moderate by four switchbacks. The trail quickly leaves the shade of trees behind as it climbs up the eastern slope of Condor Gulch. The park's idyllic stone buildings on the left at the bottom of the gulch and the surreal volcanic rock sentry looming above both create a pleasant distraction as you march up the trail. You turn on the first of four switchbacks at 0.8 mile. This is a good spot to catch your breath and have a drink of water. Three more huff and puff switchbacks and the Overlook sign appears on the left. From the edge of the overlook corralled by a metal pipe handrail, you have an up-close and personal view of the east face of the Pinnacles. In the winter and spring, a seasonal creek carves a path from the lush green base of the High Peaks down the gulch to a plunge below the overlook. This is a really great spot for a picnic in the shade of a late spring afternoon. Admire the vista across the Bear Gulch area before going back to the trailhead the way you came.

Miles and Directions

0.0 Start at the bench at the pedestrian crosswalk across from the Bear Gulch Day Use Area parking lot. Walk across the wooden bridge and up the Condor Gulch Trail.

1.0 Come to the Condor Gulch Overlook on the left. GPS: N36 29.11'/ W121 11.55'. Elevation: 1,812 feet.

2.0 Arrive back at the trailhead.

14 Condor Gulch Trail to High Peaks

The entire hike is punctuated by a series of stunning viewpoints. The 2.5 miles up Condor Gulch is a sustained, mostly exposed uphill stretch before reaching the volcanic pinnacles ridge where metal pipe handrails guide you up and down the vertical stone steps. The peaks are a prime condor-viewing area before the more gradual descent back into Bear Gulch Day Use Area.

Start: From Condor Gulch trailhead
Distance: 5.1-mile loop
Hiking time: 3 hours
Difficulty: Strenuous due to length and sustained uphill climb
Trail surface: Dirt, rock
Trailhead elevation: 1,279 feet
Highest point: 2,598 feet
Best seasons: Spring for wildflowers, late fall and winter for cooler temperatures (summer and early fall can be very hot)
Maps: USGS North Chalone Peak; Pinnacles National Park map; Tom Harrison map of Pinnacles National Park

Nearest town: Hollister
Trail contact: Pinnacles National Park, 5000 CA 146, Paicines, CA 95043-9770; (831) 389-4485 or (831) 389-4427; www.nps.gov/pinn
Trail tips: There is water, restrooms, picnic tables, and trash and recycling containers left of the trailhead in the Bear Gulch Day Use Area. The Bear Gulch Nature Center is open seasonally. There is a steep, narrow section of chiseled stone steps at the High Peaks.

Finding the trailhead: From US 101 at San Juan Bautista/Hollister exit 345 (approximately 17 miles north of Salinas and 10 miles south of Gilroy), take exit 345 and drive 7.5 miles to the Hollister turnoff on the right. Drive 3.5 miles and turn right onto CA 25. Drive 28 miles on CA 25 to the Pinnacles National Park entrance. Turn right into the park and drive 2 miles to the visitor center to pay the entrance fee and pick up a map and information. The visitor center is on your left. Return to the main park road and drive 3 more miles to the Bear Gulch Day Use Area parking lot. Walk across the road in the crosswalk to the bench and the Condor Gulch trailhead. GPS: N36 28.88' / W121 10.89'.

From US 101 at King City, take exit 282B/Broadway Street and turn right onto Broadway Street. Drive 1 mile on Broadway Street to the T intersection with First Street. Turn left onto First Street and drive 14 miles to the T intersection with CA 25. (First Street becomes Bitterwater Road at the sign for East Pinnacles.) Turn left onto CA 25 to Pinnacles and drive 14 miles to the CA 146 intersection. Turn left into Pinnacles National Park and follow directions above to the trailhead.

The Hike

This hike wastes no time getting your heart pumping with a relentless uphill as it dangles the palisade of High Peaks ahead of you like a carrot at the end of a stick for almost the first mile. Every step of huff and puff is rewarded with a promise of awesome bird's-eye views. Catch your breath on the first couple of switchbacks before coming to the Condor Gulch Overlook at 1.0 mile. You lose the peaks at 1.3 miles where views turn eastward. At 1.5 miles you're hit with a 360-degree view with a postcard shot of the High Peaks, as you turn west. The trail heads north, and at 1.7 miles Condor Gulch Trail intersects with the High Peaks Trail. Condor Gulch Trail ends; bear left on High Peaks Trail. If you look eastward, you will see something resembling the White Cliffs of Dover, which is actually a humongous slip on the face of the mountain.

At 2.0 miles the trail crests, overlooking the Balconies Cliffs to the north. The climber access at 2.2 miles reveals an even more striking view of the cliffs before the trail narrows along the corridor of boulders and towers. On the other side of this corridor, the panorama overlooks a monolithic rock wall. For a moment hikers who have been to Yosemite National Park may feel that the sheer walls before them—although relatively diminutive—share a Yosemite Valley–like perspective.

At 2.3 miles you come to a trail junction with Tunnel Trail going right. Continue walking straight on High Peaks Trail. The next 0.5 mile of trail to the crest gets narrower, with an up and down of steep stone footholds and a couple of short, cliff-side metal catwalks. There are metal pipe handrails alongside the more precarious sections, which some may find intimidating and others exciting. The soaring views and potential for condor sightings is a big payoff for a little anxiety.

The wooden bench on the saddle beneath Scout Peak as you drop down off the High Peaks is a good spot for a snack and a chance to enjoy the views straddling the

Hiking up Condor Gulch Trail toward the High Peaks

Condor Gulch Trail to High Peaks

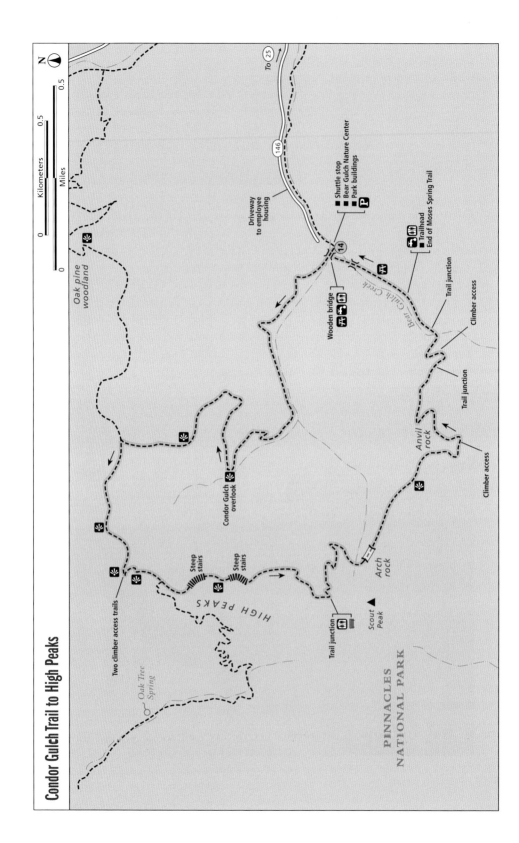

west and east side of the park. There is no water at Scout Peak, but there are two vault toilets in the small stone building to the right below the bench.

The arched rock tunnel constructed during the 1930s by the Civilian Conservation Corps (CCC) at 3.5 miles is one of the highlights of your descent. The trail eventually leaves the volcanic walls behind and opens up to a more chaparral-covered landscape with a view of the North Chalone Peak fire tower to the south before passing an anvil-shaped rock on the left and a climber access on the right.

At 4.5 miles you pass the trail junction for the Rim Trail to the reservoir on your right. Bear left and continue your descent to the Bear Gulch Day Use Area, passing a climber access on the right and the climber access to the top of Tourist Trap, which is a prominent rock formation on the left. The trail junction for the Moses Spring Trail is just ahead on the right. Continue walking down to the Moses Spring trailhead; cross the road to continue on the hiker trail through the picnic area.

At 5.05 miles you leave the large picnic area and cross a wooden footbridge. Your trailhead and end of loop are just ahead past a picnic table and restroom building on the left.

Miles and Directions

0.0 Start at the bench at the pedestrian crosswalk across from the Bear Gulch Day Use Area parking lot. Walk across the wooden bridge and up the Condor Gulch Trail.

1.0 Come to the Condor Gulch Overlook.

1.5 Soak up a 360-degree view as you approach the High Peaks and the junction for High Peaks Trail. The Condor Gulch Trail ends. Bear left on the High Peaks Trail.

2.0 The trail crests, and the view opens north across to the Balconies Cliffs.

2.2 Come to a climber access and a stunning view of the Balconies Cliffs, then emerge on the west side of a narrow corridor of sculpted rock formations with broad, soaring views. At the trail junction with the Tunnel Trail, continue walking straight on High Peaks Trail. The next 0.5 mile of trail is narrow with some sections of steep stone steps.

2.5 Begin a steep stair climb to arrive at the crest of the High Peaks Trail before a steep stair descent to the saddle beneath Scout Peak.

3.0 Come to the saddle beneath Scout Peak.

3.5 Walk through the rock tunnel.

3.8 Come to a view of the North Chalone Peak fire tower to the south.

4.0 Come to the anvil-shaped rock on the left and a climber access on the right.

4.5 Come to the trail junction for Rim Trail. Bear left down to Bear Gulch Day Use Area, passing a climber access on the right. Continue walking downhill.

4.7 Walk past the climber access to the top of Tourist Trap on the left, then come to the trail junction for Moses Spring Trail. Continue walking downhill.

4.9 Come to the Moses Spring trailhead. Walk across the road.

5.05 Walk across the wooden footbridge.

5.1 Arrive back at the trailhead.

15 Condor Gulch Trail to Chaparral Day Use Area

This is a scenic East to West Pinnacles route with a sustained, mostly exposed uphill for the first 2.5 miles, threading through an otherworldly corridor of stone towers before starting your descent along the dramatic Tunnel Trail on the west side. This hike offers multiple stunning viewpoints.

Start: From Condor Gulch trailhead
Distance: 8.2 miles out and back
Hiking time: 5 hours
Difficulty: Strenuous due to length and sustained uphill climb
Trail surface: Dirt
Trailhead elevation: 1,279 feet
Highest point: 2,552 feet
Best seasons: Spring for wildflowers, late fall and winter for cooler temperatures (summer and early fall can be very hot)
Maps: USGS North Chalone Peak; Pinnacles National Park map; Tom Harrison map of Pinnacles National Park

Nearest town: Hollister
Trail contact: Pinnacles National Park, 5000 CA 146, Paicines, CA 95043-9770; (831) 389-4485 or (831) 389-4427; www.nps.gov/pinn
Trail tips: There is water, restrooms, picnic tables, and trash and recycling containers left of the trailhead in the Bear Gulch Day Use Area. The Bear Gulch Nature Center is open seasonally. There is water, restrooms, picnic tables, grills, and trash and recycling containers in the Chaparral Day Use Area.

Finding the trailhead: From US 101 at San Juan Bautista/Hollister exit 345 (approximately 17 miles north of Salinas and 10 miles south of Gilroy), take exit 345 and drive 7.5 miles to the Hollister turnoff on the right. Drive 3.5 miles and turn right onto CA 25. Drive 28 miles on CA 25 to the Pinnacles National Park entrance. Turn right into the park and drive 2 miles to the visitor center to pay the entrance fee and pick up a map and information. The visitor center is on your left. Return to the main park road and drive 3 more miles to the Bear Gulch Day Use Area parking lot. Walk across the road in the crosswalk to the bench and the Condor Gulch trailhead. GPS: N36 28.88' / W121 10.89'.

From US 101 at King City, take exit 282B/Broadway Street and turn right onto Broadway Street. Drive 1 mile on Broadway Street to the T intersection with First Street. Turn left onto First Street and drive 14 miles to the T intersection with CA 25. (First Street becomes Bitterwater Road at the sign for East Pinnacles.) Turn left onto CA 25 to Pinnacles and drive 14 miles to the CA 146 intersection. Turn left into Pinnacles National Park and follow directions above to the trailhead.

The Hike

This hike wastes no time getting your heart pumping with a relentless uphill as it dangles the palisade of High Peaks ahead of you like a carrot at the end of a stick for almost the first mile. Every step of huff and puff is rewarded with a promise of awesome bird's-eye views. Catch your breath on the first couple of switchbacks before coming to the Condor Gulch Overlook at 1.0 mile. You lose the peaks at 1.3 miles where views

Condor Gulch Trail to Chaparral Day Use Area

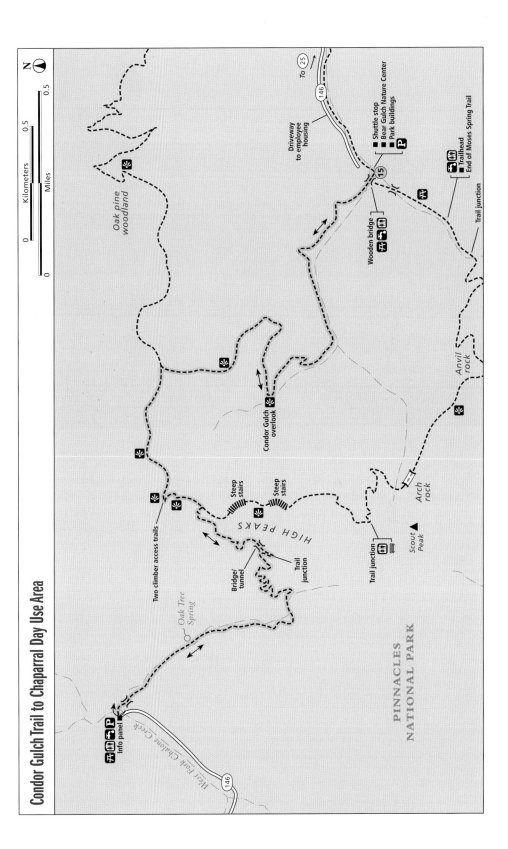

The High Peaks peering through the mist on Condor Gulch Trail

turn eastward. At 1.5 miles you're hit with a 360-degree view with a postcard shot of the High Peaks, as you turn west. The trail heads north, and at 1.7 miles Condor Gulch Trail intersects with the High Peaks Trail. Condor Gulch Trail ends; bear left on High Peaks Trail. If you look eastward, you will see something resembling the White Cliffs of Dover, which is actually a humongous slip on the face of the mountain.

At 2.0 miles the trail crests, overlooking the Balconies Cliffs to the north. The climber access at 2.2 miles reveals an even more striking view of the cliffs before the trail narrows along the corridor of boulders and towers. On the other side of this corridor, the panorama overlooks a monolithic rock wall. For a moment hikers who have been to Yosemite National Park may feel that the sheer walls before them—although relatively diminutive—share a Yosemite Valley–like perspective.

At 2.3 miles you come to a trail junction with Tunnel Trail. Turn right onto Tunnel Trail and notice the steel rod in the rock—a remnant of the CCC days when the 1930s Civilian Conservation Corps was driving these rods to break trail through the Pinnacles fortress. The trail is downhill to the Chaparral Day Use Area from here, and this section to the narrow metal bridge across the boulder-wedged ravine and to the tunnel is one of Pinnacles National Park's intensely stunning stretches of trail.

At 2.8 miles you come to the metal bridge and tunnel just short of the trail junction where the Tunnel Trail ends and you continue downhill along Juniper Canyon Trail. At 4.0 miles you cross a wooden footbridge just before the trail junction at the Condor Crags interpretive sign. Bear left along the fenced trail. You will see an entrance to the small picnic area with two picnic tables and grills on your right before you reach the Chaparral Day Use Area parking lot just across the seasonal creek, which is typically dry. There is an information map board at the trailhead and a restroom at the far end of the parking area on your right, along with trash and recycling bins at each end of the parking lot. If the small picnic area is full, there is a larger picnic area just beyond the restrooms. Take advantage of the well-developed Chaparral Day Use Area to enjoy a snack and water break to boost your energy for the return trip back the way you came.

Miles and Directions

0.0 Start at the bench at the pedestrian crosswalk across from the Bear Gulch Day Use Area parking lot. Walk across the wooden bridge and up the Condor Gulch Trail.

1.0 Come to the Condor Gulch Overlook.

1.5 Soak up a 360-degree view as you approach the High Peaks.

1.7 The Condor Gulch Trail ends at the junction with the High Peaks Trail. Bear left on the High Peaks Trail.

2.0 The trail crests, and the view opens north across to the Balconies Cliffs.

2.2 Come to a climber access and a stunning view of the Balconies Cliffs, then emerge on the west side of a narrow corridor of sculpted rock formations with broad, soaring views.

2.3 Come to the trail junction with the Tunnel Trail. Turn right onto Tunnel Trail.

2.8 Cross the metal bridge and walk through the short rock tunnel.

2.9 Tunnel Trail ends at the trail junction with the Juniper Canyon Trail. Continue walking downhill on Juniper Canyon Trail.

3.8 Walk past Oak Tree Spring on the right.

4.0 Walk across the seasonal creek on the wooden footbridge, then come to a trail junction and the Condor Crags interpretive panel. Bear left on the fenced trail.

4.1 Come to the Chaparral trailhead and parking lot. (GPS: N36 29.50'/ W121 12.56'. Elevation 1,389 feet.) Take time to enjoy an energy-boosting snack and rehydrate at the small picnic area behind the fence or in the larger Chaparral Picnic Area to the right before going back the way you came.

8.2 Arrive back at the trailhead.

16 Bear Gulch Trail

This is a "must-hike" moderate trail laced with wooden footbridges across seasonal Bear Gulch Creek, passing beautiful time- and element-sculpted boulders that tumble into cascades and waterfalls during wet winters and early spring. Even in dryer conditions, ferns and clump grass–like sedges adorn the creekbed under the canopy of sycamore, oak, and buckeye trees.

Start: From Bear Gulch Day Use Area
Distance: 2 miles out and back
Hiking time: 1 hour
Difficulty: Moderate
Trail surface: Dirt
Trailhead elevation: 1,279 feet
Highest point: 1,276 feet
Best seasons: Spring for wildflowers, late fall and winter for cooler temperatures (summer and early fall can be very hot)
Maps: USGS North Chalone Peak; Pinnacles National Park map; Tom Harrison map of Pinnacles National Park

Nearest town: Hollister
Trail contact: Pinnacles National Park, 5000 CA 146, Paicines, CA 95043-9770; (831) 389-4485 or (831) 389-4427; www.nps.gov/pinn
Trail tips: This hike begins downhill, saving the uphill for the return. Bear Gulch Day Use Area has convenient parking, a seasonal nature center, water, restrooms, picnic tables, grills, and trash and recycling containers.

Finding the trailhead: From US 101 at San Juan Bautista/Hollister exit 345 (approximately 17 miles north of Salinas and 10 miles south of Gilroy), take exit 345 and drive 7.5 miles to the Hollister turnoff on the right. Drive 3.5 miles and turn right onto CA 25. Drive 28 miles on CA 25 to the Pinnacles National Park entrance. Turn right into the park and drive 2 miles to the visitor center to pay the entrance fee and pick up a map and information. The visitor center is on your left. Return to the main park road and drive 3 more miles to the Bear Gulch Day Use Area parking lot. The trailhead is at the east end of the parking lot at the sign for Peaks View Trail. GPS: N36 28.90' / W121 10.86'.

From US 101 at King City, take exit 282B/Broadway Street and turn right onto Broadway Street. Drive 1 mile on Broadway Street to the T intersection with First Street. Turn left onto First Street and drive 14 miles to the T intersection with CA 25. (First Street becomes Bitterwater Road at the sign for East Pinnacles.) Turn left onto CA 25 to Pinnacles and drive 14 miles to the CA 146 intersection. Turn left into Pinnacles National Park and follow directions above to the trailhead.

The Hike

Popular Bear Gulch Day Use Area boasts several tempting trailheads. The Peaks View trailhead at the east end of the parking lot is the gateway to Bear Gulch Trail, one of the park's most enchanting hikes and voted one of the favorites among park employees. Bear Gulch Trail is unmarked except for the trail sign that reads "to Peaks View."

Footbridge across Bear Gulch Creek

This hike is a moderate rather than easy 2-mile out and back because what goes down must come up. It boasts six wooden footbridges, a corridor of stunning rock formations to channel seasonal Bear Gulch Creek, and about a 15-foot drop-off for the beloved waterfall effect after a rainfall.

The canopy of sycamore, buckeye, and oak makes for a shady, cool journey as your eyes feast on a garden of ferns and clump grass–like sedges in the creekbed. The creekbed fans out at the bottom of the gulch where Bear Gulch Creek flows into Chalone Creek. The several fallen trees in this wider, exposed floodplain at the end of the trail make good rest spots for a snack and water break before your return trek up to the trailhead. This is one trail that seems to end too soon, and even with the uphill the "back" is every bit as enjoyable as the downhill "out."

Miles and Directions

0.0 Start at the Peaks View trailhead at the east end of the Bear Gulch Day Use parking lot. This is the unmarked Bear Gulch Trail. Walk down the trail toward Peaks View Day Use Area. Bear Gulch Creek is on your right.

0.1 Walk across seasonal Bear Gulch Creek on a wooden footbridge, quickly followed by another footbridge crossing.

Bear Gulch Trail

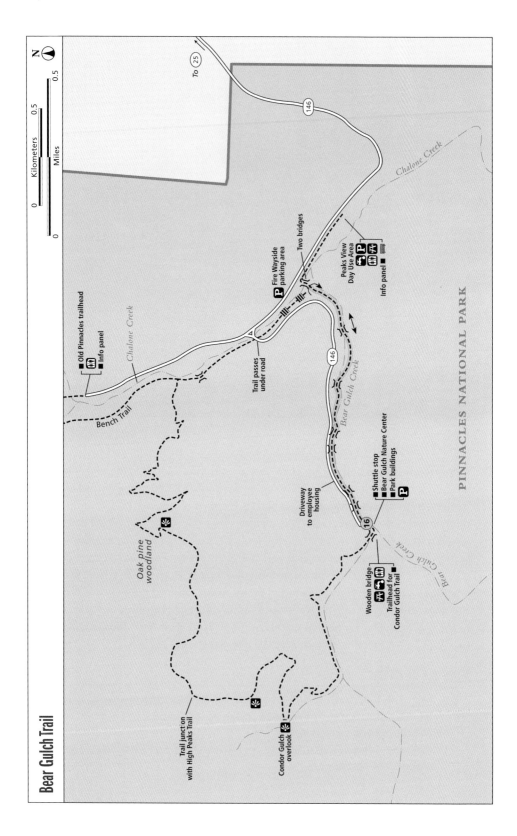

N

Kilometers
0   0.5
0   0.5
Miles

To 25

146

Chalone Creek

Old Pinnacles trailhead
Info panel

Chalone Creek

Bench Trail

Trail passes under road

Fire Wayside parking area

Two bridges

Peaks View Day Use Area

Info panel

Oak pine woodland

Driveway to employee housing

Bear Gulch Creek

146

16

Shuttle stop
Bear Gulch Nature Center
Park buildings

Wooden bridge
Trailhead for Condor Gulch Trail

Bear Gulch Creek

Trail junction with High Peaks Trail

Condor Gulch overlook

PINNACLES NATIONAL PARK

0.2 Walk across the driveway of the employee residence.

0.35 Walk across a wooden footbridge, then cross another footbridge where the trail skirts the park road.

0.6 Walk across a wooden footbridge where pools of water feed the ferns.

0.8 Walk across a wooden footbridge where the trail leaves the narrow, shaded gulch and the creekbed widens.

1.0 Bear Gulch Trail ends at the trail junction for the Bench Trail (unmarked) and the trail sign for Old Pinnacles Trail (left). (GPS: N36 29.06'/ W121 09.99'. Elevation: 984 feet.) Find a good sitting spot on one of the large fallen trees to enjoy a snack and water break before going back up to the trailhead the way you came.

2.0 Arrive back at the trailhead.

17 Bear Gulch Day Use Area to Lower Cave

It is worth noting that Pinnacles National Park has some of the most accessible talus caves in the National Park System. Cave lovers who don't have a lot of time or stamina for a long hike will love this trail. In addition to the unique rock-step climb out of the cave (flashlight required), this hike loops back along the volcanic walls of the gulch, passing Moses Spring, where you may spot the endangered red-legged frog soaking in the freshwater spring. Your passage through the cave on this route will be short but memorable. The hike begins along the picnic area's leafy corridor before the gentle climb up Moses Spring Trail into the cool moist air of the cave. This hike is also a good alternative to the more exposed hillside and Pinnacles slope trails that can get uncomfortably to dangerously hot in the summer.

Start: From Bear Gulch Day Use Area
Distance: 1.5-mile lollipop
Hiking time: 1 hour
Difficulty: Moderate
Trail surface: Dirt and rock
Trailhead elevation: 1,279 feet
Highest point: 1,606 feet
Best seasons: Spring for wildflowers, late fall and winter for cooler temperatures. Although summer and early fall can be very hot, this relatively short hike is reasonably shady and benefits from the coolness of the cave.
Maps: USGS North Chalone Peak; Pinnacles National Park map; Tom Harrison map of Pinnacles National Park

Nearest town: Hollister
Trail contact: Pinnacles National Park, 5000 CA 146, Paicines, CA 95043-9770; (831) 389-4485 or (831) 389-4427; www.nps.gov/pinn
Trail tips: Bear Gulch Day Use Area has convenient parking, a seasonal nature center, water, restrooms, picnic tables, grills, and trash and recycling containers. Check the park website for the cave's seasonal schedule, which is dependent on the bat migration. If you wear a cap with a brim, turn it backward so the brim does not obstruct your view of overhanging rocks. A flashlight or headlight is required.

Finding the trailhead: From US 101 at San Juan Bautista/Hollister exit 345 (approximately 17 miles north of Salinas and 10 miles south of Gilroy), take exit 345 and drive 7.5 miles to the Hollister turnoff on the right. Drive 3.5 miles and turn right onto CA 25. Drive 28 miles on CA 25 to the Pinnacles National Park entrance. Turn right into the park and drive 2 miles to the visitor center to pay the entrance fee and pick up a map and information. The visitor center is on your left. Return to the main park road and drive 3 more miles to the Bear Gulch Day Use Area parking lot. The trailhead is across the road from the nature center at the sign for High Peaks Trail on the left. GPS: N36 28.87' / W121 10.89'.

From US 101 at King City, take exit 282B/Broadway Street and turn right onto Broadway Street. Drive 1 mile on Broadway Street to the T intersection with First Street. Turn left onto First Street and drive 14 miles to the T intersection with CA 25. (First Street becomes Bitterwater Road at the sign for East Pinnacles.) Turn left onto CA 25 to Pinnacles and drive 14 miles to the CA 146 intersection. Turn left into Pinnacles National Park and follow directions above to the trailhead.

Trail narrows on the way to Lower Cave.

The Hike

A trip to Pinnacles National Park is not complete without a cave experience. In the winter and early spring in an average wet year, Bear Gulch Creek not only makes the gulch floor come to life with green, but also gives the volcanic palisades and the caves a voice as its water washes down the rock faces and through the boulder maze.

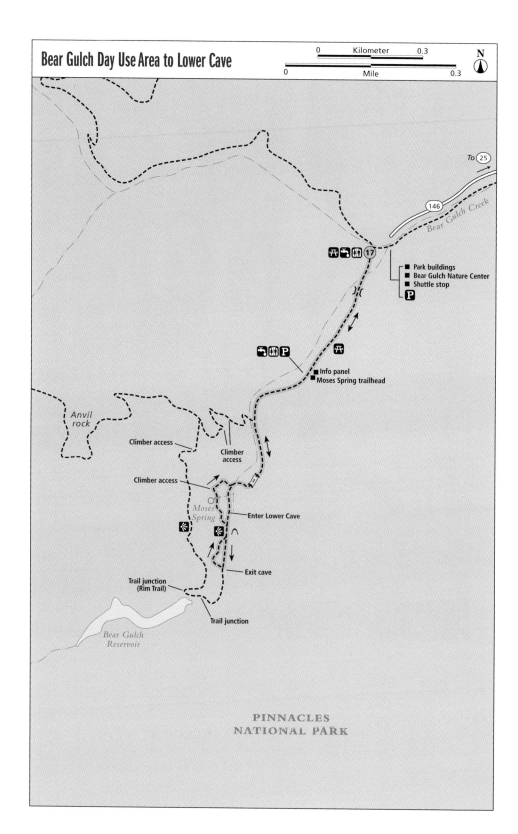

Bear Gulch Day Use Area to Lower Cave

0 Kilometer 0.3

0 Mile 0.3

N

To (25)

146

Bear Gulch Creek

(17)

■ Park buildings
■ Bear Gulch Nature Center
■ Shuttle stop

P

P

Info panel
Moses Spring trailhead

Anvil rock

Climber access

Climber access

Climber access

Moses Spring

Enter Lower Cave

Exit cave

Trail junction
(Rim Trail)

Trail junction

Bear Gulch Reservoir

PINNACLES
NATIONAL PARK

The hike begins in the Bear Gulch Day Use Area across the road from the nature center. Turn left and follow the Reservoir, Bear Gulch Caves, and High Peaks sign. The trail crosses a wooden footbridge before entering the picnic area. At 0.2 mile you come to the Moses Spring trailhead. Walk up the trail and bear left at the trail junction for High Peaks Trail to continue walking on Moses Spring Trail. This is the gateway to another realm that reveals one of the park's many faces. Seasonal Bear Gulch Creek is on your right.

At 0.45 mile you walk through one of the park's several impressive, artful rock tunnels sculpted by the Civilian Conservation Corps (CCC) in the 1930s. This particular tunnel has the distinction of being the work of an all–African American CCC crew. Just ahead is the fork in the trail where you turn left into Bear Gulch Caves. Turn on your flashlight and prepare to be awed by the masonry work of chiseled stone steps (over 150) that lead you out of the cave and back on Moses Spring Trail. Turn right and walk past a climber access on the left.

At 0.9 mile you come to Moses Spring, where a large fern thrives at the edge of a grotto; it may be your lucky day to spot the endangered red-legged frog where the spring percolates to the surface. Just ahead is a climber access trail on the left. This is the close of your lollipop. Bear left and continue down the trail back to the trailhead the way you came.

Miles and Directions

0.0 Start at the Picnic Area, Bear Gulch Caves, Reservoir, and High Peaks Trail sign across from the Bear Gulch Nature Center.

0.05 Walk left across the wooden footbridge and enter the picnic area.

0.2 Come to the Moses Spring trailhead.

0.3 Come to the trail junction for the High Peaks Trail. Bear left and walk uphill on the Moses Spring Trail.

0.45 Walk through the rock tunnel.

0.5 Come to a fork in the trail signed Reservoir via Moses Spring Trail to the right. Bear left for the reservoir via Bear Gulch Caves. This is where you will return to close your lollipop.

0.6 Enter Lower Cave.

0.75 Exit Lower Cave and turn right onto Moses Spring Trail.

0.85 Come to a viewpoint.

0.9 Come to Moses Spring, with the fern and grotto on the left.

0.95 Walk past a climber access on the left.

1.0 Come to the trail junction with Bear Gulch Cave Trail on the right. This is the close of your lollipop. Bear left and continue down Moses Spring Trail back to the trailhead the way you came.

1.5 Arrive back at the trailhead.

18 Bear Gulch Day Use Area to Lower and Upper Caves

Rarely does such a short little hike pack so much adventure. This is one of the many unique and distinct worlds within Pinnacles National Park, which has some of the most accessible talus caves in the National Park System. The catch is that you must be sure-footed and comfortable in dark, tight spaces. If you meet those criteria, this hike through one of the park's most extensive talus caves will astonish you.

Start: From Bear Gulch Day Use Area
Distance: 1.9 miles out and back
Hiking time: 1.5 hours
Difficulty: Moderate due to terrain
Trail surface: Dirt and rock
Trailhead elevation: 1,279 feet
Highest point: 1,620 feet
Best seasons: Pinnacles boasts wildflowers in the spring, but this hike highlights the caves. Late fall, winter, and spring are cooler than summer and early fall, which can be very hot in the park. Luckily the shady corridor to the caves and the cooler environment of the caves themselves make this hike more comfortable than most for hiking in the warmer seasons.
Maps: USGS North Chalone Peak; Pinnacles National Park map; Tom Harrison map of Pinnacles National Park

Nearest town: Hollister
Trail contact: Pinnacles National Park, 5000 CA 146, Paicines, CA 95043-9770; (831) 389-4485 or (831) 389-4427; www.nps.gov/pinn
Trail tips: Bear Gulch Day Use Area has convenient parking, a seasonal nature center, water, restrooms, picnic tables, grills, and trash and recycling containers. This hike can be challenging due to the slippery surface and intimidating because of the constricting conditions. Check the park website for the cave's seasonal schedule, which is dependent on the bat migration. If you wear a cap with a brim, turn it backward so the brim does not obstruct your view of overhanging rocks. A flashlight or headlight is required.

Finding the trailhead: From US 101 at San Juan Bautista/Hollister exit 345 (approximately 17 miles north of Salinas and 10 miles south of Gilroy), take exit 345 and drive 7.5 miles to the Hollister turnoff on the right. Drive 3.5 miles and turn right onto CA 25. Drive 28 miles on CA 25 to the Pinnacles National Park entrance. Turn right into the park and drive 2 miles to the visitor center to pay the entrance fee and pick up a map and information. The visitor center is on your left. Return to the main park road and drive 3 more miles to the Bear Gulch Day Use Area parking lot. The trailhead is across the road from the nature center at the sign for High Peaks Trail on the left. GPS: N36 28.87' / W121 10.89'.

From US 101 at King City, take exit 282B/Broadway Street and turn right onto Broadway Street. Drive 1 mile on Broadway Street to the T intersection with First Street. Turn left onto First Street and drive 14 miles to the T intersection with CA 25. (First Street becomes Bitterwater Road at the sign for East Pinnacles.) Turn left onto CA 25 to Pinnacles and drive 14 miles to the CA 146 intersection. Turn left into Pinnacles National Park and follow directions above to the trailhead.

Horizontal bars on the gate between Lower and Upper Caves allow bats to fly through.

Bear Gulch Caves happen to also be the home of bats. Bear Gulch Caves are "bat caves" of sorts. Park biologists specifically monitor the Townsend's big-eared bat population and their migration patterns to determine which caves to close when and for how long, so the public can have access to parts of the talus caves (if not both Lower and Upper Caves) without risk of disturbing the breeding, birthing, and rearing process. The caves are closed specifically for colonies of state-listed Townsend's big-eared bats, which are in particularly large concentrations in the talus caves. The Lower Cave becomes a bat maternity ward part of the year when female bats give birth to their young.

At some point the baby bats are strong enough to ride on mom's back, and she migrates to the Upper Cave, where baby bats become young bats strong enough to fly off with mom. The caves are usually fully open for a short time in March or April and again in October. These are windows of opportunity for hikers to experience the full cave adventure. The cave closure schedule is posted on the park website and updated regularly.

If you should be so lucky as to find yourself in the park when both caves are open to the public, don't miss your chance to travel through this challenging maze of boulder tunnels and talus caves. Pinnacles has some of the most accessible talus caves in the National Park System. This is one of the park's coolest hikes, and I mean cool in both senses of the word.

The first 350 yards of this hike is pleasantly tame as you walk across a wooden footbridge and enter the nicely developed picnic area across the road from the Bear Gulch Nature Center parking lot. Bear Gulch Creek will be gurgling on the right if you are here in winter or spring. You come to the Moses Spring trailhead at the west end of the shady picnic area. Walk up Moses Spring Trail and bear left to stay on Moses Spring at the trail junction with High Peaks Trail. The minute you leave that junction, you enter a special realm as the trail meanders up between velvety green boulders and towering rock walls to a hollowed-out rock tunnel. Walk through the short tunnel and to the fork in the trail signed Reservoir via Moses Spring Trail to the right and Reservoir via Bear Gulch Caves to the left. Bear left for the adventure via Bear Gulch Caves.

Have your flashlight ready as you enter the Lower Cave. Don't be surprised to see, hear, and step in water in the winter and spring. The uneven volcanic rock floor becomes even slipperier in dark, wet conditions. Be prepared to walk slowly and cautiously.

Shortly after entering and navigating the narrow passage, you walk up about 155 stone steps—guided by a metal pipe handrail—to a junction. The metal gate to the Upper Cave is on your right. This is the gate that is closed and locked when the Upper Cave is the bat maternity ward. (You are on this hike because the Upper Cave is open.) You will have to do a lot of stooping and scooching in this section; keep

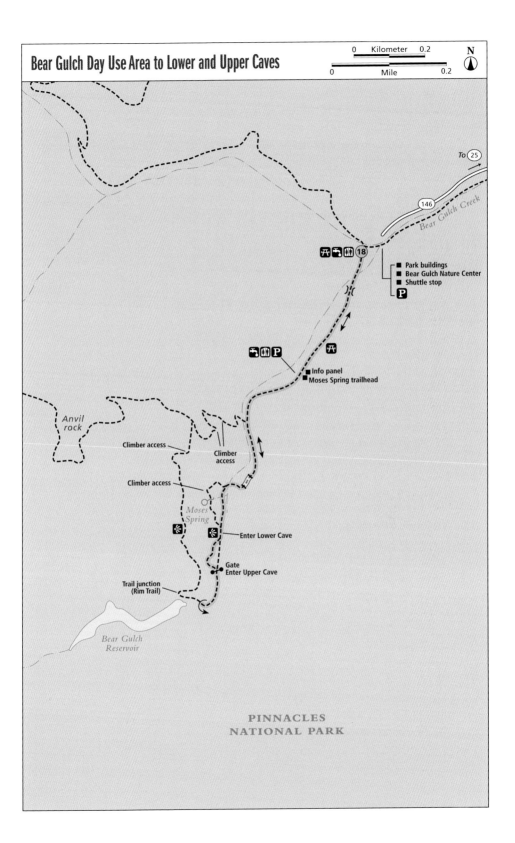

Bear Gulch Day Use Area to Lower and Upper Caves

0 Kilometer 0.2
0 Mile 0.2

N

To 25

146

Bear Gulch Creek

18

■ Park buildings
■ Bear Gulch Nature Center
■ Shuttle stop

P

■ Info panel
Moses Spring trailhead

Anvil rock

Climber access

Climber access

Climber access

Moses Spring

Enter Lower Cave

Gate
Enter Upper Cave

Trail junction
(Rim Trail)

Bear Gulch Reservoir

PINNACLES
NATIONAL PARK

your flashlight scanning for the white arrows on the walls pointing you in the correct direction. There are a couple of chambers tall enough for you to stand. You exit the Upper Cave through a second open gate, where you merge onto the Moses Spring Trail coming in from the left. Head toward daylight and walk up 75 stone steps to the head of the reservoir.

The caves will seem like a portal to another world as you stand on the concrete walkway looking at the long body of water hugging the volcanic walls ahead of you and the boulder cave opening below and behind you. There is an interpretive panel about the endangered red-legged frog at the head of the reservoir to the right. Take in the view and open air before turning around to go back the way you came.

Miles and Directions

0.0 Start at the Picnic Area, Bear Gulch Caves, Reservoir, and High Peaks Trail sign across from the Bear Gulch Nature Center.

0.05 Walk left across the wooden footbridge and enter the picnic area.

0.2 Come to the Moses Spring trailhead.

0.3 Come to the trail junction for the High Peaks Trail. Bear left and walk uphill on the Moses Spring Trail.

0.45 Walk through the rock tunnel, then come to a fork in the trail signed Reservoir via Moses Spring Trail to the right. Bear left for the reservoir via Bear Gulch Caves.

0.6 Enter Lower Cave.

0.75 Come to a fork after climbing approximately 155 stone steps. Bear right and walk through the open gate into Upper Cave, exploring the narrow and low-ceilinged passages.

0.9 Exit through a gate and rejoin Moses Spring Trail. Walk up 75 rock steps.

0.95 Arrive at the reservoir. (GPS: N36 28.37'/ W121 11.25'. Elevation: 1,620 feet.) Breathe, look around, read the interpretive panel about red-legged frogs, and turn around to go back down the rock steps the way you came.

1.9 Arrive back at the trailhead.

19 Bear Gulch Day Use Area to Rim Trail via Reservoir

Moses Spring Trail is a cornucopia of sights and experiences. This sweet trail traces volcanic cliff walls where an underground spring feeds verdant ferns and the cool moist air lets velvety green moss drape boulders like wallpaper. The last stretch of seventy-five rock-etched steps out of a boulder tunnel feel like the portal to a hidden world as you emerge at the head of the reservoir. There is an interpretive panel about the threatened red-legged frog (largest native frog in the western United States) at the reservoir.

Start: From Bear Gulch Day Use Area
Distance: 1.95-mile lollipop
Hiking time: 1.5 hours
Difficulty: Moderate
Trail surface: Dirt and rock
Trailhead Elevation: 1,279 feet
Highest point: 1,721 feet
Best seasons: Although summer can be hot, most of this trail has the advantage of shade, and the cave stays cool. Flowing water adds another dimension after a winter rain or spring shower.
Maps: USGS North Chalone Peak; Pinnacles National Park map; Tom Harrison map of Pinnacles National Park
Nearest town: Hollister

Trail contact: Pinnacles National Park, 5000 CA 146, Paicines, CA 95043-9770; (831) 389-4485 or (831) 389-4427; www.nps.gov/pinn
Trail tips: There is a parking lot with 10 spaces at the Moses Spring trailhead at the end of the paved road, which would shorten this hike by 0.3 mile. But this small lot is one of the first to fill up early on weekends in the spring, especially when rock climbers are present. There are restrooms at the Bear Gulch Day Use Area parking lot as well as at the Moses Spring lot, and a picnic area with tables, water, and grills between the Bear Gulch parking lot and the Moses Spring lot. Carry a flashlight for the short cave section.

Finding the trailhead: From US 101 at San Juan Bautista/Hollister exit 345 (approximately 17 miles north of Salinas and 10 miles south of Gilroy), take exit 345 and drive 7.5 miles to the Hollister turnoff on the right. Drive 3.5 miles and turn right onto CA 25. Drive 28 miles on CA 25 to the Pinnacles National Park entrance. Turn right into the park and drive 2 miles to the visitor center to pay the entrance fee and pick up a map and information. The visitor center is on your left. Return to the main park road and drive 3 more miles to the Bear Gulch Day Use Area parking lot. The trailhead is across the road from the nature center at the sign for High Peaks Trail on the left. GPS: N36 28.87' / W121 10.89'.

From US 101 at King City, take exit 282B/Broadway Street and turn right onto Broadway Street. Drive 1 mile on Broadway Street to the T intersection with First Street. Turn left onto First Street and drive 14 miles to the T intersection with CA 25. (First Street becomes Bitterwater Road at the sign for East Pinnacles.) Turn left onto CA 25 to Pinnacles and drive 14 miles to the CA 146 intersection. Turn left into Pinnacles National Park and follow directions above to the trailhead.

Bear Gulch Reservoir is an unexpected surprise along the trail.

The Hike

The Bear Gulch Day Use Area is a popular starting point for several hikes. Besides the fact that it has water, restrooms, and a nicely developed picnic area with grills, the small historic stone buildings housing the seasonal Bear Gulch Nature Center, park headquarter offices, and employee residences seem to be a natural fit in the shadow of volcanic sentinels and leafy woodlands fed by the seasonal Bear Gulch Creek.

The trail begins across from the nature center parking area at the Reservoir, Bear Gulch Cave and High Peaks sign. The walk through the shaded picnic area to the Moses Spring Trailhead is a pleasant flat beginning to the hike. The trail climbs gently from the trailhead as you bear left, entering a boulder passage with the creekbed on your right. During the winter and spring wet season, the creek flows happily, and you can hear and see curtains and veils of water washing the volcanic walls.

At 0.5 mile you come to a fork in the trail signed Reservoir via Bear Gulch Caves to the left. Bear right to continue walking on Moses Spring Trail, passing a climber access on the right before coming to a grotto scooped out by time and the elements and Moses Spring, which feeds the flourishing ferns. Just ahead, Moses Spring Trail treats hikers to a front-row view of the gargantuan rock known as the Monolith. Looking left into the gulch as you continue up the trail, notice how Mother Nature and the tectonic movement of the volcanic field created this cascade of boulders that is part of the Pinnacles' unique geology.

At 0.8 mile you pass two climber access trails just before entering the boulder cave that is your portal to the reservoir up the seventy-five narrow stone steps to the

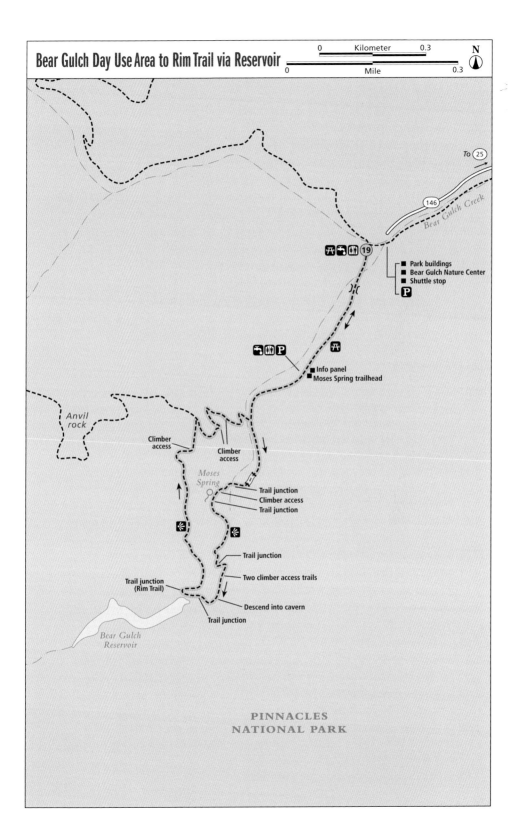

Bear Gulch Day Use Area to Rim Trail via Reservoir

0   Kilometer   0.3

0   Mile   0.3

N

To 25

146

Bear Gulch Creek

19

■ Park buildings
■ Bear Gulch Nature Center
■ Shuttle stop

P

P

■ Info panel
■ Moses Spring trailhead

Anvil rock

Climber access

Climber access

Moses Spring

Trail junction
Climber access
Trail junction

Trail junction

Two climber access trails

Trail junction (Rim Trail)

Descend into cavern

Trail junction

Bear Gulch Reservoir

PINNACLES
NATIONAL PARK

surface. Pull out your flashlight before proceeding through this short cave-like passage; use caution and step slowly along the uneven cave floor, which can be slippery in wet weather.

At 0.95 mile you come to the reservoir and a trail junction for North Chalone Peak to the left across the head of the stone dam and the Rim Trail straight ahead. Don't leave the dam without soaking up the otherworldly setting of this body of water and reading the interpretive panel about the endangered red-legged frog that makes this area home.

The Rim Trail route skirts the top of the gulch with expansive views toward the Bear Gulch Day Use Area from the crest. At 1.3 miles you pass a climber access trail on the right just before the junction with High Peaks Trail. Rim Trail ends at this junction. Turn right and continue walking downhill on High Peaks Trail. You pass two more climber accesses: Discovery Wall (name is not on the post) on the right, and the top to Tourist Trap climber access on the left.

At 1.65 miles High Peaks Trail ends, merging into the Moses Spring Trail where you close your lollipop. Continue down the trail the way you came back to the trailhead, which is 0.3 mile ahead back in the Bear Gulch Day Use Area.

Miles and Directions

0.0 Start at the Picnic Area, Bear Gulch Cave, Reservoir, and High Peaks Trail sign across from the Bear Gulch Nature Center. Walk left across the wooden footbridge and enter the picnic area. At the Moses Spring trailhead, walk uphill and continue on walking on Moses Spring Trail and bear left at the trail junction for High Peaks Trail. This is where you will close your lollipop on the way down.

0.45 Walk through the rock tunnel, then come to a fork in the trail signed Reservoir via Bear Gulch Caves to the left. Bear right and continue walking on the Moses Spring Trail. Immediately come to a climber access on the right.

0.6 Walk past Moses Spring with its ferns and grotto, then come to a viewpoint of the volcanic Monolith.

0.75 Walk past the climber access on the right and stairway to Lower Cave on the left.

0.8 Walk past two climber access trails on the right, then enter the cave-like tunnel ahead.

0.9 The Upper Cave trail is on the right. Bear left and walk up seventy-five rock-etched steps.

0.95 Arrive at the reservoir and trail junction for the North Chalone Peak and Rim Trail. Moses Spring Trail ends here. Continue up the Rim Trail.

1.15 Come to the crest of the Rim Trail and view up Bear Gulch to the east.

1.3 Walk past a climber access on the right, then come to the trail junction with High Peaks Trail. Rim Trail ends. Turn right onto High Peaks Trail and walk downhill to Bear Gulch.

1.45 Walk past a climber access on the right, and in 0.1 mile come to the climber access to the top of Tourist Trap on the left.

1.65 Come to the trail junction for the Moses Spring Trail. This is the close of the lollipop and where High Peaks Trail ends. Continue walking down Moses Spring Trail the way you came back to the trailhead.

1.95 Arrive back at the trailhead.

20 Bear Gulch Day Use Area to Reservoir via Rim Trail

This is a sweet trail that combines shade and a moderate incline to open views of striking volcanic formations contrasted by the oasis feel of the unlikely body of water at the foot of Chalone Peak's more arid chaparral zone. The trail then loops through an enchanting boulder tunnel and cliff-shouldered corridor back into Bear Gulch.

Start: From Bear Gulch Day Use Area.
Distance: 1.95-mile lollipop
Hiking time: 1.5 hours
Difficulty: Moderate
Trail surface: Dirt and rock
Trailhead elevation: 1,279 feet
Highest point: 1,721 feet
Best seasons: Spring for wildflowers, late fall and winter for cooler temperatures (summer and early fall can be very hot)
Maps: USGS North Chalone Peak; Pinnacles National Park map; Tom Harrison map of Pinnacles National Park

Nearest town: Hollister
Trail contact: Pinnacles National Park, 5000 CA 146, Paicines, CA 95043-9770; (831) 389-4485 or (831) 389-4427; www.nps.gov/pinn
Trail tips: Bear Gulch Day Use Area has convenient parking, a seasonal nature center, water, restrooms, picnic tables, grills, and trash and recycling containers. Although the hike is relatively short, the cave section on the way back from the reservoir requires some fancy footwork in narrow areas. Carry a flashlight.

Finding the trailhead: From US 101 at San Juan Bautista/Hollister exit 345 (approximately 17 miles north of Salinas and 10 miles south of Gilroy), take exit 345 and drive 7.5 miles to the Hollister turnoff on the right. Drive 3.5 miles and turn right onto CA 25. Drive 28 miles on CA 25 to the Pinnacles National Park entrance. Turn right into the park and drive 2 miles to the visitor center to pay the entrance fee and pick up a map and information. The visitor center is on your left. Return to the main park road and drive 3 more miles to the Bear Gulch Day Use Area parking lot. The trailhead is across the road from the nature center at the sign for High Peaks Trail on the left. GPS: N36 28.87' / W121 10.89'.

From US 101 at King City, take exit 282B/Broadway Street and turn right onto Broadway Street. Drive 1 mile on Broadway Street to the T intersection with First Street. Turn left onto First Street and drive 14 miles to the T intersection with CA 25. (First Street becomes Bitterwater Road at the sign for East Pinnacles.) Turn left onto CA 25 to Pinnacles and drive 14 miles to the CA 146 intersection. Turn left into Pinnacles National Park and follow directions above to the trailhead.

The Hike

Within 250 feet from the trailhead, the trail cuts through a shady picnic area before reaching the Moses Spring parking area and another trailhead sign for the High Peaks. Note that although you can park here to hike to the High Peaks, there are only ten spaces, and they typically fill up with rock climbers getting an early start, especially on weekends. The trail continues across the parking entrance at the Moses Spring trailhead and information panel with a sign for High Peaks 1.9 and Reservoir Caves 0.7.

Springtime waterfall along Moses Spring Trail

Approximately 500 feet up the trail, you come to a trail junction for the Moses Spring Trail going left and the High Peaks Trail continuing to the right. Bear right and continue walking uphill along the High Peaks Trail. This is the trail junction where you will close your lollipop on Moses Spring Trail on your return to the trailhead.

Pinnacles National Park was a favorite of rock climbers long before its status changed from monument to national park. The Tourist Trap, on your right where the trail begins to rise out of the gulch, is a very popular climb. On weekends especially, keep your eyes open for climbers perched on massive boulders or dangling from ropes on the right side of the trail.

At 0.5 mile you pass another climber access on the left. Continue walking on High Peaks Trail to the right until you come to the trail junction signed Rim Trail to Reservoir. Bear left and walk up Rim Trail. The trail sits on a volcanic rock rim above the caves and tunnels in the gulch below to your left. Shortly after passing a climber access on your left, the trail crests, revealing splendid views of distant rolling hills to the east behind you. As the trail begins to slope gently downward, the rock dam at the head of the reservoir built by the 1930s Civilian Conservation Corps (CCC) will come into view.

At 1.0 mile you reach the reservoir. The Rim Trail ends at the junction for North Chalone Peak across the dam and the signed Bear Gulch Area via Moses Spring Trail.

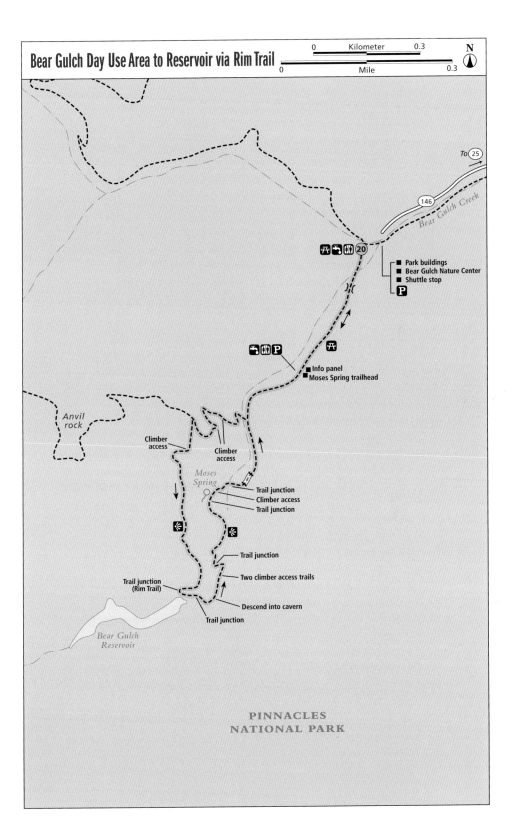

Bear Gulch Day Use Area to Reservoir via Rim Trail

0   Kilometer   0.3

0   Mile   0.3

N

To 25

146

Bear Gulch Creek

20

■ Park buildings
■ Bear Gulch Nature Center
■ Shuttle stop

P

P

■ Info panel
■ Moses Spring trailhead

Anvil rock

Climber access

Climber access

Moses Spring

Trail junction
Climber access
Trail junction

Trail junction

Two climber access trails

Trail junction (Rim Trail)

Descend into cavern

Trail junction

Bear Gulch Reservoir

PINNACLES
NATIONAL PARK

Bear left and follow the trail down the steps cut into the rock; use the metal handrail on the right. This section of the trail winds along towering volcanic rock walls and through a phenomenal cave-like talus tunnel. It is safer to use a flashlight in this section. There is something beautifully primeval about this trail, especially after a winter or spring rain when the rock walls are draped in waterfalls. Several of the wedged boulders act as bridges over rock crevices.

At 1.1 miles you exit the cavern and pass two climber access trails just before the trail junction for the Lower Cave on the right. The viewpoint ahead showcases a couple of these stunning post-rain waterfalls before passing by Moses Spring and the first fern on the left. It is possible to spot a typically nocturnal red-legged frog sitting in the shallow water that pools at Moses Spring.

You pass one last climber access on the left and the trail junction signed Reservoir via Bear Gulch Caves on the right. Continue along the Moses Spring Trail through a carved-out rock tunnel and come to the trail junction for the High Peaks Trail. This is the end of your lollipop. Bear right downhill back to the trailhead the way you came.

Miles and Directions

0.0 Start at the High Peaks Trail sign across from the Bear Gulch Nature Center and turn left to walk across the wooden footbridge and through the shaded picnic area to the Moses Spring trailhead, information board, and sign for High Peaks 1.9 and Reservoir Caves 0.7.

0.3 Come to the trail junction for Moses Spring Trail going left and High Peaks Trail going right. Bear right on High Peaks Trail and walk past the climber access trail for Tourist Trap on the right.

0.5 Come to a T-junction and trail marker for a climber access trail to the left and the High Peaks Trail to the right. Continue walking on High Peaks Trail to a trail junction signed Rim Trail to Reservoir to the left. Bear left on Rim Trail and immediately pass a climber access on the left.

1.0 Arrive at the reservoir and the trail junction signed Bear Gulch via Moses Spring Trail. Bear left and walk down the stone staircase.

1.05 Come to the trail junction for Upper Cave to the left. Bear right to continue on Moses Spring Trail through a cavern-like chamber.

1.1 Exit the cavern, then come to two climber access trails on the left.

1.2 Come to the trail junction for Lower Cave descending to the right. There is a climber access to the left. Continue walking straight on Moses Spring Trail toward Bear Gulch Day Use Area.

1.3 Come to a viewpoint, then arrive at Moses Spring with its ferns and grotto on the left.

1.4 Pass a climber access on the left and immediately come to a trail junction signed Reservoir via Bear Gulch Caves on the right. Bear left and continue walking on Moses Spring Trail.

1.5 Walk through a carved-out rock tunnel.

1.65 Come to the trail junction for the High Peaks Trail. This is the end of the lollipop. Continue walking down to the trailhead the way you came.

1.95 Arrive back at the trailhead.

21 Bear Gulch Day Use Area to Chalone Peaks

This hike is the shortest route to the Chalone Peaks. On a warm day it is also the coolest route to the reservoir on the way to the peaks. The hike climbs out of shady Bear Gulch and along Moses Spring Trail's picturesque rock tunnels and passages before reaching the reservoir's edge and the interpretive panel about the threatened red-legged frog. From here it's a steady, sweeping climb up the exposed, chaparral-covered slopes of the South Gabilan Range away from the towering volcanic stone outcrop. The cardio pump to the fire tower on the top of North Chalone Peak is rewarded with breathtaking views across the valley's farmland and vineyards all the way west to the Santa Lucia Range. Ambitious hikers who want to rack up more miles and sweat can continue to lower South Chalone Peak. You won't get any views worth remembering on South Chalone, but you'll be able to say that you hiked to the southernmost destination in the park.

Start: From Bear Gulch Day Use Area
Distance: 11.7 miles out and back
Hiking time: 6 hours
Difficulty: Strenuous
Trail surface: Dirt and rock
Trailhead elevation: 1,279 feet
Highest point: 3,304 feet
Best seasons: Spring for wildflowers, late fall and winter for cooler temperatures (summer and early fall can be very hot, especially on these exposed slopes)
Maps: USGS North Chalone Peak; Pinnacles National Park map; Tom Harrison map of Pinnacles National Park

Nearest town: Hollister
Trail contact: Pinnacles National Park, 5000 CA 146, Paicines, CA 95043-9770; (831) 389-4485 or (831) 389-4427; www.nps.gov/pinn
Trail tips: Bear Gulch Day Use Area has convenient parking, a seasonal nature center, water, restrooms, picnic tables, grills, and trash and recycling containers. There is no water past Bear Gulch; make sure you bring plenty of water for the hot dry climb from the reservoir.

Finding the trailhead: From US 101 at San Juan Bautista/Hollister exit 345 (approximately 17 miles north of Salinas and 10 miles south of Gilroy), take exit 345 and drive 7.5 miles to the Hollister turnoff on the right. Drive 3.5 miles and turn right onto CA 25. Drive 28 miles on CA 25 to the Pinnacles National Park entrance. Turn right into the park and drive 2 miles to the visitor center to pay the entrance fee and pick up a map and information. The visitor center is on your left. Return to the main park road and drive 3 more miles to the Bear Gulch Day Use Area parking lot. The trailhead is across the road from the nature center at the sign for High Peaks Trail on the left. GPS: N36 28.87' / W121 10.89'.

From US 101 at King City, take exit 282B/Broadway Street and turn right onto Broadway Street. Drive 1 mile on Broadway Street to the T intersection with First Street. Turn left onto First Street and drive 14 miles to the T intersection with CA 25. (First Street becomes Bitterwater Road at the sign for East Pinnacles.) Turn left onto CA 25 to Pinnacles and drive 14 miles to the CA 146 intersection. Turn left into Pinnacles National Park and follow directions above to the trailhead.

The Hike

Bear Gulch with its seasonal creeks, woodlands, and cool moss-draped boulder gardens is a bit of an oasis compared to the rest of the park. The hike up to North and South Chalone Peaks lets you sample some of the park's contrasts as you leave the lush, cool zones of the gulch for the dry, exposed chaparral peaks. The views from North Chalone Peak are the most panoramic in the park, and the once operational fire tower on North Chalone adds a romantic dimension to this hike. The original fire tower was built in 1935 and replaced in 1952 following a fire the previous year; it has not been staffed since 1991. The structure remains one of the most prominent landmarks in the park second to the Pinnacles. South Chalone Peak Trail goes down below North Chalone and up again for 1.6 miles past the fire tower. But if you are expecting dramatic views from South Chalone, you will be disappointed. The trail ends on a chamise-covered knoll with a small cluster of volcanic rock below a higher chamise-blanketed summit. This is the southernmost point in the park and will give you the satisfaction of checking that destination off your list if you decide to tear yourself away from the top-of-the-world feel of North Chalone Peak.

The trail begins across from the nature center at the Picnic Area, Bear Gulch Cave, Reservoir and High Peaks sign. Follow the arrow up the hiker trail across the wooden footbridge and through the shaded picnic area to the Moses Spring trailhead. The trail climbs gently from the trailhead as you bear left to stay on Moses Spring Trail and enter a spectacular boulder passage with the creekbed on your right. During the winter and spring wet season, the creek flows happily, and you can hear and see curtains and veils of water washing the volcanic walls.

At 0.5 mile you come to a fork in the trail signed Reservoir via Bear Gulch Caves to the left. Bear right to continue walking on Moses Spring Trail, passing a climber access on the right before coming to a grotto scooped out by time and the elements and Moses Spring, which feeds the flourishing ferns. Just ahead, Moses Spring Trail treats hikers to a front-row view of the gargantuan rock known as the Monolith. Looking left into the gulch as you continue up the trail, notice how Mother Nature and the tectonic movement of the volcanic field created this cascade of boulders that is part of the Pinnacles' unique geology.

At 0.8 mile you pass two climber access trails just before entering the boulder cave that is your portal to the reservoir up the seventy-five narrow rock steps to the surface. It is safer to carry a flashlight through this short cave-like passage where the uneven rock floor can be slippery in wet weather.

At 0.95 mile you come to the reservoir and a trail junction for North Chalone Peak to the left across the head of the stone dam and the Rim Trail straight ahead. Moses Spring Trail ends here, and you will turn left and walk across the concrete walkway at the head of the dam. But don't leave the dam without soaking up the otherworldly setting of this body of water and reading the interpretive panel about the endangered red-legged frog that makes this area home.

Historic stone restroom on North Chalone Peak with South Chalone Peak in the distance

The trail passes a couple of climber access trails before transitioning from volcanic terrain to exposed, dry chaparral hillsides. The only shade you can expect on your way up to North Chalone Peak and the fire tower is from the shadow of the tall chamise.

At 1.55 miles you get an unobstructed view of the High Peaks as you look back. In about half a mile, where the trail crests and levels for a short distance, the fire tower comes into view ahead; the High Peaks remain in view on your right.

At 3.45 miles you come to a wire fence. This is the pig fence built to protect the main park area from the rooting damage of nonnative pigs. There is a trail sign for North Chalone Peak 0.8 at the fence. Use the wooden pedestrian access stile to climb over the fence. The trail merges with a service road and just ahead is a gate and a pedestrian access over another wooden stile. The trail junction and sign for South Chalone Peak 1.6 is on your right at 4.05 miles. This is where you will turn to go to South Chalone Peak on your way back down from the fire tower on North Chalone Peak. Continue walking up the service road about 350 yards, then be amazed by the commanding 360-degree view, which is truly the highlight of this hike.

The green fire tower is nonoperational, but its fabulous location remains a hiker's treat. On a clear day you can almost see Monterey Bay on the northern horizon and

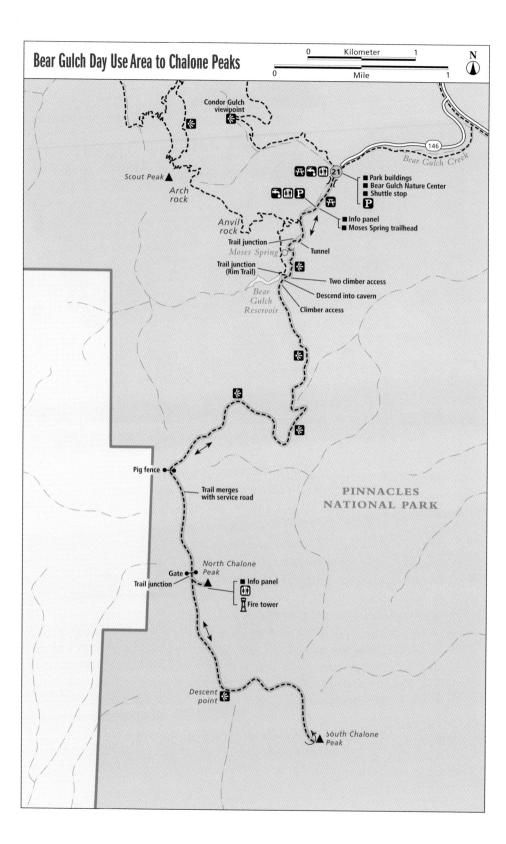

Bear Gulch Day Use Area to Chalone Peaks

0   Kilometer   1

0   Mile   1

N

Condor Gulch viewpoint

146

Bear Gulch Creek

Scout Peak ▲

Arch rock

21

Park buildings
Bear Gulch Nature Center
Shuttle stop

P

Anvil rock

Info panel
Moses Spring trailhead

Trail junction

Moses Spring

Tunnel

Trail junction (Rim Trail)

Two climber access

Bear Gulch Reservoir

Descend into cavern

Climber access

Pig fence

Trail merges with service road

PINNACLES NATIONAL PARK

North Chalone Peak

Gate

Trail junction

▲

Info panel

Fire tower

Descent point

South Chalone Peak ▲

across to the coastal Santa Lucia Range to the west, with the San Andreas Fault rift zone to the east and vineyard and agricultural valleys running north and south.

There is an air quality monitoring station and interpretive sign at the peak along with two vault toilets in a Civilian Conservation Corps (CCC)–built stone building on a volcanic perch just below the tower off a spur trail to the east. The fire tower is a great destination to end your hike on a high note. If you are focused on South Chalone Peak, however, North Chalone and the fire tower are a must-stop for the views and a great spot for a water break and refueling snack.

Retrace your steps back down the service road to the trail junction and trail sign for South Chalone Peak 1.6. Turn left at the junction and walk along the narrow trail on the slope. The fire tower is above on your left, and the pig fence is on your right. At the foot of the mountain in the distance you can see the hint of CA 146 tracing the landscape behind a rust-roofed barn. The trail is exposed here, and the breeze fluttering through the occasional pine is the only sound to break the silence.

The trail bottoms out in about a mile and then climbs up again to South Chalone Peak from the backside, veering away from the pig fence. The North Chalone Peak fire tower is visible on your left and behind you as you reach the chamise-covered ridge where the trail ends in a clearing at just over 6 miles. Reaching South Chalone Peak will be anticlimactic if you are expecting grand views. The reward for your accomplishment is the knowledge that you have hiked to the southernmost point in the park—and a good snack. Thread your way through a few bushes to the volcanic outcrop in the clearing and sit down to savor your favorite treat before you head back to the trailhead the way you came.

Miles and Directions

0.0 Start at the Picnic Area, Bear Gulch Cave, Reservoir, and High Peaks Trail sign across from the Bear Gulch Nature Center and walk left across wooden footbridge through the picinic area to the Moses Spring trailhead.

0.3 Walk up Moses Spring Trail and bear left at the High Peaks Trail junction.

0.45 Walk through the rock tunnel, then come to a fork in the trail signed Reservoir via Bear Gulch Caves to the left. Bear right and continue walking on the Moses Spring Trail. Immediately come to a climber access ahead on the right.

0.6 Walk past Moses Spring with its ferns and grotto, then come to a viewpoint of the volcanic Monolith.

0.75 Walk past the climber access trail on the right and stairway to Lower Cave on the left.

0.8 Walk past two climber accesses on the right, then enter the cave-like tunnel ahead (flashlight recommended). Bear left at the trail junction for Upper Cave on the right and walk up 75 rock-etched stairs.

0.95 Arrive at the Bear Gulch Reservoir and trail junction for North Chalone Peak and Rim Trail. Moses Spring Trail ends here. Walk across the dam on the concrete path to continue to North Chalone Peak. Shortly pass two climber access trails on the left.

1.55 Come to a viewpoint looking back at the High Peaks.

2.15 Come to a viewpoint looking toward the fire tower on North Chalone Peak. Another view-point is 0.6 mile farther.

3.45 Come to the pig fence and trail sign for North Chalone Peak 0.8. Climb over the fence on the wooden stile.

3.55 The trail merges with the gravel service road coming up from the left. Continue walking uphill on the service road.

4.05 Come to a gate and wooden stile for pedestrian access over the gate. The trail junction signed South Chalone Peak 1.6 is on the right. Continue up the service road to the fire tower on North Chalone Peak.

4.25 Arrive on North Chalone Peak at the fire tower. Soak up the views, use the vault toilet, and read the air quality interpretive sign. This makes a great destination if you are in it for the views. If your goal is to make it to South Chalone Peak to reach the southernmost point in the park, then hydrate and retrace your steps back to the junction for South Chalone Peak and turn left onto the narrow South Chalone Peak trail going downhill.

4.45 Come to the trail junction for South Chalone Peak. Turn left and walk downhill for about three quarters of a mile and continue uphill on the trail where it veers left away from the pig fence.

6.05 Arrive at the end of the trail in a clearing surrounded by chamise. (GPS: N36 26.14'/ W121 10.96'. Elevation: 3,269 feet.) Sit on the volcanic outcrop in a clearing obscured by chamise bushes and catch your breath. Hydrate and enjoy a high-energy treat before retracing your steps back to the trailhead.

11.7 Arrive back at the trailhead.

22 Bear Gulch Day Use Area to Scout Peak

This is a very popular trail to the Pinnacles saddle that straddles the east and west sides of Pinnacles National Park. The trail climbs out of a shaded gulch overlooking the chaparral landscape, and switchbacks up the backside of the volcanic sentinels to the saddle at the base of Scout Peak.

Start: From Bear Gulch Day Use Area
Distance: 4.2 miles out and back
Hiking time: 3 hours
Difficulty: Strenuous due to uphill
Trail surface: Dirt and rock
Trailhead elevation: 1,279 feet
Highest point: 2,478 feet
Best seasons: Spring for wildflowers, late fall and winter for cooler temperatures (summer and early fall can be very hot)

Maps: USGS North Chalone Peak; Pinnacles National Park map; Tom Harrison map of Pinnacles National Park
Nearest town: Hollister
Trail contact: Pinnacles National Park, 5000 CA 146, Paicines, CA 95043-9770; (831) 389-4485 or (831) 389-4427; www.nps.gov/pinn
Trail tips: Bear Gulch Day Use Area has convenient parking, a seasonal nature center, water, restrooms, picnic tables, grills, and trash and recycling containers.

Finding the trailhead: From US 101 at San Juan Bautista/Hollister exit 345 (approximately 17 miles north of Salinas and 10 miles south of Gilroy), take exit 345 and drive 7.5 miles to the Hollister turnoff on the right. Drive 3.5 miles and turn right onto CA 25. Drive 28 miles on CA 25 to the Pinnacles National Park entrance. Turn right into the park and drive 2 miles to the visitor center to pay the entrance fee and pick up a map and information. The visitor center is on your left. Return to the main park road and drive 3 more miles to the Bear Gulch Day Use Area parking lot. The trailhead is across the road from the nature center at the sign for High Peaks Trail on the left. GPS: N36 28.87' / W121 10.89'.

From US 101 at King City, take exit 282B/Broadway Street and turn right onto Broadway Street. Drive 1 mile on Broadway Street to the T intersection with First Street. Turn left onto First Street and drive 14 miles to the T intersection with CA 25. (First Street becomes Bitterwater Road at the sign for East Pinnacles.) Turn left onto CA 25 to Pinnacles and drive 14 miles to the CA 146 intersection. Turn left into Pinnacles National Park and follow directions above to the trailhead.

The Hike

Within 350 yards from the trailhead, the trail cuts through a shady picnic area before reaching the Moses Spring parking area and another trailhead sign for the High Peaks. Note that although you can park here to hike to the High Peaks, there are only ten spaces, and they typically fill up with rock climbers getting an early start, especially on weekends. The trail continues across the parking entrance at the Moses Spring trailhead information panel and sign for High Peaks 1.9 and Reservoir Caves 0.7.

High Peaks Trail passes the Tourist Trap rock formation, a favorite with rock climbers.

Just 0.2 mile up the trail you come to a trail junction for the Moses Spring Trail going left and the High Peaks Trail continuing to the right. This is the head of the gulch, where the trail to the High Peaks begins a very gradual climb for the first 0.5 mile before it transitions to switchbacks in more exposed chaparral terrain, overlooking giant boulder and slab tumbles in the shadow of the park's volcanic stone towers and crags. Pinnacles National Park was a favorite of rock climbers long before its status changed from monument to park. The Tourist Trap, on your right where the trail begins to rise out of the gulch, is a very popular climb. On weekends especially, keep your eyes open for climbers perched on massive boulders or dangling from ropes on the right side of the trail.

At 0.75 mile the stretch of terraced stone steps is a welcome change to the frequently uneven rock surface as you continue to switchback out of the gulch. At about 1.1 miles the trail offers a natural viewpoint toward the High Peaks to the west and an unobstructed view of the trail tracing the open ridge ahead. Manzanita and chamise dominate the landscape beneath the peaks, but the most enchanting feature of this hike—and a great photo spot—is the stone-arched tunnel at 1.6 miles. The last 0.5 mile of sweeping switchbacks is one of the more dramatic sections of the hike. As you make the last turn, you will see a small stone building housing the vault toilets

Bear Gulch Day Use Area to Scout Peak

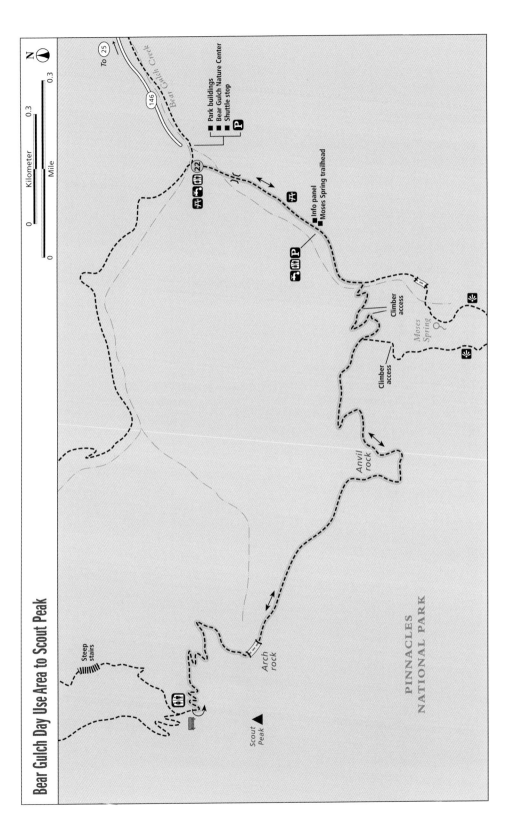

Steep stairs

Scout Peak

Arch rock

Anvil rock

PINNACLES NATIONAL PARK

Climber access

Climber access

Moses Spring

Info panel
Moses Spring trailhead

Park buildings
Bear Gulch Nature Center
Shuttle stop
P

22

146

To 25

Bear Gulch Creek

N

Kilometer
0   0.3

Mile
0   0.3

on your left; the bench on the saddle above is your destination beneath Scout Peak. Enjoy the soaring views and a well-deserved picnic break straddling the East and West Pinnacles before going back down to the trailhead the way you came.

Miles and Directions

0.0 Start at the High Peaks Trail sign across from the Bear Gulch Nature Center.

0.05 Walk left across the wooden footbridge and through the shaded picnic area.

0.2 Come to the Moses Spring trailhead, information board, and sign for High Peaks 1.9 and Reservoir Caves 0.7.

0.3 Come to the trail junction for Moses Spring Trail going left and High Peaks Trail going right. Bear right on High Peaks Trail.

0.4 Come to the climber access trail for Tourist Trap.

0.5 Come to a T-junction and trail marker for a climber access trail to the left and the High Peaks Trail to the right. Continue walking on High Peaks Trail.

0.6 Come to a trail junction signed Rim Trail to Reservoir to the left. Continue walking to the right on High Peaks Trail.

1.1 Arrive at a climber access trail on the left and continue walking past the anvil-shaped rock on the right. Views open to the west.

1.6 Walk through the arch tunnel rock.

2.1 Arrive at your destination at the High Peaks bench below Scout Peak. (GPS: N36 28.89'/ W121 11.96'. Elevation 2,478 feet.) Soak up the soaring views on the saddle straddling the East and West Pinnacles. Go back to the trailhead the way you came.

4.2 Arrive back at the trailhead.

23 Bear Gulch Day Use Area to High Peaks

This is one of the classic hikes in Pinnacles National Park, with almost half a mile of intimidating, steep, narrow chiseled rock steps, sometimes assisted by metal pipe handrails on the rock faces. The scenic trail climbs out of leafy Bear Gulch up to the Pinnacles saddle straddling the east and west sides of the park beneath Scout Peak, before looping around the panoramic High Peaks where condors love to soar. The loop closes back at the saddle.

Start: From Bear Gulch Day Use Area.
Distance: 6.1-mile lollipop
Hiking time: 4 hours
Difficulty: Strenuous due to uphill and challenging High Peaks loop
Trail surface: Dirt and rock
Trailhead elevation: 1,279 feet
Highest point: 2,598 feet
Best seasons: Spring for wildflowers, late fall and winter for cooler temperatures (summer and early fall can be very hot)
Maps: USGS North Chalone Peak; Pinnacles National Park map; Tom Harrison map of Pinnacles National Park
Nearest town: Hollister

Trail contact: Pinnacles National Park, 5000 CA 146, Paicines, CA 95043-9770; (831) 389-4485 or (831) 389-4427; www.nps.gov/pinn
Trail tips: Bear Gulch Day Use Area has convenient parking, a seasonal nature center, water, restrooms, picnic tables, grills, and trash and recycling containers. There is about a 300 yard stretch of narrow rock steps that are steep enough to require metal pipe handrails in some sections on the High Peaks loop part of the hike. This can be too intimidating to someone with a fear of heights and too challenging for anyone with knee issues.

Finding the trailhead: From US 101 at San Juan Bautista/Hollister exit 345 (approximately 17 miles north of Salinas and 10 miles south of Gilroy), take exit 345 and drive 7.5 miles to the Hollister turnoff on the right. Drive 3.5 miles and turn right onto CA 25. Drive 28 miles on CA 25 to the Pinnacles National Park entrance. Turn right into the park and drive 2 miles to the visitor center to pay the entrance fee and pick up a map and information. The visitor center is on your left. Return to the main park road and drive 3 more miles to the Bear Gulch Day Use Area parking lot. The trailhead is across the road from the nature center at the sign for High Peaks Trail on the left. GPS: N36 28.87' / W121 10.89'.

From US 101 at King City, take exit 282B/Broadway Street and turn right onto Broadway Street. Drive 1 mile on Broadway Street to the T intersection with First Street. Turn left onto First Street and drive 14 miles to the T intersection with CA 25. (First Street becomes Bitterwater Road at the sign for East Pinnacles.) Turn left onto CA 25 to Pinnacles and drive 14 miles to the CA 146 intersection. Turn left into Pinnacles National Park and follow directions above to the trailhead.

The Hike

Within 350 yards from the trailhead, the trail cuts through a shady picnic area before reaching the Moses Spring trailhead and a parking area and sign for the High Peaks.

At 0.2 mile up the trail you come to a trail junction for the Moses Spring Trail to the left and the High Peaks Trail to the right. Bear right on the High Peaks Trail for the 0.5-mile-long gradual climb before the trail transitions to switchbacks in more exposed chaparral terrain, overlooking giant boulder and slab tumbles in the shadow of the park's volcanic stone towers and crags. On weekends especially, keep your eyes open for climbers perched on massive boulders or dangling from ropes on the right side of the trail.

At 0.75 mile the stretch of terraced stone steps is a welcome change to the frequently uneven rock surface as you continue to switchback out of the gulch. The green of spring also comes with the bloom of burgundy Indian warrior flowers on this stretch up to about 1.1 miles, where the trail offers a natural viewpoint toward the High Peaks to the west and an unobstructed view of the trail tracing the open ridge ahead. Manzanita and chamise dominate the landscape beneath the peaks, but the most enchanting feature of this hike—and a great photo spot—is the stone-arched tunnel at 1.6 miles. The last 0.5 mile of views from the sweeping switchbacks before the bench that straddles the East and West Pinnacles at the base of Scout Peak is a prelude to the grander panorama ahead on the High Peaks Trail. As you make the last turn to the bench and saddle, you will pass a small stone building housing the vault toilets on your left. Enjoy the soaring views and a well-deserved water break at the bench.

From the bench High Peaks Trail turns northward uphill. Notice the Steep and Narrow sign. The trail begins to climb gently on the west slope, then switchbacks downhill overlooking the east side of the park. At about 500 yards from the bench, the trail starts its tricky, challenging steep sections of primitive single-foot, rock-chipped steps and metal pipe handrails along narrow ledges. If your friends call you "big foot," the shallow chiseled steps may be more like "toe" holds than "foot" holds. At 2.5 miles the trail crests and rewards you with striking views of the Diablo Range on the northern and eastern horizon. The white streaks and blots on the rocky ledges as you look left indicate where condors and other birds nest and roost. To the southeast is an obvious swirl of eroded sediment on the face of a rock wall. North Chalone Peak and the fire tower dominate to the south. The wide rock slab at the crest is a great spot to enjoy a snack while scanning the horizon for condors.

The trail continues down more rock steps, hugging rock faces along wooden catwalks with steel pipe handrails. At 2.8 miles you come to a trail intersection for the Tunnel Trail on the west slope of the peaks. Bear left on Tunnel Trail and walk downhill across a metal walkway that bridges the short, narrow ravine before walking through the stone tunnel built by the Civilian Conservation Corps in the 1930s.

Just past the tunnel you come to the trail junction signed High Peaks via Juniper Canyon Trail Hollister side. Turn left and walk uphill on Juniper Canyon Trail back up

Spring wildflowers enhance the trail to the High Peaks.

Bear Gulch Day Use Area to High Peaks

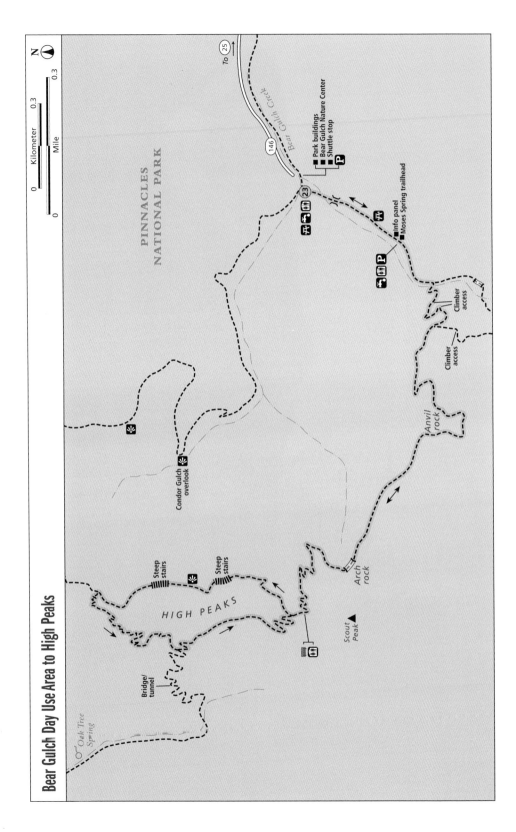

to the bench beneath Scout Peak. At 4.0 miles you reach the bench and the close of your lollipop. Breathe in the views before going back down to the trailhead the way you came.

Miles and Directions

0.0 Start at the High Peaks Trail sign across from the Bear Gulch Nature Center and walk left across the wooden footbridge and through the shaded picnic area to the Moses Spring trailhead, information board, and sign for High Peaks 1.9 and Reservoir Caves 0.7.

0.3 Come to the trail junction for Moses Spring Trail going left and High Peaks Trail going right. Bear right on High Peaks Trail and pass the climber access trail for Tourist Trap.

0.5 Come to a T-junction and trail marker for a climber access trail to the left and the High Peaks Trail to the right. Continue walking on High Peaks Trail past a trail junction signed Rim Trail to Reservoir to the left. Continue walking to the right on High Peaks Trail.

1.1 Arrive at a climber access trail on the left and continue walking past the anvil-shaped rock on the right. Views open to the west.

1.6 Walk through the arch tunnel rock.

2.1 Arrive at the High Peaks bench below Scout Peak. Soak up the soaring views on the saddle straddling the East and West Pinnacles. Walk northward uphill on the High Peaks Trail.

2.4 Come to the beginning of the rock steps, with metal pipe handrails assisting the narrower and steeper stretches.

2.5 The trail crests on the High Peaks with soaring views north, east, and south. Watch for condors before descending the last stretch of the steep, narrow rock steps.

2.8 Come to a trail junction for Tunnel Trail. Bear left on Tunnel Trail.

3.3 Come to a metal walkway over the ravine and a rock tunnel. Turn left at the trail junction for Juniper Canyon trail after the rock tunnel and walk uphill on Juniper Canyon Trail.

4.0 Arrive back at the bench below Scout Peak and the close of the lollipop. Go back to the trailhead the way you came.

6.1 Arrive back at the trailhead.

24 Bear Gulch Day Use Area to Chaparral Day Use Area via High Peaks Trail

The out-and-back hike from one side of the park to the other is for the hardy hiker. This is a scenic but strenuous traverse from east to west up a shady gulch hugging the exposed volcanic rock palisades of the park. Once over the top the descent traces the impressive rock face of the west flank down shady Juniper Canyon to an expansive, well-developed picnic area.

Start: From Bear Gulch Day Use Area
Distance: 7.8 miles out and back
Hiking time: 5 hours
Difficulty: Strenuous
Trail surface: Dirt, gravel, and rock
Trailhead elevation: 1,279 feet
Highest point: 2,478 feet
Best seasons: Spring for wildflowers, late fall and winter for cooler temperatures (summer and early fall can be very hot)
Maps: USGS North Chalone Peak; Pinnacles National Park map; Tom Harrison map of Pinnacles National Park
Nearest town: Hollister

Trail contact: Pinnacles National Park, 5000 CA 146, Paicines, CA 95043-9770; (831) 389-4485 or (831) 389-4427; www.nps.gov/pinn
Trail tips: Bear Gulch Day Use Area has convenient parking, a seasonal nature center, water, restrooms, picnic tables, grills, and trash and recycling containers. There is no water along the hike, but you will find 2 vault toilets on the saddle before dropping down to the west side. Chaparral Day Use Area has water, restrooms, picnic tables, grills, and trash and recycling containers.

Finding the trailhead: From US 101 at San Juan Bautista/Hollister exit 345 (approximately 17 miles north of Salinas and 10 miles south of Gilroy), take exit 345 and drive 7.5 miles to the Hollister turnoff on the right. Drive 3.5 miles and turn right onto CA 25. Drive 28 miles on CA 25 to the Pinnacles National Park entrance. Turn right into the park and drive 2 miles to the visitor center to pay the entrance fee and pick up a map and information. The visitor center is on your left. Return to the main park road and drive 3 more miles to the Bear Gulch Day Use Area parking lot. The trailhead is across the road from the nature center at the sign for High Peaks Trail on the left. GPS: N36 28.87' / W121 10.89'.

From US 101 at King City, take exit 282B/Broadway Street and turn right onto Broadway Street. Drive 1 mile on Broadway Street to the T intersection with First Street. Turn left onto First Street and drive 14 miles to the T intersection with CA 25. (First Street becomes Bitterwater Road at the sign for East Pinnacles.) Turn left onto CA 25 to Pinnacles and drive 14 miles to the CA 146 intersection. Turn left into Pinnacles National Park and follow directions above to the trailhead.

The Hike

Historic stone buildings, seasonal creeks, shady groves, caves, a reservoir, stunning rock formations, and several trailheads, not to mention a campground 3 miles down the road,

Pines and sticky-monkey blooms along the High Peaks Trail

make the Bear Gulch area "hike central" on the east side of Pinnacles National Park. The west side, where farmland and vineyards unfurl north toward the Pacific Coast between the ancient volcanic Pinnacles and the coastal range, boasts its own special cave, seasonal creeks, dramatic cliffs, and a wilderness for those seeking more solitude. There are no roads within the park connecting the distinctly unique east and west sides, and the shortest hiking route is both the most scenic and the most strenuous. This is a hike that makes you feel like an explorer and rewards you with panoramic views.

Your hike begins through the shady picnic area across from the Bear Gulch Nature Center and begins the sinewy climb up the High Peaks Trail at the Moses Spring trailhead. In the winter and early spring, Bear Gulch Creek gurgles on the right through the picnic area and partway up High Peaks Trail. Bear right at the Moses Spring Trail junction, and soon you trade the leafy gulch and cool, velvety, moss-covered boulders for manzanita shrubs as the trail traces the base of the towering rock spires past climber access trails. Keep an eye out for climbers dangling from ropes like marionettes or sitting on top of precipitous cliffs.

Bear Gulch Day Use Area to Chaparral Day Use Area via High Peaks Trail

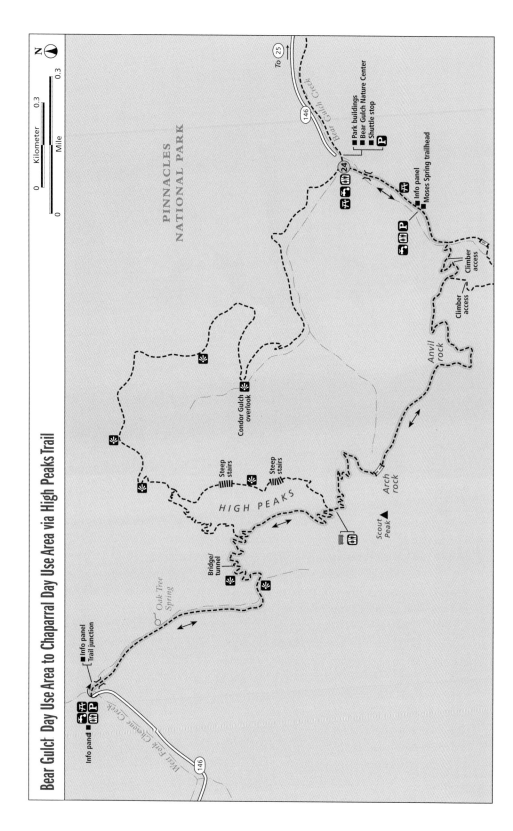

Info panel
Info panel
Trail junction

West Fork Chalone Creek

146

Oak Tree Spring

Bridge/tunnel

HIGH PEAKS

Steep stairs

Steep stairs

Condor Gulch overlook

Scout Peak

Arch rock

Anvil rock

Climber access

Climber access

Info panel
Moses Spring trailhead

■ Park buildings
■ Bear Gulch Nature Center
■ Shuttle stop

24

146

Bear Gulch Creek

To 25

PINNACLES NATIONAL PARK

N

Kilometer
0   0.3   0.3

Mile
0   0.3

At about 1.1 miles up the trail, after passing an anvil-shaped rock on the right, the views open south toward the chaparral slopes of North Chalone Peak and the fire tower. The trail then veers away from this dry, exposed saddle and goes back to hugging the towering volcanic outcroppings. At 1.6 miles you walk through one of several rock tunnels in the park constructed by Civilian Conservation Corps (CCC) crews during the 1930s. The trail continues to climb into the heart of this amazing geologic realm until you reach the ridge at the wooden bench straddling the East and West Pinnacles at 2.1 miles. The setting and views are nothing short of humbling. You come to a trail junction for High Peaks going up on the right and Chaparral Picnic Area via Juniper Canyon on the left. Bear left and begin your descent down Juniper Canyon.

At 2.7 miles you come to the junction for the High Peaks via Tunnel Trail. Bear left and continue down Juniper Canyon. The Balconies Cliffs come into view on your right at about 3.0 miles, just before the trail turns for a close-up view of the rock face across Juniper Canyon. The trail transitions from switchbacks to a gentler grade under the canopy of junipers and oaks. At 3.6 miles you pass unmarked Oak Tree Spring on the right. During a normal wet season, the narrow canyon is alive with ribbons of water babbling beneath the large trailside boulders.

The trail levels out at 3.8 miles, where you walk over a wooden footbridge and bear left at the Condor interpretive sign. At 3.9 miles you reach the Chaparral Picnic Area parking lot and trail information board. Take advantage of the restrooms with flush toilets, drinking fountain and developed picnic area on the right at the north end of the parking lot. Rest and refuel before going back over to the east side the way you came.

Miles and Directions

0.0 Start at the High Peaks Trail sign across from the Bear Gulch Nature Center and walk left across the wooden footbridge and through the shaded picnic area to the Moses Spring trailhead, information board, and sign for High Peaks 1.9 and Reservoir Caves 0.7. Walk uphill on Moses Spring Trail.

0.3 Come to the trail junction for Moses Spring Trail going left and High Peaks Trail going right. Bear right on High Peaks Trail and walk past the climber access trail for Tourist Trap on the right.

0.5 Come to a T-junction and trail marker for a climber access trail to the left and the High Peaks Trail to the right. Continue walking on High Peaks Trail.

0.6 Come to a trail junction signed Rim Trail to Reservoir to the left. Continue walking to the right on High Peaks Trail.

1.1 Arrive at a climber access trail on the left and continue walking past the anvil-shaped rock on the right. Views open to the west.

1.6 Walk through the arch tunnel rock.

2.1 Come to the bench on the saddle straddling the East and West Pinnacles below Scout Peak and a fork in the trail. Bear left and walk down the west slope along Juniper Canyon Trail.

2.7 Come to the trail junction for High Peaks via Tunnel Trail. Bear left and continue walking down toward the Chaparral Picnic Area.

3.0 Come to a viewpoint of the Balconies Cliffs to the north. In another 0.2 mile come to a viewpoint looking across Juniper Canyon.

3.6 Come to unmarked Oak Tree Spring on your left.

3.8 Come to a fork and cross a wooden footbridge, then bear left at the Condor interpretive sign.

3.9 Arrive at the Chaparral Picnic Area parking area and information board. (GPS: N36 29.50'/ W121 12.56'. Elevation: 1,389 feet.) Restrooms, a drinking fountain, and grills are in the large picnic area to the right at the north end of the parking area. Refuel with a snack and water in the picnic area before going back to the trailhead on the east side the way you came.

7.8 Arrive back at the trailhead.

25 Bear Gulch Day Use Area to Bear Gulch Caves and Balconies Cave

Pinnacles National Park has some of the most accessible talus caves in the National Park System. This hike is a "cave fest" for cave lovers but comes with both bad news and good news. The bad news is that the two sets of caves are on opposite sides of the park, so you will have to climb up the east side from the Bear Gulch Caves to get down to the Balconies Cave on the west side. The good news is that the loop back to the trailhead is mostly on flat terrain except for the last mile uphill along lovely Bear Gulch Creek.

Start: From Bear Gulch Day Use Area
Distance: 9.65-mile loop
Hiking time: 6 hours
Difficulty: Strenuous
Trail surface: Dirt, rock, and possible water in the caves
Trailhead elevation: 1,279 feet
Highest point: 2,478 feet
Best seasons: Spring for wildflowers, late fall and winter for cooler temperatures (summer and early fall can be very hot); cool in the caves
Maps: USGS North Chalone Peak; Pinnacles National Park map; Tom Harrison map of Pinnacles National Park
Nearest town: Hollister

Trail contact: Pinnacles National Park, 5000 CA 146, Paicines, CA 95043-9770; (831) 389-4485 or (831) 389-4427; www.nps.gov/pinn
Trail tips: Bear Gulch Day Use Area has convenient parking, a seasonal nature center, water, restrooms, picnic tables, grills, and trash and recycling containers. Check the park website for up-to-date information about cave closures. You need a flashlight or headlamp for the caves. The caves are a cool escape when outside temperatures are high, but bring ample water for this hike's long, exposed stretches. You can take a short spur to refill your water in the Chaparral Day Use Area before continuing to Balconies Cave.

Finding the trailhead: From US 101 at San Juan Bautista/Hollister exit 345 (approximately 17 miles north of Salinas and 10 miles south of Gilroy), take exit 345 and drive 7.5 miles to the Hollister turnoff on the right. Drive 3.5 miles and turn right onto CA 25. Drive 28 miles on CA 25 to the Pinnacles National Park entrance. Turn right into the park and drive 2 miles to the visitor center to pay the entrance fee and pick up a map and information. The visitor center is on your left. Return to the main park road and drive 3 more miles to the Bear Gulch Day Use Area parking lot. The trailhead is across the road from the nature center at the sign for High Peaks Trail on the left. GPS: N36 28.87' / W121 10.89'.

From US 101 at King City, take exit 282B/Broadway Street and turn right onto Broadway Street. Drive 1 mile on Broadway Street to the T intersection with First Street. Turn left onto First Street and drive 14 miles to the T intersection with CA 25. (First Street becomes Bitterwater Road at the sign for East Pinnacles.) Turn left onto CA 25 to Pinnacles and drive 14 miles to the CA 146 intersection. Turn left into Pinnacles National Park and follow directions above to the trailhead.

The Hike

The east- and west-side talus "caves" are a definite highlight in Pinnacles National Park. The "caves" are actually boulder-roofed tunnels. Looking at the cave entrances, it appears as if a cataclysmic event triggered an avalanche of rock, some of gargantuan proportions, that toppled, wedged, and stacked up, forming gulches, skinny canyons, and narrow, irregular maze-like corridors, intricate passages, and chambers. The caves have an entrance and exit point that can be traveled in either direction with a flashlight. There are white arrows painted at strategic locations on the rock walls to help guide you through the dark maze. The distance from entrance to exit is short, approximately 1,400 feet in the longest stretch for Lower and Upper Bear Gulch Caves. But because you are in the dark watching your footing on sometimes very slippery wet surfaces every inch of the way when you are not squeezing and stooping, the journey (at least the first time) may seem longer. Each cave presents its own challenges and unique characteristics.

There is no road connecting the east and west sides of the park, so hiking the caves on both sides in one day requires at least one strenuous uphill to the Pinnacles saddle and down the other side.

Bear Gulch Caves, the first caves you come to from the trailhead, happen to also be the home of bats. Bear Gulch Caves are "bat caves" of sorts. The park biologists monitor the bat population and their migration patterns in and out of the caves to determine which caves to close when and for how long, so the public can have access to parts of the caves (if not both Lower and Upper Caves) without risk of disturbing the breeding, birthing, and rearing process. The Lower Cave becomes the main bat maternity ward part of the year (warmer months) when female bats give birth to their young.

At some point the baby bats are strong enough to ride on mom's back, and she migrates to the Upper Cave (cooler months) where baby bats become young bats strong enough to fly off with mom. Sometime, usually in March or April and again in October, there is a short window of opportunity to open both caves to the public, and that is when hikers can experience the full cave adventure. The cave closure schedule is posted on the park website and updated regularly. The Bear Gulch Caves route (Upper and Lower) joins the Moses Spring Trail for the last section of about seventy-five rock steps that emerge at Bear Gulch Reservoir. Although the hike described here applies to when the Lower and Upper Caves route are both open, don't be deterred from committing to the East/West cave-fest hike if the Upper section is closed and the Lower is open. The East/West cave hike will be a memorable notch in your cave belt. The main factor that could interfere with your double caves excursion (East/West) is if Balconies Cave is closed due to flooding. Even in a drought year with minimal storm activity, the Balconies Cave is a funnel for water and floods easily. The surrounding seasonal streams can be ridiculously low, but Balconies Cave can remain closed for a week at a time while the water level drops from thigh-high to ankle-deep.

Entering the Balconies Cave

Check the park website and call the ranger station ahead of time to avoid disappointment if your heart is set on "all caves"-only day.

Be aware that even a light film of moisture on the cave floor can be treacherous. Wet, slippery rocks as you are climbing up and down with one hand gripping a flashlight and the other a hiking stick or feeling for a rock handhold can make the path very precarious. But all that is also what makes a Pinnacles caves hike a fun agility and flexibility course and a satisfying adventure.

The first 350 yards of this hike is pleasantly tame as you walk across a wooden footbridge and enter the nicely developed picnic area across the road from the Bear Gulch Nature Center parking lot. Bear Gulch Creek will be gurgling on the right if you are here in winter or spring. You come to the Moses Spring trailhead at the west end of the shady picnic area. Walk up Moses Spring Trail and bear left to stay on Moses Spring at the junction with High Peaks Trail. The minute you leave that junction, you enter a special realm as the trail meanders up between velvety green boulders and towering rock walls to a hollowed-out rock tunnel. Walk through the short tunnel and to the fork in the trail signed Reservoir via Moses Spring Trail to the right and Reservoir via Bear Gulch Caves to the left. Bear left for the adventure via Bear Gulch Caves.

Have your flashlight ready as you enter the Lower Cave. Don't be surprised to see, hear, and step in water in the winter and spring. The uneven volcanic rock floor becomes even slipperier in dark, wet conditions. The entire route through the Lower and Upper Caves is about 1,400 feet but will feel much longer if this is your first time, because the going is slow and deliberate.

Shortly after entering and navigating the narrow passage you will walk up 135 rock steps guided by a metal pipe handrail to a junction. The metal gate to the Upper Cave is on your right up another 20 steps. This is the gate that is closed and locked when the Upper Cave is the bat maternity ward. (You are on this hike because the Upper Cave is open.) You will have to do a lot of stooping and scooching in this section; keep your flashlight scanning for the white arrows on the walls pointing you in the correct direction. There are a couple of chambers tall enough for you to stand. You exit the Upper Cave through a second open gate, where you merge onto the Moses Spring Trail coming in from the left. Head toward the light and walk up 75 rock steps to the head of the reservoir.

At 0.95 mile you come to Bear Gulch Reservoir and the trail junction for the North Chalone Peak to the left across the head of the stone dam and the Rim Trail straight ahead. Don't leave the dam without soaking up the otherworldly setting of this body of water and reading the interpretive sign about the endangered red-legged frog that makes this area home.

The Rim Trail route skirts the top of the gulch with expansive views toward the Bear Gulch Day Use Area from the crest. At almost 1.3 miles you pass a climber access on the right just before the trail junction with High Peaks Trail. Rim Trail ends at this junction. Turn left onto High Peaks Trail. At almost 2 miles up the trail, after passing an anvil-shaped rock on the right, the views open south toward the chaparral slopes of North Chalone Peak and the fire tower. The trail then veers away from this dry, exposed saddle and goes back to hugging the towering volcanic outcroppings. At 2.35 miles you walk through one of several rock tunnels in the park constructed by Civilian Conservation Corps (CCC) crews during the 1930s. The trail continues to climb into the heart of this amazing geologic realm, and you reach the ridge at the wooden bench straddling the East and West Pinnacles at almost 3 miles. There is no water here, but the small stone building on the left before you reach the bench has two vault toilets. The setting and views are nothing short of humbling.

The trail junction for High Peaks goes up on the right, and Chaparral Picnic Area via Juniper Canyon goes down on the left. Bear left and begin your descent down Juniper Canyon. At 3.45 miles you come to the junction for the High Peaks via Tunnel Trail. Bear left and continue down Juniper Canyon. The Balconies Cliffs come into view on your right just before the trail turns for a close-up view of the rock face across Juniper Canyon. The trail transitions from switchbacks to a gentler grade under the canopy of junipers and oaks. At 4.35 miles you pass unmarked Oak Tree Spring on the right. During a normal wet season, the narrow canyon is alive with ribbons of water babbling beneath the large trailside boulders.

The trail levels out at 4.55 miles at a fork where you walk over a wooden footbridge and past the Condor interpretive sign on the right. Continue walking straight with the fence on your left. You will see the Chaparral Picnic Area and trailhead parking across the way on the left. There is a restroom and drinking water here, the last before you end your loop back at the trailhead. You may want to fill up your water bottle and take a break for a snack before continuing any farther.

Just ahead, the trail from the Chaparral Picnic Area merges from the left. There is another interpretive sign and a trail sign for Balconies Cave 0.6 and Old Pinnacles Trailhead 3.3. Turn right toward the Old Pinnacles trailhead. The trail heads toward a canyon with Machete Ridge on your right and the Flume rock formation on your left. The landscape is mostly buckwheat shrub and some pine trees at the head of the canyon. You walk across five wooden footbridges over seasonal West Fork Chalone Creek and pass several climber access trail spurs before the trail narrows into the canyon and you come to the junction for the Balconies Cliff Trail. Turn right at the junction and continue walking in the canyon to the Balconies Cave.

At 5.4 miles you come to the entrance of the Balconies Cave and an open gate. The gate would be locked shut if the cave were closed due to flooding from West Fork Chalone Creek. Use your flashlight to light your path through the cave. The path begins between towering boulder walls before you reach the dark, cave-like entrance. You have to step down and ease yourself slowly down a slab before continuing on the cave floor. From here on, the short journey requires some crawling and sideways slithering.

Exit back in the canyon and continue on the trail to a junction where the Balconies Cliffs Trail merges from the left. Bear right at the sign for Pinnacles Campground 3.7 and Pinnacles Visitor Center 4.1. Although it is not marked as such, you are now on the Old Pinnacles Trail. The trail crosses West Fork Chalone Creek seven times until you come to the junction with the North Wilderness Trail on the left. Continue walking straight toward the Old Pinnacles trailhead. Chalone Creek is on your left. At 7.5 miles come to the interpretive sign for the Chalone Creek Restoration project.

Bear Gulch Day Use Area to Bear Gulch Caves and Balconies Cave

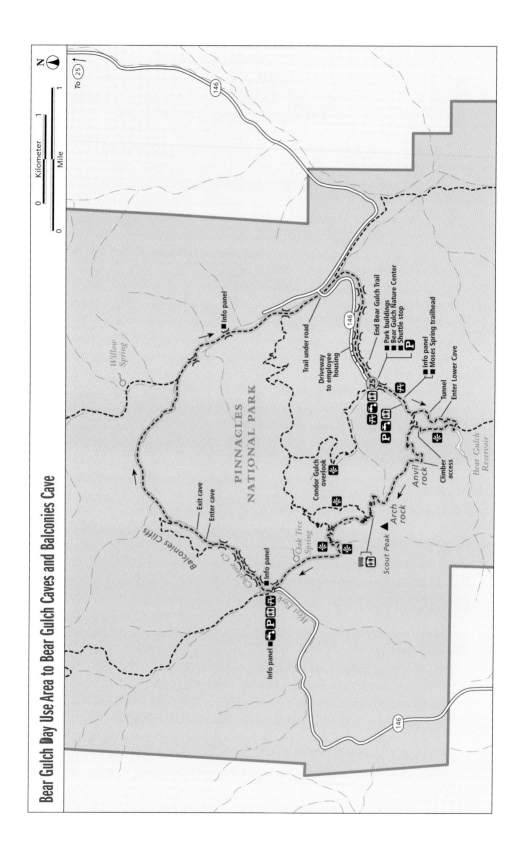

Come to the Bench Trail junction and turn right onto Bench Trail, then walk across seasonal Chalone Creek on a wooden footbridge.

Walk past the junction for High Peaks Trail on the right and cross another wooden footbridge before the Bench Trail passes under the road overpass. You walk on two sections of boardwalk over an eroded section of the Chalone Creek on your left before coming to the trail junction for the unmarked Bear Gulch Trail. This is where Bench Trail continues to the left across a double wooden footbridge, but you will turn right toward Bear Gulch Day Use Area. Just 1 mile remains on your long haul back to the trailhead. Although the last mile is uphill, the trail traces idyllic Bear Gulch Creek with its creekbed ferns and clump grasses under canopies of buckeye in the spring and sycamore later in the season. In an average wet season, Bear Gulch Creek tumbles over boulders and even plunges into a small waterfall on its way to meet Chalone Creek.

Stop to admire the setting as you cross the six wooden footbridges up to the trailhead. The trail steepens briefly between bridges #2 and #3 but plateaus just past the employee residence driveway at 9.6 miles in time to catch your breath before the end of your excursion at 9.65 miles back at the trailhead across from the Bear Gulch Nature Center.

Miles and Directions

0.0 Start at the Picnic Area, Bear Gulch Caves, Reservoir, and High Peaks Trail sign across from the Bear Gulch Nature Center and walk across the wooden footbridge through the picnic area to the Moses Spring trailhead.

0.3 Come to the trail junction for the High Peaks Trail. Bear left and walk uphill on the Moses Spring Trail.

0.45 Walk through the rock tunnel.

0.5 Come to a fork in the trail signed Reservoir via Moses Spring Trail to the right. Bear left for the reservoir via Bear Gulch Caves.

0.6 Enter the Lower Cave. There are 135 rock-chiseled stairs ahead.

0.75 Come to an unmarked fork where going left takes you out of the caves. Bear right and walk up 20 rock steps through a gate into Upper Cave's narrow and low-ceilinged passages.

0.9 Exit through a gate and rejoin Moses Spring Trail. Walk up 75 rock steps to Bear Gulch Reservoir. Breathe and take time to look around. Moses Spring Trail ends here. Turn right to continue walking up on Rim Trail.

1.15 Come to the crest of the Rim Trail and a view up Bear Gulch to the east.

1.35 Come to the trail junction for High Peaks Trail. Rim Trail ends. Turn left onto High Peaks Trail.

1.85 Arrive at a climber access on the left and continue walking past the anvil-shaped rock on the right. Views open to the west.

2.35 Walk through the arch tunnel rock.

2.85 Come to the bench on the saddle straddling the East and West Pinnacles below Scout Peak and a fork in the trail. Bear left and walk down the west slope along Juniper Canyon Trail.

3.45 Come to the trail junction for High Peaks via Tunnel Trail. Bear left and continue walking down toward the Chaparral Picnic Area.

3.95 Come to a viewpoint looking across Juniper Canyon.

4.35 Come to unmarked Oak Tree Spring on your right.

4.55 Come to a fork and cross a wooden footbridge. Continue walking straight at the trail junction for the Chaparral Picnic Area parking lot with restroom and drinking fountain. A Condor interpretive sign is on the right.

4.7 Come to a trail junction where the Chaparral Picnic Area trail merges from the left. Bear right and continue toward the sign for Balconies Cave 0.6 and Old Pinnacles Trailhead 3.3. Come to a map board and interpretive sign and continue on the trail to cross the West Fork Chalone Creek on a footbridge. Shortly cross another footbridge to the trail junction and a sign on the right for the climber access trail to Elephant Rock and The Citadel. Bear left and walk under the gargantuan boulder arch.

5.1 Cross two more footbridges in quick succession over West Fork Chalone Creek.

5.3 Walk across another footbridge to the trail junction for Balconies Cliffs Trail and Balconies Cave. Machete Ridge and a climber access trail are on your right. Turn right to Balconies Cave and immediately walk across the creek to the entrance of Balconies Cave. Turn on your flashlight to continue into the cave. You exit Balconies Cave in 0.1 mile.

5.7 Come to the trail junction for Balconies Cliffs Trail. Bear right on unmarked Old Pinnacles Trail.

6.0 Walk across West Fork Chalone Creek. You will cross the creek five more times in the next 0.7 mile.

7.0 Come to the trail junction with the North Wilderness Trail. Continue walking straight to the Old Pinnacles trailhead. Chalone Creek is on your left and you will cross Chalone Creek on a footbridge about 350 yards up the trail.

7.5 Come to an interpretive sign about the Chalone Creek Restoration project and a trail junction with Bench Trail. Bear right on Bench Trail and cross Chalone Creek on a wooden footbridge.

8.0 Come to the trail junction with High Peaks Trail on the right. Continue walking straight on Bench Trail, then shortly cross the creek on a wooden footbridge.

8.3 Walk under the park road overpass. In 0.2 mile walk on two closely spaced boardwalks along an eroded section of Chalone Creek.

8.6 Come to the trail junction with the unmarked Bear Gulch Trail and a trail sign for Bear Gulch Day Use Area. Bench Trail continues left. Bear right and walk up Bear Gulch Trail along Bear Gulch Creek toward the day-use area.

8.8 Walk across a wooden footbridge. Cross three more footbridges in the next 0.5 mile.

9.4 Walk across the driveway at the employee residence, then walk across two more footbridges in quick succession. Park buildings are on the left.

9.6 Reach the end of Bear Gulch Trail. Follow the sidewalk to the crosswalk. Cross the road in the crosswalk.

9.65 Arrive back at the trailhead.

26 Bear Gulch Day Use Area to North Wilderness via High Peaks

If you thrive on the exhilaration and exertion of climbing to feast on soaring views, and the thrill of navigating steep and narrow trails chiseled in volcanic rock, but also enjoy the solitude of long meanders across the California chaparral landscape, then this hike is for you. Just when you think the day couldn't get any better, the last mile of trail climbs up picturesque Bear Gulch, following the seasonal gurgles and cascades of Bear Gulch Creek across six wooden footbridges.

Start: From Bear Gulch Day Use Area
Distance: 14.2-mile loop
Hiking time: 8 hours
Difficulty: Strenuous
Trail surface: Dirt, rock, and gravel
Trailhead elevation: 1,279 feet
Highest point: 2,598 feet
Best seasons: Spring for wildflowers, late fall and winter for cooler temperatures (summer and early fall can be very hot)
Maps: USGS North Chalone Peak; Pinnacles National Park map; Tom Harrison map of Pinnacles National Park

Nearest town: Hollister
Trail contact: Pinnacles National Park, 5000 CA 146, Paicines, CA 95043-9770; (831) 389-4485 or (831) 389-4427; www.nps.gov/pinn
Trail tips: Bear Gulch Day Use Area has convenient parking, a seasonal nature center, water, restrooms, picnic tables, grills, and trash and recycling containers. Make sure you refill your water in the Chaparral Day Use Area. Once you start on the North Wilderness Trail it will be about 10 miles before you come to water (back at the trailhead).

Finding the trailhead: From US 101 at San Juan Bautista/Hollister exit 345 (approximately 17 miles north of Salinas and 10 miles south of Gilroy), take exit 345 and drive 7.5 miles to the Hollister turnoff on the right. Drive 3.5 miles and turn right onto CA 25. Drive 28 miles on CA 25 to the Pinnacles National Park entrance. Turn right into the park and drive 2 miles to the visitor center to pay the entrance fee and pick up a map and information. The visitor center is on your left. Return to the main park road and drive 3 more miles to the Bear Gulch Day Use Area parking lot. The trailhead is across the road from the nature center at the sign for High Peaks Trail on the left. GPS: N36 28.87' / W121 10.89'.

From US 101 at King City, take exit 282B/Broadway Street and turn right onto Broadway Street. Drive 1 mile on Broadway Street to the T intersection with First Street. Turn left onto First Street and drive 14 miles to the T intersection with CA 25. (First Street becomes Bitterwater Road at the sign for East Pinnacles.) Turn left onto CA 25 to Pinnacles and drive 14 miles to the CA 146 intersection. Turn left into Pinnacles National Park and follow directions above to the trailhead.

The Hike

Within 250 feet from the trailhead, the trail cuts through a shady picnic area before reaching the Moses Spring trailhead and parking area and a sign for the High Peaks.

At 0.2 mile up the trail, you come to a trail junction for the Moses Spring Trail to the left and the High Peaks Trail to the right. Bear right on the High Peaks Trail for the 0.5-mile-long gradual climb before the trail transitions to switchbacks in more exposed chaparral terrain, overlooking giant boulder and slab tumbles in the shadow of the park's volcanic stone towers and crags. On weekends especially, keep your eyes open for climbers perched on massive boulders or dangling from ropes on the right side of the trail.

At 0.75 mile the stretch of terraced stone steps is a welcome change to the frequently uneven rock surface as you continue to switchback out of the gulch. At about 1.1 miles the trail offers a natural viewpoint toward the High Peaks to the west and an unobstructed view of the trail tracing the open ridge ahead. Manzanita and chamise dominate the landscape beneath the peaks, but the most enchanting feature of this hike—and a great photo spot—is the stone-arched tunnel at 1.6 miles. The last 0.5 mile of views from the sweeping switchbacks before the bench straddling the East and West Pinnacles at the base of Scout Peak is a prelude to the grander panorama ahead on the High Peaks Trail. As you make the last turn to the bench and saddle, you pass a small stone building housing the vault toilets on your left. There is no water up here, and the next opportunity for restrooms with water is down in the Chaparral Picnic Area. Enjoy the soaring views and a well-deserved picnic break at the saddle.

From the bench High Peaks Trail turns northward uphill. Notice the Steep and Narrow sign. The trail begins to climb gently on the west slope, then switchbacks downhill overlooking the east side of the park. Less than 0.5 mile from the bench, the trail starts its tricky, challenging steep sections of primitive single-foot, rock-chipped steps and metal pipe handrails along narrow ledges. If your friends call you "big foot," the shallow-chiseled steps may be more like "toe" holds than "foot" holds.

At 2.5 miles the trail crests and rewards you with striking views of the Diablo Range on the northern and eastern horizon. The white streaks and blots on the rocky ledges as you look left indicate where condors and other birds nest and roost. To the southeast is an obvious swirl of eroded sediment on the face of a rock wall. North Chalone Peak and the fire tower dominate to the south. The trail continues down more rock steps, hugging rock faces along wooden catwalks with steel pipe handrails.

At 2.8 miles you come to a trail intersection for the Tunnel Trail on the west slope of the peaks. Bear left to the Chaparral Picnic Area via Tunnel Trail and walk downhill across a metal walkway that bridges the short, narrow ravine before walking through the stone tunnel built by the Civilian Conservation Corps in the 1930s.

Just past the tunnel you come to the trail junction for Juniper Canyon Trail. Tunnel Trail ends here. Bear right and continue walking down to the Chaparral Picnic Area via Juniper Canyon Trail. Less than 0.5 mile down, notice the viewpoint looking down and across Juniper Canyon. At 4.3 miles you pass the unmarked Oak Tree Spring on the right, which puddles at the base of an oak tree. At the fork just ahead on the trail, walk straight across the wooden footbridge and bear left at the Condor Crags interpretive panel to the Chaparral trailhead in the parking area. Turn left and

Volcanic rock formations along the North Wilderness Trail

walk to the north end of the parking lot into the nicely developed picnic area complete with grills and recycling and trash containers. A restroom with flush toilets is on the right and a drinking fountain is on the left. After almost 5 miles, this is the perfect stopover for a picnic and refilling your water bottle before heading out on the North Wilderness Trail at the far end of the picnic area.

Just 0.2 mile out from the North Wilderness trailhead you cross a seasonal creek at a large boulder where the trail cuts through a pleasant meadow. The trail climbs gently, but the undulation is punctuated by steeper stretches until you reach the best view of the West Pinnacles volcanic palisades and crags on the higher of two knolls at 6.25 miles. Walk 50 feet to the right on the spur trail in the chamise clearing for one of the best vantage points to appreciate the scope of this geologic phenomenon.

Approximately 250 feet ahead, the trail drops down in a southwest direction, placing the Pinnacles on your left. Just ahead, you come to a marker at an elbow in the trail. Turn right to continue on the North Wilderness Trail, which follows a swale for almost a mile down to the seasonal North Fork Chalone Creek. Walk across the creek to one of many stacks of rock cairns that will guide you along the more primitive stretches of the trail as it zigzags in and out of the creekbed and along woodlands over the next 3 miles, where little bees keep busy pollinating spring wildflowers.

Bear Gulch Day Use Area to North Wilderness via High Peaks

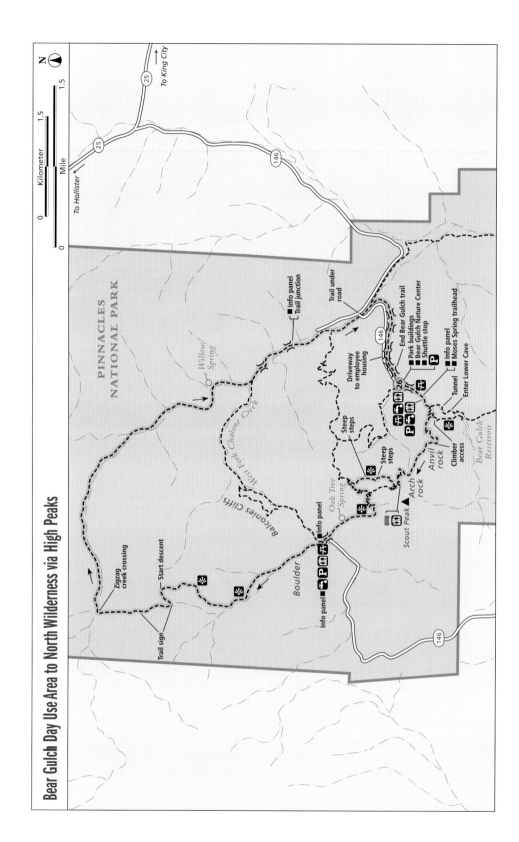

At 11.05 miles you cross the unmarked trickling Willow Spring, a welcome sight in dry years. The spring feeds a riparian habitat of willows and California blackberry vines in the pine and oak woodland for about half a mile before its waters in North Fork Chalone Creek merge with the seasonal West Fork Chalone Creek to become Chalone Creek.

At 11.55 miles North Wilderness Trail ends, and you cross West Fork Chalone Creek just before the junction for Old Pinnacles Trail. Turn left toward the Old Pinnacles trailhead and cross the footbridge ahead over Chalone Creek. At 12.05 miles turn right onto Bench Trail at the junction, then walk across a wooden footbridge and continue on Bench Trail past the junction for High Peaks Trail. You cross another wooden footbridge before the Bench Trail passes under the road overpass. Walk on two sections of boardwalk over an eroded section of Chalone Creek on your left before coming to the trail junction for the unmarked Bear Gulch Trail. Bench Trail continues to the left across a double wooden footbridge, but you turn right toward Bear Gulch Day Use Area. This last mile of trail is a really sweet way to complete your loop at the end of your long over-hill-and-dale journey. The gulch narrows soon after you turn right. Bear Gulch Creek, or the dry creekbed (depending on the season), is on your left. Bear Gulch Creek flows into Chalone Creek.

Although Bear Gulch Creek is seasonal, you will see ferns and clump grass–like sedge being happily nourished by enough water at the bottom of the creek to make sections of the creek a year-round riparian habitat. You cross six idyllic wooden footbridges under leafy canopies of buckeye in early spring and oak and sycamore later in the season. During the wetter winter and early spring, the real prize are the tumbling cascades draping boulders and a waterfall between bridges #2 and #3, where the trail steepens briefly to kick up your cardio one last time. At 13.95 miles the trail crosses the employee residence driveway and plateaus across a meadow before the last two footbridges and the trail's end at the Bear Gulch Day Use Area parking area. The seasonally open nature center is on the left and is a must-do if it is open when you are there. Walk across the road in the pedestrian crosswalk and arrive back at your trailhead on the left.

Miles and Directions

0.0 Start at the High Peaks Trail sign across from the Bear Gulch Nature Center and walk left across the wooden footbridge and through the shaded picnic area to the Moses Spring trailhead, information board, and sign for High Peaks 1.9 and Reservoir Caves 0.7.

0.3 Come to the trail junction for Moses Spring Trail going left and High Peaks Trail going right. Bear right on High Peaks Trail and walk past the climber access trail for Tourist Trap on the right.

0.5 Come to a T-junction and trail marker for a climber access trail to the left and the High Peaks Trail to the right. Continue walking on High Peaks Trail.

0.6 Come to a trail junction signed Rim Trail to Reservoir to the left. Continue walking to the right on High Peaks Trail.

1.1 Arrive at a climber access trail on the left and continue walking past the anvil-shaped rock on the right. Views open to the west.

1.6 Walk through the arch tunnel rock.

2.1 Arrive at the High Peaks bench below Scout Peak. Soak up the soaring views on the saddle straddling the East and West Pinnacles. Walk northward uphill on the High Peaks Trail.

2.4 Come to narrow rock steps leading to the crest of the High Peaks. Watch for condors as the views open north, east and south. In 0.1 mile come to steep rock stairs going down.

2.8 Come to a trail junction at Tunnel Trail. Bear left and walk down to the Chaparral Picnic Area via Tunnel Trail.

3.3 Come to a metal walkway over the ravine and a rock tunnel.

3.4 Come to the trail junction for Juniper Canyon Trail. Bear right and walk to the Chaparral Picnic Area via Juniper Canyon Trail.

3.7 Come to a viewpoint looking down Juniper Canyon.

4.3 Come to unmarked Oak Tree Spring on the right.

4.5 Trail forks. Walk straight across the wooden footbridge, then bear left at the Condor Crags interpretive panel to the Chaparral parking area and trailhead. Turn right and walk to the north end of the parking area. Walk past the restroom and stop at the water fountain to fill your water before continuing to the north end of picnic area.

4.75 Come to the North Wilderness trailhead. In 0.2 mile walk across a seasonal creek at the boulder.

5.65 The trail crests, and views open briefly southward to North Chalone Peak and the fire tower behind you.

6.25 Come to a knoll and spur trail to the right. Walk 50 feet on the spur trail for the view of the West Pinnacles volcanic palisades and peaks and the North Chalone Peak fire tower.

6.65 The trail descends and changes direction toward the southwest. The Pinnacles are on your left. In 0.2 mile come to a trail marker and turn right to continue walking on the North Wilderness Trail at the elbow.

7.65 Reach the seasonal North Fork Chalone Creek. Walk across the creek to the stack of cairns. The trail becomes more primitive. In 0.1 mile crossNorth Fork Chalone Creek again at an almost 90-degree angle east to cairns across the creek and toward the rock outcrop.

7.95 Come to the rock outcrop on your left. The trail continues to zigzag along the creekbed with stacks of cairns guiding you along a well-defined but more primitive stretch.

11.05 Come to a faint trickle in the dry season. This trickle is known as Willow Spring. Walk across the trickle. In 0.3 mile come to another Willow Spring crossing, threading through the willows in the pine woodland.

11.55 Cross West Fork Chalone Creek and come to a trail junction for Old Pinnacles Trail; turn left toward the Old Pinnacles trailhead.

11.75 Walk across seasonal Chalone Creek on a wooden footbridge. In less than one third of a mile come to a trail junction, bear right on Bench Trail, and walk across a wooden footbridge.

12.55 Come to a T-junction with High Peaks Trail on the right. Continue walking straight on Bench Trail, then shortly walk across the seasonal creek on the wooden footbridge.

12.85 Walk under the park road overpass. In 0.2 mile walk on two closely spaced boardwalks along an eroded section of Chalone Creek.

13.15 Come to the trail junction with the unmarked Bear Gulch Trail and a trail sign for Bear Gulch Day Use Area. Bench Trail continues left. Bear right and walk up Bear Gulch Trail along Bear Gulch Creek toward the day-use area.

13.35 Walk across a wooden footbridge. Cross three more footbridges in the next 0.5 mile.

13.95 Walk across the driveway at the employee residence, then walk across two more footbridges in quick succession. Park buildings are on the left.

14.15 Reach the end of Bear Gulch Trail at Bear Gulch Day Use Area.

14.2 Walk across the road in the pedestrian crosswalk, turn left, and arrive back at the trailhead.

East Pinnacles Regional Information and Recreation

At the north end and closest to the park's East Entrance are Tres Pinos, Hollister, and San Juan Bautista.

Tres Pinos

Tres Pinos is a small community 5 miles south of Hollister.

Dining

Tres Pinos Inn, 6991 Airline Hwy., Tres Pinos, CA 95075; (831) 628-3320. The rustic Tres Pinos Inn, a national historic landmark, was built in 1880. Dinner is served Tuesday through Sunday from 5 p.m. to 10 p.m.

Hollister

Hollister, 30 miles north of Pinnacles National Park, is the main town outside of the park's East Entrance for visitors to find lodging, dining, services, and markets for provisions. Wine lovers will be pleased with San Benito County's fertile vineyard country. Visit sanbenitocounty.com and outandaboutmagazine.com.

Lodging

Best Western San Benito Inn, 660 San Felipe Rd., Hollister, CA 95023; (831) 637-9248. Complimentary continental breakfast, no pets. The pool is a plus in hot weather.

Casa de Fruta Inn, 10021 Pacheco Pass/CA 152, Hollister, CA 95023; (408) 842-7282; casadefruta.com. RV campground, 24-hour restaurant, fruit stand, market, gift shop, and amusements. From the first orchard planted by an Italian in 1908 this establishment became a full-blown bustling family business and roadside oasis. Check out their news/events page for a monthly calendar. The Northern California Renaissance Faire is an annual fall favorite.

Hollister Inn, 152 San Felipe Rd., Hollister, CA 95023; (831) 637-1641; hollister inn.com. Complimentary continental breakfast, pet friendly, no pool.

Joshua Inn B&B, 712 West St., Hollister, CA 95023; (831) 265-7829. The Queen Anne–style home was built in 1902. Greg and Tricia and the inn's canine mascot "Sugar Bear," a four-year-old Shih Tzu, welcome visitors in their home's five guest rooms (some with private baths).

Wiebe Motel, 1271 San Felipe Rd., Hollister, CA 95023; (831) 637-5801; wiebe motel.com. The pool is a plus in hot weather.

Dining

Casa de Coffee, 10021 Pacheco Pass/CA 152, Hollister, CA 95023; (408) 842-7282; casadefruta.com. This is a 24-hour restaurant located at the Casa de Fruta Inn.

Ella's Italian Restaurant, 1709 Airline Hwy., Hollister, CA 95023; (831) 638-0338. Thin-crust pizza, caprese salad, and seasonal dishes.

Grillin and Chillin, 3650 San Juan Rd., Hollister, CA 95023; (831) 636-1010; relaxgrillinchillin.com. Succulent freshly ground burgers and thirty beers on tap among other taste-bud teasers.

Running Rooster, 800 San Felipe Rd., Hollister, CA 95023; (831) 634-0135; running rooster.com. Great salads and beer on tap.

San Juan Bautista

San Juan Bautista (san-juan-bautista.ca.us), off US 101, is about 40 miles north of Pinnacles National Park and on the National Register of Historical Places. It boasts frontier character and Spanish colonial history preserved as a state historic park around the plaza and the Old Mission San Juan Bautista, the fifteenth and largest in the California Mission system along the Camino Real (Royal Highway). The mission overlooks the San Andreas Fault. Shops and courtyard restaurants housed in buildings dating back to the mid- and late 1800s are the centerpiece to the town's vibrant cultural history.

Lodging

Posada De San Juan, 310 4th St., San Juan Bautista, CA, 95045; (831) 623-4030; posadadesanjuanbautistaca.com

San Juan Inn, 410 The Alameda, #156, San Juan Bautista, CA 95045; (831) 623-4380; sanjuaninn.com. Pet-friendly rooms.

Dining

Dona Esther Mexican Restaurant, 25 Franklin St., San Juan Bautista, CA 95045; (831) 623-2518; donaesthermexicanrestaurant.com. A favorite for thirty years with a popular Sunday buffet brunch.

Jardine's, 115 3rd St., San Juan Bautista, CA, 95045; (831) 623-4466; jardines restaurant.com. Garden courtyard setting.

JJ's Burgers, 100 Alameda, San Juan Bautista, CA, 95045; (831) 623-1748; jjshome madeburgers.com. Shakes, burgers, and fries on the dog-friendly patio.

Recreation

Fremont Peak State Park, San Juan Bautista, www.parks.ca.gov/?page_id=564. Hiking with views of the Monterey Bay, camping and an astronomical observatory.

Juan Bautista De Anza National Trail, San Juan Bautista, nps.gov/juba. Dog-friendly hiking trail with views.

Laguna Mountain, blm.gov/ca/st/en/fo/hollister/recreation/Laguna.print.html. Dispersed and developed camping and hiking.

San Benito County Parks, cosb.us/county-departments/parks-recreation

West Pinnacles– Soledad Gateway

Although the park is open 24 hours a day, the automatic gate at the west-side entrance closes at 8 p.m. for incoming traffic and reopens at 7:30 a.m. Vehicles can exit the park after 8 p.m., which allows for late hiking and climbing.

The West Pinnacles Visitor Contact Station at the West Entrance has restrooms, water, exhibits, and a small bookstore. It is 2 miles to the Chaparral Day Use Area and the three trailheads (Juniper Canyon, Balconies Caves and Balconies Cliffs, and North Wilderness) that will launch you on a Pinnacles National Park adventure through an ancient talus cave, offer you solitude in unspoiled wilderness, or kick your cardio and test your nerve on the peaks of the volcanic fortress.

The Balconies Cave route is the flattest access to the east side. The Balconies Cliffs route is an alternate, moderately uphill route to the east side if the cave is closed. The Juniper Canyon route is the steepest and most scenic access to the east side. The North Wilderness route is mostly flat, but is the longest route.

The Balconies Cave and Cliffs and Juniper Canyon trailheads may seem a bit confusing at first because of a couple of merging spurs in the picnic area and parking lot. At the time of publication, there was discussion about simplifying access by eliminating the trailhead at the entrance to the Chaparral parking area and making the existing Balconies trailhead in the picnic area at the far end of the parking lot the primary trailhead, with a junction for the Juniper Canyon Trail.

There is an overflow parking area just short of the main paved Chaparral trailhead and picnic area parking lot. The Chaparral Day Use Area has a self-pay station, restrooms, water, picnic tables, grills, and trash and recycling containers, but no phones.

27 Visitor Contact Station to Vista Point

This very short, flat and narrow, unmarked dirt trail is as rich in views as it is poor in challenge. It's too convenient to the West Pinnacles Visitor Contact Station to miss as you drive into the park, and it is spectacular at sunset. At the time of publication, this portal to stunning views was slated for improvement per the ADA (Americans with Disabilities Act).

Start: From West Pinnacles Visitor Contact Station
Distance: 0.1 mile out and back
Hiking time: 15 minutes
Difficulty: Easy
Trail surface: Dirt
Trailhead elevation: 1,954 feet
Highest point: 1,961 feet
Best seasons: Year-round
Maps: USGS North Chalone Peak; Pinnacles National Park map; Tom Harrison map of Pinnacles National Park

Nearest town: Soledad
Trail contact: Pinnacles National Park, 5000 CA 146, Paicines, CA 95043-9770; (831) 389-4485 or (831) 389-4427; www.nps.gov/pinn
Trail tips: Restrooms, water, and trash and recycling containers are at the visitor contact station. Sunset is spectacular from this vantage point. Catch a full moonrise if you can.

Finding the trailhead: From US 101 at Soledad, take exit 302/CA 146 and drive 0.3 mile to the traffic signal. Follow the signs for West Pinnacles. Turn left onto Front Street and drive 0.3 mile to East Street. Turn right onto East Street and drive 0.2 mile to Metz Road/CA 146. Turn right onto Metz Road/CA 146, drive 2.5 miles to the Pinnacles National Park sign, and turn left. The road becomes narrower and winding. Drive 5.8 miles on CA 146 to the intersection of Stonewall Canyon Road (left) and CA 146 (right). Bear right and continue on CA 146 for 0.8 mile to the Pinnacles National Park entrance/gate. Drive 0.2 mile to the West Pinnacles Visitor Contact Station parking lot. Walk in front of the contact station along the row of interpretive signs to the east, to the start of the unmarked dirt trail. GPS: N36 28.65' / W121 13.53'.

The Hike

If ever a hike in the park epitomized "short and sweet," this unmarked trail is it. Just 120 feet from the Contact Station, it is the most easily accessed trail offering an unobstructed and stunning view of the unusual volcanic outcrop after which the park is named. The postcard view opens up 500 feet up the trail across grassy meadows and chamise-covered ridges. It is a great way to begin a visit in the park and offers an unforgettable last view at sunset.

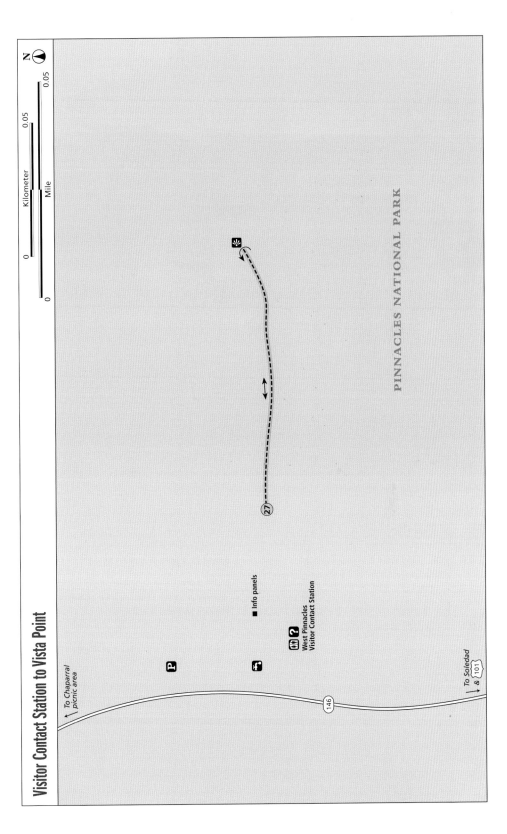

Visitor Contact Station to Vista Point

Info panels

West Pinnacles
Visitor Contact Station

To Chaparral
picnic area

146

To Soledad
& 101

PINNACLES NATIONAL PARK

27

N

Kilometer
0   0.05

Mile
0   0.05

Trailhead at the far end of the West Pinnacles Visitor Contact Station

Miles and Directions

0.0 Start at the West Pinnacles Contact Visitor Station and walk 120 feet east to the unmarked trailhead at the far end of the concrete patio.

0.05 The view opens up toward the rocky pinnacles. (GPS: N36 28.66'/ W121 13.47'. Elevation: 1,961 feet.) Soak up the panorama and go back the way you came.

0.1 Arrive back at the trailhead.

28 Juniper Canyon Trail to Scout Peak

The hike begins in a moderately shaded gray pine and juniper canyon before climbing up exposed switchbacks against scenic towering rock walls to a panoramic saddle straddling the east and west sides of Pinnacles National Park.

Start: From the wooden Trailhead sign in the Chaparral Picnic Area and trailhead parking lot
Distance: 3.6 miles out and back
Hiking time: 2 hours
Difficulty: Strenuous due to sustained uphill climb
Trail surface: Dirt and rock
Trailhead elevation: 1,389 feet
Highest point: 2,478 feet
Best seasons: Spring for wildflowers, late fall and winter for cooler temperatures (summer and early fall can be very hot)

Maps: USGS North Chalone Peak; Pinnacles National Park map; Tom Harrison map of Pinnacles National Park
Nearest town: Soledad
Trail contact: Pinnacles National Park, 5000 CA 146, Paicines, CA 95043-9770; (831) 389-4485 or (831) 389-4427; www.nps.gov/pinn
Trail tips: There are trash and recycling receptacles, flush toilets, and a drinking fountain between the parking lot and the developed picnic area. Each picnic site has a table and grill. There are "self-pay" envelopes and maps by the fee box in the parking lot.

Finding the trailhead: From US 101 at Soledad, take exit 302/CA 146 and drive 0.3 mile to the traffic signal. Follow the signs for West Pinnacles. Turn left onto Front Street and drive 0.3 mile to East Street. Turn right onto East Street and drive 0.2 mile to Metz Road/CA 146. Turn right onto Metz Road/CA 146, drive 2.5 miles to the Pinnacles National Park sign, and turn left. The road becomes narrower and winding. Drive 5.8 miles on CA 146 to the intersection of Stonewall Canyon Road (left) and CA 146 (right). Bear right and continue on CA 146 for 0.8 mile to the Pinnacles National Park entrance/gate. Drive 0.2 mile to the West Pinnacles Visitor Contact Station parking lot. Stop in the contact station to pay the park entrance fee and pick up a map and information. Take the time to view the park film and look at the various exhibits before driving 2 miles to the end of the road in the Chaparral Picnic Area and trailhead parking lot. (If the station is closed, maps and envelopes are at the self-pay fee box in the parking lot.) The trail begins at the wooden Trailhead sign at the head of the parking lot to the right of the information and map board. GPS: N36 29.50' / W121 12.56'.

Note: In winter to early spring, if Chalone Creek is running too high for a dry crossing, you can walk 250 feet to the right (south) and bypass the creek crossing to join up with the trail. There is also an alternate trailhead marked Balconies Trail at the far end of the large picnic area past the parking area. A junction for Juniper Canyon is on the right off the Balconies Trail just a few hundred yards up the trail. You can see that short alternate route above the parking lot.

Juniper Canyon Trail to Scout Peak

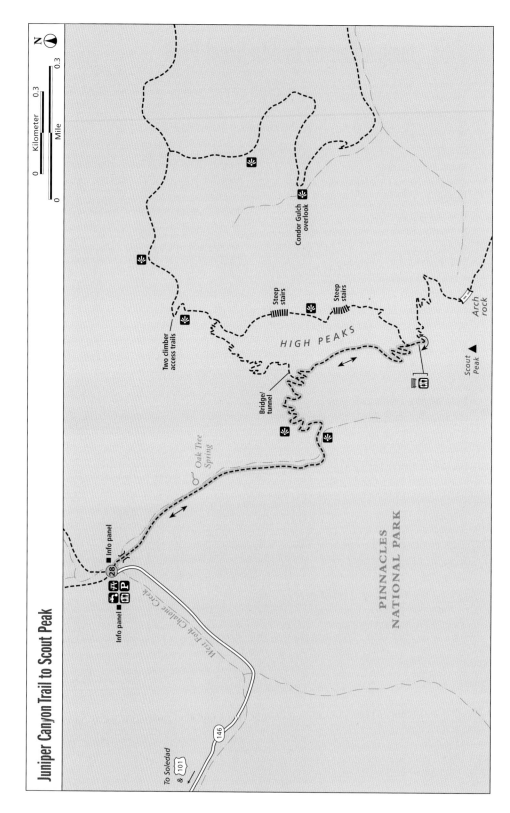

N

0   Kilometer   0.3

0   Mile   0.3

Info panel ■

Info panel ■

28

To Soledad
& 101

146

West Fork Chalone Creek

Oak Tree
Spring

Two climber
access trails

Bridge/
tunnel

HIGH PEAKS

Steep
stairs

Steep
stairs

Condor Gulch
overlook

Arch
rock

Scout
Peak

PINNACLES
NATIONAL PARK

The Hike

True to its name, the hike begins in a canyon cooled by a creekbed lined with juniper shrubs and trees. You cross a typically dry creek at the trailhead and walk 150 feet to the first junction and the Condor Crags interpretive panel. Turn right at the interpretive panel and walk 250 feet to a seasonal creek; cross on the wooden footbridge. At 0.3 mile the unmarked Oak Tree Spring feeds the seasonal creek on the right. The next 0.5 mile benefits from a shady canopy among valley oaks and some gray pines before the trail begins to climb up the exposed rocky flanks. The switchbacks quickly reveal expansive views of hilly California chaparral and Pinnacles wilderness.

At 1.2 miles you come to a trail junction for the High Peaks via Tunnel Trail. Bear right to continue on the Juniper Canyon Trail. The trail narrows, tracing the foot of colossal stone knuckles, towers, and volcanic spirals sculpted by wind, water, and time. The views just get grander as you approach the "Continental Divide" of Pinnacles

Footbridge across a seasonal creek on Juniper Canyon Trail

National Park at 1.8 miles. This is the saddle beneath Scout Peak, where you can sit on a bench straddling the east and west side of Pinnacles National Park; it's a perfect perch for a picnic lunch while you watch condors soar. Although this seems like an unlikely place, there are two vault toilets in the small stone building beyond the bench to the left. Go back to the trailhead the way you came.

Miles and Directions

0.0 Start at the wooden Trailhead sign in the Chaparral Picnic Area parking lot. Walk across the typically dry West Fork Chalone Creek and follow the fenced trail for 150 feet to the T-junction and the Condor Crags interpretive panel. Turn right, walk 250 feet to a seasonal creek, and cross the wooden footbridge.

0.3 Come to Oak Tree Spring on the left of the trail, which feeds the seasonal creek.

0.7 The trail becomes more exposed, rewarding you with an embracing view of Juniper Canyon below.

0.9 The trail reveals expansive views northward as it begins a series of switchbacks.

1.2 Come to the junction with Tunnel Trail. Bear right and continue walking up Juniper Canyon Trail.

1.8 Arrive at a bench and the saddle straddling the east and west sides of Pinnacles National Park just below Scout Peak. (GPS: N36 28.89'/ W121 11.96'. Elevation: 2,478 feet.) This is the perfect perch to soak up the stunning views with a picnic lunch while hoping for condors to glide by. Go back to the trailhead the way you came.

3.6 Arrive back at the trailhead.

29 Juniper Canyon Trail to High Peaks

If you have already hiked among the rock formations on other trails in the park, you may think this trail starts out a little ho–hum as you hike through the chaparral flatlands staring up at the base of more towering rock palisades. The best is yet to come. The Civil Conservation Corps' engineering feat of metal catwalks, steep Inca pyramid–like footholds picked out of the rock, and metal pipe handrails on the High Peaks' narrow ledges has an almost Italian Dolomites Via Ferrata flair that will charge your adrenaline batteries. You might even be rewarded with spotting condors on their midday soar.

Start: From the wooden Trailhead sign in the Chaparral Picnic Area and trailhead parking lot
Distance: 4.3-mile lollipop
Hiking time: 3 hours
Difficulty: Strenuous due to uphill climb and steep precarious sections
Trail surface: Dirt and rock
Trailhead elevation: 1,389 feet
Highest point: 2,598 feet
Best seasons: Spring for wildflowers, late fall and winter for cooler temperatures (summers and early fall can be very hot)

Maps: USGS North Chalone Peak; Pinnacles National Park map; Tom Harrison map of Pinnacles National Park
Nearest town: Soledad
Trail contact: Pinnacles National Park, 5000 CA 146, Paicines, CA 95043-9770; (831) 389-4485 or (831) 389-4427; www.nps.gov/pinn
Trail tips: There are trash and recycling receptacles, restrooms with flush toilets, and a drinking fountain between the parking lot and the developed picnic area. Each picnic site has a table and grill. The steep rock-chipped stairs at the High Peaks can be intimidating.

Finding the trailhead: From US 101 at Soledad, take exit 302/CA 146 and drive 0.3 mile to the traffic signal. Follow the signs for West Pinnacles. Turn left onto Front Street and drive 0.3 mile to East Street. Turn right onto East Street and drive 0.2 mile to Metz Road/CA 146. Turn right onto Metz Road/CA 146, drive 2.5 miles to the Pinnacles National Park sign, and turn left. The road becomes narrower and winding. Drive 5.8 miles on CA 146 to the intersection of Stonewall Canyon Road (left) and CA 146 (right). Bear right and continue on CA 146 for 0.8 mile to the Pinnacles National Park entrance/gate. Drive 0.2 mile to the West Pinnacles Visitor Contact Station parking lot. Stop in the contact station to pay the park entrance fee and pick up a map and information. Take the time to view the park film and look at the various exhibits before driving 2 miles to the end of the road in the Chaparral Picnic Area and trailhead parking lot. (If the station is closed, maps and envelopes are at the self-pay fee box in the parking lot.) The trail begins at the wooden Trailhead sign at the head of the parking lot to the right of the information and map board. GPS: N36 29.50' / W121 12.56'.

Note: In winter to early spring, if Chalone Creek is running too high for a dry crossing, you can walk 250 feet to the right (south) and bypass the creek crossing to join up with the trail. There is also an alternate trailhead marked Balconies Trail at the far end of the large picnic area past the parking area. A junction for Juniper Canyon is on the right off the Balconies Trail just a few hundred yards up the trail. You can see that short alternate route above the parking lot.

The Hike

The trail begins in open chaparral terrain by the information panel. Walk 150 feet up the trail in the fenced trail corridor to the Condor Crags interpretive panel and turn right. Walk 250 feet and cross the footbridge over the seasonal creek. Enjoy the wispy shade of the juniper and gray pines spread among the buckeye trees for the first mile.

A whimsical rock formation on the way to the High Peaks

Juniper Canyon Trail to High Peaks

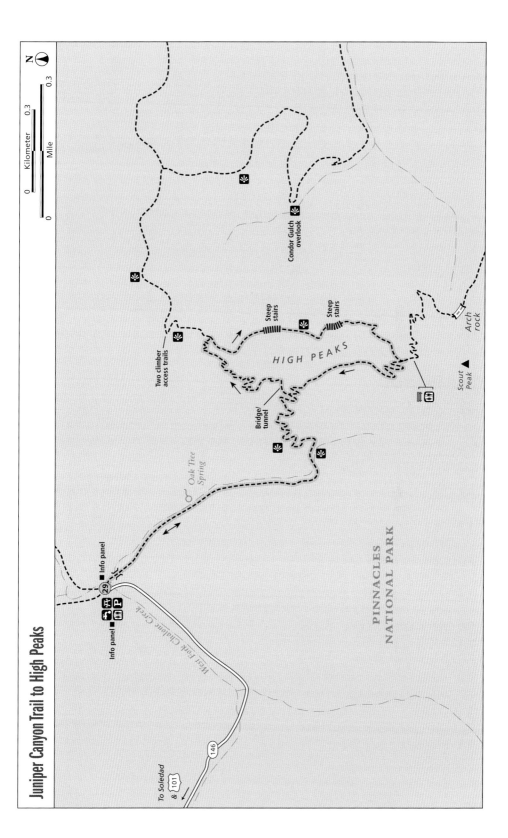

From here on, the trail climbs up the exposed rocky flanks, treating you to views of various element-sculpted volcanic rock monuments.

The trail is at its most challenging, unique, and precipitously exciting from the High Peaks via Tunnel Trail junction at 1.2 miles for almost 2 more miles. On this section you will use rock-chiseled footholds and metal pipe handrails installed by the Civilian Conservation Corps during the 1930s. The views are breathtaking; the trail itself is a heart thumper and not for the timid or anyone fearful of heights.

At 2.1 miles you have your best chance for condor sightings and may have the privilege of running into staff or volunteers tracking condors with spotting scopes and receiving signals from transmitters placed on the condors' wings. This summit-like area is a good spot for a picnic break sitting on a rock scanning for condors and falcons. The descent continues to be narrow with metal pipe handrail assists along the steepest sections.

At 2.5 miles you come to the trail junction for the Chaparral Picnic Area via Juniper Canyon Trail. There is a bench at the base of Scout Peak for a rest and two vault toilets off the spur on the left. Turn right to walk down Juniper Canyon Trail. Close your lollipop at 3.1 miles at the trail junction for Tunnel Trail. Continue walking downhill on Juniper Canyon Trail back to the trailhead at 4.3 miles.

Miles and Directions

0.0 Start at the wooden Trailhead sign in the Chaparral Picnic Area parking lot. Walk across the typically dry West Fork Chalone Creek and follow the fenced trail for 150 feet to the T-junction and the Condor Crags interpretive panel. Turn right, walk 250 feet to a seasonal creek, and cross the wooden footbridge.

0.3 Come to the unmarked Oak Tree Spring, which feeds the seasonal creek on your right.

0.7 The trail becomes more exposed, rewarding you with an embracing view of Juniper Canyon below before revealing expansive views northward on the switchbacks ahead.

1.2 Come to the trail junction with Tunnel Trail. Bear left to High Peaks via Tunnel Trail. This junction is where you will return from the right to close your lollipop.

1.3 Come to the tunnel built by the Civilian Conservation Corps in the 1930s. Walk through the tunnel and across the concrete footbridge over the ravine.

1.7 Come to a view of the Balconies Cliffs north on the left and turn right at the T-junction and onto the High Peaks Trail at the Steep and Narrow sign.

2.0 Start of steep rock stairs going up.

2.1 Come to a good condor-viewing site. Enjoy a snack and water break with a view before the descent down the steep rock stairs.

2.5 Come to a trail junction with Juniper Canyon Trail and a bench on the saddle at the base of Scout Peak. Turn right to return to the Chaparral Picnic Area via Juniper Canyon Trail.

3.1 Come to a T-junction with Tunnel Trail and the close of your lollipop. Continue walking downhill on Juniper Canyon Trail.

4.3 Arrive back at the trailhead.

30 Juniper Canyon Trail to Bear Gulch Day Use Area

The hike begins in a moderately shaded gray pine and juniper canyon before climbing up exposed switchbacks against scenic towering rock walls up to a panoramic saddle straddling the east and west sides of Pinnacles National Park. You will descend along the volcanic flank of the East Pinnacles along a scenic gulch, enjoying views of North Chalone Peak and passing climber access spur trails to unusual solitary rock outcrops before arriving at the Bear Gulch Nature Center.

Start: From the wooden Trailhead sign in the Chaparral Picnic Area and trailhead parking lot
Distance: 7.8 miles out and back
Hiking time: 5 hours
Difficulty: Strenuous due to sustained uphill climb
Trail surface: Dirt and rock
Trailhead elevation: 1,389 feet
Highest point: 2,478 feet
Best seasons: Spring for wildflowers, late fall and winter for cooler temperatures (summer and early fall can be very hot)
Maps: USGS North Chalone Peak; Pinnacles National Park map; Tom Harrison map of Pinnacles National Park

Nearest town: Soledad
Trail contact: Pinnacles National Park, 5000 CA 146, Paicines, CA 95043-9770; (831) 389-4485 or (831) 389-4427; www.nps.gov/pinn
Trail tips: There are trash and recycling receptacles, flush toilets, and a drinking fountain between the parking lot and the developed picnic area. Each picnic site has a table and grill. There are "self-pay" envelopes and maps by the fee box in the parking lot. The Bear Gulch Nature Center is open seasonally.

Finding the trailhead: From US 101 at Soledad, take exit 302/CA 146 and drive 0.3 mile to the traffic signal. Follow the signs for West Pinnacles. Turn left onto Front Street and drive 0.3 mile to East Street. Turn right onto East Street and drive 0.2 mile to Metz Road/CA 146. Turn right onto Metz Road/CA 146, drive 2.5 miles to the Pinnacles National Park sign, and turn left. The road becomes narrower and winding. Drive 5.8 miles on CA 146 to the intersection of Stonewall Canyon Road (left) and CA 146 (right). Bear right and continue on CA 146 for 0.8 mile to the Pinnacles National Park entrance/gate. Drive 0.2 mile to the West Pinnacles Visitor Contact Station parking lot. Stop in the contact station to pay the park entrance fee and pick up a map and information. Take the time to view the park film and look at the various exhibits before driving 2 miles to the end of the road in the Chaparral Picnic Area and trailhead parking lot. (If the station is closed, maps and envelopes are at the self-pay fee box in the parking lot.) The trail begins at the wooden Trailhead sign at the head of the parking lot to the right of the information and map board. GPS: N36 29.50' / W121 12.56'.

Note: In winter to early spring, if Chalone Creek is running too high for a dry crossing, you can walk 250 feet to the right (south) and bypass the creek crossing to join up with the trail. There is also an alternate trailhead marked Balconies Trail at the far end of the large picnic area past the parking area. A junction for Juniper Canyon is on the right off the Balconies Trail just a few hundred yards up the trail. You can see that short alternate route above the parking lot.

The Hike

True to its name, the hike begins in a canyon cooled by a creekbed lined with juniper shrubs and trees. You cross a typically dry creek at the trailhead and walk 150 feet to the first junction and the Condor Crags interpretive panel. Turn right at the interpretive sign and walk 250 feet to a seasonal creek; cross on the wooden footbridge.

The next 0.5 mile benefits from a shady canopy among valley oaks and some gray pines before the trail begins to climb up the exposed rocky flanks. The switchbacks quickly reveal expansive views of hilly California chaparral and Pinnacles wilderness. At 1.2 miles you come to a trail junction for the High Peaks via Tunnel Trail. Bear right to continue on the Juniper Canyon Trail. The trail narrows, tracing the foot of colossal stone knuckles, towers, and volcanic spirals sculpted by wind, water, and time. The views just get grander as you approach the "Continental Divide" of Pinnacles National Park at 1.8 miles. This is the saddle beneath Scout Peak, where you can sit on a bench straddling the east and west sides of Pinnacles National Park; it's a perfect perch for a picnic break. You may get lucky and spot condors riding the thermals in the early afternoon.

Looking eastward the trail bears left just below the bench where the spur trail leads to a stone building with toilets. Walk down to the trail, bear left at the marker, and follow the trail downhill toward the Bear Gulch area on the east side. Looking at the cluster of rock on your right is like peering into the giant molar of a prehistoric animal. Farther down on your right, the landscape changes to a steep stadium of stone knolls and pinnacles dotted with gray pine trees.

The trail traces the base of the stone palisades as you continue walking downhill. At 2.3 miles you walk through a short tunnel carved out of the volcanic rock. Take time to admire this one of many trail-building and sculpting marvels accomplished by the Civilian Conservation Corps (CCC) between 1933 and 1938. Just ahead the trail levels off, and the canyon on your left softens into more of a swale.

At 2.6 miles the trail comes to a wide saddle with views opening southward up the chaparral-covered slopes of the Gabilan Range toward North Chalone Peak and the fire tower. You can see the outline of the Salinas Mountains in the distance and the ridge of the San Lucia Range on the far western horizon.

Just past the lone anvil-shaped rock on your left is a climber access spur trail to another rock outcrop at 2.8 miles. The trail hugs left and sweeps back down along the canyon. This is one of many areas where the CCC terraced the volcanic terrain to construct the park's tapestry of trails and unique hiking routes.

At 3.3 miles you come to a trail junction signed Rim Trail to Reservoir on your right. Bear left and continue walking down to the Bear Gulch area. Just ahead is a spur to the right for a climber access trail. Bear left toward Bear Gulch.

At 3.5 miles you come to the climber access to the top of Tourist Trap on your left. This is the last climber access trail on this hike. Watch for dangling rock climbers as switchbacks take you down the gulch.

Soaking up the view across Juniper Canyon

At 3.6 miles you come to a trail junction for the Moses Spring Trail to the right. This is the end of the High Peaks Trail. Continue walking downhill on Moses Spring Trail to the Moses Spring trailhead at the paved road. There is a parking lot on your left and a restroom. Walk across the paved road and continue along the hiker trail through the developed picnic area (tables, grills, water, recycling and trash bins).

At 3.85 miles bear left and walk across the wooden footbridge. Walk 250 feet and arrive at the Bear Gulch Day Use Area. There is a restroom, a picnic table, and recycling and trash bins on your left. The Bear Gulch Nature Center is across the road.

Walk across the road in the pedestrian crosswalk and enjoy browsing the exhibits if the nature center is open. Notice the row of small stone buildings. These were built by the CCC and are on the National Register of Historic Places. There are a couple of picnic tables in the parking area by the nature center. Pick a spot for a rest and refueling break before going back the way you came.

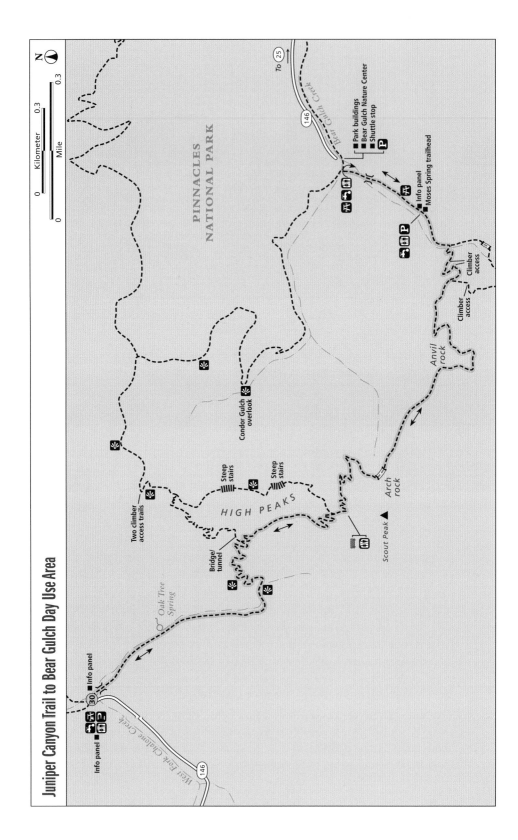

Juniper Canyon Trail to Bear Gulch Day Use Area

PINNACLES
NATIONAL PARK

HIGH PEAKS

Condor Gulch
overlook

Two climber
access trails

Steep stairs

Steep stairs

Oak Tree
Spring

Bridge/
tunnel

Scout Peak

Arch
rock

Anvil
rock

Climber
access

Climber
access

West Fork Chalone Creek

Info panel

Info panel

Bear Gulch Creek

To 25

146

146

30

Park buildings
Bear Gulch Nature Center
Shuttle stop

Info panel
Moses Spring trailhead

N

0   Kilometer   0.3

0   Mile   0.3

Miles and Directions

0.0 Start at the wooden Trailhead sign in the Chaparral Picnic Area parking lot. Walk across the typically dry West Fork Chalone Creek and follow the fenced trail for 150 feet to the T-junction and the Condor Crags interpretive panel Turn right, walk 250 feet to a seasonal creek, and cross the wooden footbridge.

0.3 Come to the unmarked Oak Tree Spring, which feeds the seasonal creek on the right.

0.7 The trail becomes more exposed, rewarding you with an embracing view of Juniper Canyon below.

0.9 The trail reveals expansive views northward as it begins a series of switchbacks.

1.2 Come to the junction with Tunnel Trail. Bear right and continue walking up Juniper Canyon Trail.

1.8 Arrive at a bench and the saddle straddling the east and west sides of Pinnacles National Park just below Scout Peak. This is the perfect perch to take a water break and soak up the stunning views while hoping for condors to glide by. Continue on the trail below the bench on the east side toward the spur trail going to the toilets in the stone building. Bear left to Bear Gulch at the spur intersection and begin walking downhill.

2.3 Walk through a short but impressive stone tunnel.

2.6 The exposed trail offers expansive southward views toward North Chalone Peak and the fire tower.

2.8 Come to an anvil-shaped rock formation on your left with a spur trail to a climber access to another rock outcrop just ahead on your right.

3.3 Come to a trail junction signed Rim Trail to Reservoir. Bear left and continue walking down-hill toward Bear Gulch Day Use Area.

3.4 Come to a spur trail on your right for climber access. Bear left. In 0.1 mile come to another climber access to the top of Tourist Trap on the left.

3.6 Come to the trail junction for the Moses Spring Trail. High Peaks Trail ends and merges with Moses Spring Trail. Continue walking downhill.

3.7 Arrive at the Moses Spring trailhead, with a parking lot and restroom on the left and a paved road. Walk across the paved road and continue walking on the hiker trail through the picnic area.

3.85 Bear left and walk across the wooden footbridge.

3.9 Arrive at the parking area, restroom, and picnic table across from the Bear Gulch Nature Center. (GPS: N36 28.87'/ W121 10.89'. Elevation: 1,279 feet.) Walk across the road at the crosswalk ahead. Enjoy the exhibits if the nature center is open. Take time to refuel with snacks and water and relax at a picnic table before going back the way you came.

7.8 Arrive back at the trailhead.

31 Juniper Canyon Trail to Bear Gulch Day Use Area via High Peaks

This is a challenging clockwise circuit hike from the Chaparral Picnic Area on the west side over the High Peaks down to Bear Gulch on the east side and looping back over the top at the base of Scout Peak to close the loop and lollipop back down to the trailhead. This hike boasts great views on the way up and down with perspectives unique to both the east and west sides. There is an Anasazi cliff-dwelling feel to the up-close and personal experience of threading along the volcanic towers and rock monoliths. The "steep and narrow" stretch of trail in the High Peaks includes single footsteps etched in the rock. If you like your Stairmaster sessions at the gym, you will love the High Peaks. This is not the trail to test new knees and hips. For some, walking along rock catwalk ledges with steel pipe handrails as an assist will be fun, and for others it may be more thrilling than they want.

Start: From the wooden Trailhead sign in the Chaparral Picnic Area and trailhead parking lot
Distance: 8.7-mile lollipop
Hiking time: 5.5 hours
Difficulty: Strenuous due to length and double uphill climb
Trail surface: Dirt and rock
Trailhead elevation: 1,389 feet
Highest point: 2,598 feet
Best seasons: Spring for wildflowers, late fall and winter for cooler temperatures (summer and early fall can be very hot)
Maps: USGS North Chalone Peak; Pinnacles National Park map; Tom Harrison map of Pinnacles National Park
Nearest town: Soledad

Trail contact: Pinnacles National Park, 5000 CA 146, Paicines, CA 95043-9770; (831) 389-4485 or (831) 389-4427; www.nps.gov/pinn
Trail tips: There are trash and recycling receptacles, flush toilets, and a drinking fountain between the parking lot and the developed picnic area. Each picnic site has a table and grill. There are "self-pay" envelopes and maps by the fee box in the parking lot. Allow more time on weekends for the single file of people on High Peaks. Drinking water is available only at the trailhead and 2 places in Bear Gulch. There are vault toilets below Scout Peak but no water.

Finding the trailhead: From US 101 at Soledad, take exit 302/CA 146 and drive 0.3 mile to the traffic signal. Follow the signs for West Pinnacles. Turn left onto Front Street and drive 0.3 mile to East Street. Turn right onto East Street and drive 0.2 mile to Metz Road/CA 146. Turn right onto Metz Road/CA 146, drive 2.5 miles to the Pinnacles National Park sign, and turn left. The road becomes narrower and winding. Drive 5.8 miles on CA 146 to the intersection of Stonewall Canyon Road (left) and CA 146 (right). Bear right and continue on CA 146 for 0.8 mile to the Pinnacles National Park entrance/gate. Drive 0.2 mile to the West Pinnacles Visitor Contact Station parking lot. Stop in the contact station to pay the park entrance fee and pick up a map and information. Take the time to view the park film and look at the various exhibits before driving 2 miles to the end of the road in the Chaparral Picnic Area and trailhead parking lot. (If the station is closed, maps and envelopes are at the self-pay fee box in the parking lot.) The trail begins at the wooden Trailhead sign at the head of the parking lot to the right of the information and map board. GPS: N36 29.50' / W121 12.56'.

Note: In winter to early spring, if Chalone Creek is running too high for a dry crossing, you can walk 250 feet to the right (south) and bypass the creek crossing to join up with the trail. There is also an alternate trailhead marked Balconies Trail at the far end of the large picnic area past the parking area. A junction for Juniper Canyon is on the right off the Balconies Trail just a few hundred yards up the trail. You can see that short alternate route above the parking lot.

The Hike

The hike begins in a canyon cooled by a creekbed lined with juniper shrubs and trees. You cross a typically dry creek at the trailhead and walk 150 feet to the first junction and the Condor Crags interpretive sign. Turn right at the interpretive panel and walk 250 feet to a seasonal creek; cross on the wooden footbridge. The next 0.5 mile benefits from a shady canopy among valley oaks and some gray pines before the trail begins to climb up the exposed rocky flanks. The switchbacks quickly reveal expansive views of hilly California chaparral and Pinnacles wilderness.

At 1.2 miles you come to a trail junction for the High Peaks via Tunnel Trail. Bear right to continue on the Juniper Canyon Trail. The trail narrows, tracing the foot of colossal stone knuckles, towers, and volcanic spirals sculpted by wind, water, and time. The views just get grander as you approach the "Continental Divide" of Pinnacles National Park at 1.8 miles. This is the saddle beneath Scout Peak, where you can sit on a bench straddling the east and west sides of Pinnacles National Park; it's a perfect perch for a water break while you catch your breath and scan the skies for condors. There is a small stone building with two vault toilets off a spur trail past the bench; this is the only toilet until you get down into Bear Gulch.

From the bench you turn northward uphill on the High Peaks Trail. Notice the Steep and Narrow sign. The trail begins to climb gently, then switchbacks downhill overlooking the east side of the park. Less than 350 yards from the bench, the trail starts its tricky, challenging steep sections of primitive single-foot, rock-chipped steps and steel pipe handrails along narrow ledges. What is dramatic to some may be intimidating and too frightening for others.

At 2.2 miles the trail crests, revealing sweeping views south toward North Chalone Peak and the fire tower. Looking north you see a white cliff created by a landslide and the Diablo Range across the horizon. The white streaks and blots on the rocky ledges as you look left indicate where condors and other birds nest and roost. To the southeast is an obvious swirl of ancient sediment on the face of a rock wall. The trail continues down more rock steps, navigating around rock faces along catwalks with steel pipe handrails.

At 2.5 miles you come to a trail intersection for the Tunnel Trail on the left. Bear right uphill. You come to a switchback a short distance ahead; if you look northward you can see the Balconies Cliffs across the canyon and the pale line of the trail that traces the base of the cliffs, where raptors nest. Just past this viewpoint you walk past two climber access trails on your left. As you leave the stone tower corridor behind and the white cliffs slide into view again, the trail levels on a saddle cradled by chamise and manzanita shrubland on both sides.

At 3.1 miles you come to a trail junction where the High Peaks Trail continues left to Bench Trail. Although unmarked, this is the junction for the Condor Gulch Trail heading down to Bear Gulch. Bear right. The High Peaks are at your back as you walk the gulch. At 3.8 miles you arrive at the Condor Gulch Overlook, which is a nice spot for a water break before the last mile down to Bear Gulch where you will find restrooms, a drinking fountain to fill up your bottle, picnic tables, and trash and recycling containers.

At 4.8 miles you drop down to the Bear Gulch Nature Center parking lot. The administrative offices are housed in the small historic buildings to the left of the seasonally open nature center across the road. There is a telephone, first aid, and a ranger for emergencies at the nature center.

You come to a footbridge and a bench at the bottom of Condor Gulch Trail. Walk across the wooden footbridge and along the concrete path across the parking area (restrooms are on your right) to the High Peaks trailhead. Continue walking a few hundred feet across another wooden footbridge as you enter the picnic area set in a pine and oak woodland. Listen for the rat-tat of woodpeckers on some of the dry, barren limbs above and the rustling of scurrying quails below. At the other end of the picnic area, you come to a paved road entrance to the parking lot at the Moses Spring trailhead. Take advantage of the restroom and water fountain at the back of the parking lot. There are two vault toilets at Scout Peak, 2 miles up the trail, where you will close your lollipop, but this is the last chance for drinking water with almost 4 miles left to go until you get back to the trailhead.

Walk across the road to the Moses Spring trailhead and information board and start up the trail to High Peaks. At the junction for the Moses Spring Trail, bear right and continue walking on High Peaks Trail. You come to the climber access trail to the top of Tourist Trap on your right as the switchbacks begin, shortly before the trail junction for another climber access on the left. Bear right to High Peaks and come to the trail junction signed Rim Trail to Reservoir on your left. Continue to bear right and walk uphill to High Peaks.

At about 5.9 miles you see an apple core–like rock formation on the left and an anvil-shaped rock outcrop on the right of the chaparral ridge. You'll see climber access trails as you pass these rocks. The trail sweeps onto a saddle between a ravine on your left and Bear Gulch on your right. Scout Peak's volcanic towers are ahead. At about 6.4 miles the trail traces the rock wall on your left with Bear Gulch on your right. The sculpted arch tunnel ahead is one of the most enchanting features on this last stretch of the climb to the base of Scout Peak before your descent back to the trailhead.

At 6.9 miles you make your last turn up to the bench on the ridge below Scout Peak, where you close the loop part of the lollipop. The vault toilet stone building

Descending from the High Peaks

is on your left. Reward your last 2-mile cardio workout with a snack while feasting on the east to west panorama. Rehydrate and walk to the trail junction just past the bench. Bear left on Juniper Canyon Trail to start the downhill walk back to the trailhead the way you came.

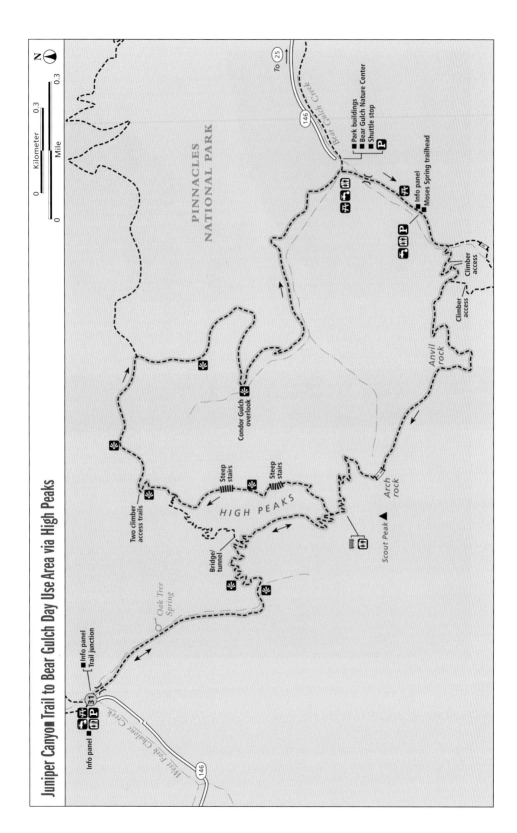

Juniper Canyon Trail to Bear Gulch Day Use Area via High Peaks

PINNACLES NATIONAL PARK

N

0   Kilometer   0.3

0   Mile   0.3

To 25

146

Bear Gulch Creek

Park buildings
Bear Gulch Nature Center
Shuttle stop
P

Info panel
Moses Spring trailhead

P

Climber access

Anvil rock

Climber access

Condor Gulch overlook

Two climber access trails

Steep stairs

Steep stairs

HIGH PEAKS

Bridge/tunnel

Oak Tree Spring

Arch rock

Scout Peak

Info panel
Trail junction

31

Info panel

West Fork Chalone Creek

146

Miles and Directions

0.0 Start at the wooden Trailhead sign in the Chaparral Picnic Area parking lot. Walk across the typically dry West Fork Chalone Creek and follow the fenced trail for 150 feet to the T-junction and the Condor Crags interpretive panel. Turn right, walk 250 feet to a seasonal creek, and cross on the wooden footbridge.

0.3 Come to the unmarked Oak Tree Spring, which feeds the seasonal creek on the right.

0.7 The trail becomes more exposed, with an embracing view of Juniper Canyon Trail before starting up a series of switchbacks.

1.2 Come to the junction with Tunnel Trail. Bear right and continue walking up Juniper Canyon Trail.

1.8 Juniper Canyon Trail ends here. Arrive at a bench and the saddle straddling the east and west sides of Pinnacles National Park just below Scout Peak. This is the perfect perch to soak up the stunning views and rehydrate before continuing uphill on the steep and narrow trail section to the High Peaks. This is also a good condor-spotting bench. Walk northward uphill on the High Peaks Trail.

2.1 Come to narrow rock steps going up. In 0.1 mile the trail crests on the High Peaks with soaring views north, east, and south. Watch for condors.

2.3 Come to steep rock stairs going down.

2.5 Come to a trail junction at Tunnel Trail on your left. Bear right uphill and immediately come to a viewpoint looking across to the Balconies Cliffs and the trail beneath the cliffs. Come to two climber access trails just below the viewpoint.

2.8 Arrive at a viewpoint looking back toward Balconies Cliffs.

3.1 Come to a trail junction where the High Peaks Trail goes left to Bench Trail and the unmarked Condor Gulch Trail goes right down to the Bear Gulch Day Use Area. Bear right on Condor Gulch Trail.

3.8 Come to Condor Gulch Overlook.

4.8 Arrive in Bear Gulch Day Use Area and walk across the wooden footbridge just before the bench and concrete path at the parking lot with restrooms and picnic tables. Walk to the other side of the parking area to the dirt trail and sign with an arrow for the Picnic Area, Bear Gulch Caves Reservoir, and High Peaks Trail. Immediately cross a wooden footbridge and walk through the wooded picnic area to the Moses Spring trailhead and information board where you start up the trail to High Peaks.

5.1 Come to the junction for High Peaks Trail. Bear right and continue on High Peaks Trail past a climber access to the top of Tourist Trap on the right. In 0.1 mile come to another climber access spur trail on the left. Bear right and continue walking to High Peaks.

5.4 Come to the trail junction signed Rim Trail to Reservoir on the left. Bear right and continue walking uphill to High Peaks.

5.9 Come to a climber access trail on the left and one on the right just ahead for two distinctive rock outcrops.

6.4 Come to the arched rock tunnel.

6.9 Come to a bench on the saddle at the base of Scout Peak, where you close the loop of your lollipop at the junction with Juniper Canyon Trail. Bear left on Juniper Canyon Trail to go back to the trailhead the way you came.

8.7 Arrive back at the trailhead.

32 Juniper Canyon Trail to Reservoir and Moses Spring

This hike highlights the contrasts in Pinnacles National Park. It climbs out of a shaded canyon to a panoramic saddle before descending along the volcanic east flank for North Chalone Peak views and then opening to a freshwater reservoir. The trail loops down into the surreal world of boulder-tunneled cave passages and a spring feeding a fern grotto before the climb back up over the saddle straddling the East and West Pinnacles.

Start: From the wooden trailhead sign in the Chaparral Picnic Area and trailhead parking lot
Distance: 7.95-mile lollipop
Hiking time: 4.5 hours
Difficulty: Strenuous
Trail surface: Dirt and rock
Trailhead elevation: 1,389 feet
Highest point: 2,478 feet
Best seasons: Spring for wildflowers, late fall and winter for cooler temperatures (summer and early fall can be very hot)
Maps: USGS North Chalone Peak; Pinnacles National Park map; Tom Harrison map of Pinnacles National Park

Nearest town: Soledad
Trail contact: Pinnacles National Park, 5000 CA 146, Paicines, CA 95043-9770; (831) 389-4485 or (831) 389-4427; www.nps.gov/pinn
Trail tips: There are trash and recycling receptacles, flush toilets, and a drinking fountain between the parking lot and the developed picnic area. Each picnic site has a table and grill. There are "self-pay" envelopes and maps by the fee box in the parking lot. Carry a flashlight to enhance visibility through the boulder cavern passage below the reservoir.

Finding the trailhead: From US 101 at Soledad, take exit 302/CA 146 and drive 0.3 mile to the traffic signal. Follow the signs for West Pinnacles. Turn left onto Front Street and drive 0.3 mile to East Street. Turn right onto East Street and drive 0.2 mile to Metz Road/CA 146. Turn right onto Metz Road/CA 146, drive 2.5 miles to the Pinnacles National Park sign, and turn left. The road becomes narrower and winding. Drive 5.8 miles on CA 146 to the intersection of Stonewall Canyon Road (left) and CA 146 (right). Bear right and continue on CA 146 for 0.8 mile to the Pinnacles National Park entrance/gate. Drive 0.2 mile to the West Pinnacles Visitor Contact Station parking lot. Stop in the contact station to pay the park entrance fee and pick up a map and information. Take the time to view the park film and look at the various exhibits before driving 2 miles to the end of the road in the Chaparral Picnic Area and trailhead parking lot. (If the station is closed, maps and envelopes are at the self-pay fee box in the parking lot.) The trail begins at the wooden Trailhead sign at the head of the parking lot to the right of the information and map board. GPS: N36 29.50' / W121 12.56'.

Note: In winter to early spring, if Chalone Creek is running too high for a dry crossing, you can walk 250 feet to the right (south) and bypass the creek crossing to join up with the trail. There is also an alternate trailhead marked Balconies Trail at the far end of the large picnic area past the parking area. A junction for Juniper Canyon is on the right off the Balconies Trail just a few hundred yards up the trail. You can see that short alternate route above the parking lot.

The Hike

True to its name, the hike begins in a canyon cooled by a creekbed lined with juniper shrubs and trees. You cross a typically dry creek at the trailhead and walk 150 feet to the first junction and the Condor Crags interpretive panel. Turn right at the interpretive sign and walk 250 feet to a seasonal creek; cross on the wooden footbridge.

The next 0.5 mile benefits from a shady canopy among valley oaks and some gray pines before the trail begins to climb up the exposed rocky flanks. The switchbacks quickly reveal expansive views of hilly California chaparral and Pinnacles wilderness. At 1.2 miles you come to a trail junction for the High Peaks via Tunnel Trail. Bear right to continue on the Juniper Canyon Trail. The trail narrows, tracing the foot of colossal stone knuckles, towers, and volcanic spirals sculpted by wind, water, and time. The views just get grander as you approach the "Continental Divide" of Pinnacles National Park at 1.8 miles. This is the saddle beneath Scout Peak where you can sit on a bench straddling the east and west sides of Pinnacles National Park; it's a perfect perch for a picnic break. You may get lucky and spot condors riding the thermals in the early afternoon.

Looking eastward the trail bears left just below the bench where the spur trail leads to a stone building with toilets on the right. Walk down to the trail, bear left at the marker, and follow the trail downhill to the Bear Gulch area on the east side.

Ferns thrive on the waters of Moses Spring.

Looking at the cluster of rock on your right is like peering into the giant molar of a prehistoric animal. Farther down on your right the landscape changes to a steep stadium of stone knolls and pinnacles dotted with gray pine trees.

The trail traces the base of the stone palisades as you continue walking downhill. At 2.3 miles you walk through a short tunnel carved out of the volcanic rock. Take time to admire this one of many trail-building and sculpting marvels accomplished by the Civilian Conservation Corps (CCC) between 1933 and 1938. Just ahead the trail levels off, and the canyon on your left softens into more of a swale.

At 2.6 miles the trail comes to a wide saddle with views opening southward up the chaparral-covered slopes of the Gabilan Range toward North Chalone Peak and the fire tower. You can see the outline of the Salinas Mountains in the distance and the ridge of the San Lucia Range on the far western horizon.

Just past the lone anvil-shaped rock on your left is a climber access spur trail to another rock outcrop at 2.8 miles. The trail hugs left and sweeps back down along the canyon. This is one of many areas where the CCC terraced the volcanic terrain to construct the park's tapestry of trails and unique hiking routes.

At 3.3 miles you come to a trail junction signed Rim Trail to Reservoir on your right. Bear right uphill on the Rim Trail. You pass an unnamed climber access trail just ahead on your left. Rim Trail approaches the crest, where a splendid view opens above Bear Gulch. You begin a gradual downhill and pass through a rock corridor. The head of the stone dam built by the CCC in the 1930s comes into view with the reservoir behind it. At about 3.7 miles you arrive at the reservoir, a trail junction for North Chalone Peak across the dam, and the Bear Gulch Day Use Area via Bear Gulch Caves and Moses Spring Trail going left and downhill. There is an interpretive panel about the threatened red-legged frog on the right. Walk down the narrow, Inca-like rock steps with the metal pipe handrail on your right. You are entering a phenomenal boulder-tunnel canyon. At 3.85 miles you pass two climber access trails on your left. The trail junction for the Lower Cave is just ahead on the right. Continue walking downhill. The rock passages and the cliff-dwelling feel of this section of the trail is one of several highlights of this hike. At 4.05 miles the unexpected ferns fed by Moses Spring are a nourishing contrast to the surrounding rock landscape, especially in the drier dormant season.

The climber access ahead on your left is missing the carabiner marker on the post. Bear right downhill past that spur and come to a trail junction signed Reservoir via Bear Gulch Caves.

Bear left past the junction and continue downhill to the trail junction for the High Peaks Trail. Turn left and walk uphill on the High Peaks Trail. Just ahead on your right is the climber access to the top of Tourist Trap. Walk past another climber access on your left and notice the view down Bear Gulch with the nature center's stone building in the distance through a clearing in the trees.

At 4.65 miles you come to the trail junction with the Rim Trail, which closes the loop of your lollipop. Continue walking uphill toward the High Peaks and the Pinnacles saddle, returning to the trailhead the way you came.

Juniper Canyon Trail to Reservoir and Moses Spring

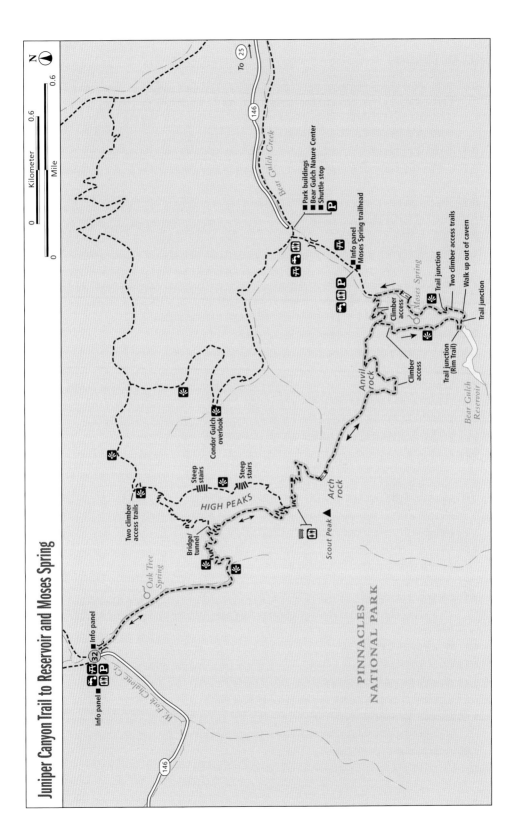

Miles and Directions

0.0   Start at the wooden Trailhead sign in the Chaparral Picnic Area parking lot. Walk across the typically dry West Fork Chalone Creek and follow the fenced trail for 150 feet to the T-junction and the Condor Crags interpretive panel. Turn right, walk 250 feet to a seasonal creek, and cross the wooden footbridge.

0.3   Come to unmarked Oak Tree Spring, which feeds the seasonal creek on the right.

0.7   The trail becomes more exposed, rewarding you with an embracing view of Juniper Canyon below.

0.9   The trail reveals expansive views northward as it begins a series of switchbacks.

1.2   Come to the junction with Tunnel Trail. Bear right and continue walking up Juniper Canyon Trail.

1.8   Arrive at a bench and the saddle straddling the east and west sides of Pinnacles National Park just below Scout Peak. This is the perfect perch to take a water break and soak up the stunning views while hoping for condors to glide by. Continue on the trail below the bench on the east side toward the spur trail going to the toilets in the stone building. Bear left to Bear Gulch at the spur intersection and begin walking downhill.

2.3   Walk through a short but impressive stone tunnel.

2.6   The exposed trail offers expansive southward views toward North Chalone Peak and the fire tower.

2.8   Come to an anvil-shaped rock formation on your left with a spur trail to a climber access to another rock outcrop just ahead on your right.

3.3   Come to a trail junction signed Rim Trail to Reservoir. Bear right uphill on the Rim Trail. Immediately come to an unnamed climber access trail on the left.

3.5   Arrive at the crest and walk downhill to the reservoir. The bouldery head of the reservoir comes into view a few feet ahead.

3.7   Arrive at the reservoir and a trail junction signed North Chalone Peak, Moses Spring Trail, and Bear Gulch via Cave. Rim Trail ends. Walk down the rock steps on Moses Springs Trail and come to the trail junction for Upper Cave on the left. Bear right through the boulder tunnel. In 0.1 mile pass two climber access trails on the left.

3.9   Come to a trail junction for Lower Cave to the right and a climber access. Continue downhill to a viewpoint down Bear Gulch, then pass by Moses Spring with its ferns and grotto on your left.

4.1   Come to a climber access spur on the left. Bear right and continue walking downhill to the trail junction signed Reservoir via Bear Gulch Caves. Bear left and continue walking downhill.

4.2   Walk through a rock tunnel.

4.35 Come to the trail junction for High Peaks Trail. Turn left and walk uphill on High Peaks Trail.

4.45 Come to the climber access trail to the top of Tourist Trap on the right, followed quickly by a climber access on the left and a view down Bear Gulch.

4.65 Come to the trail intersection with the Rim Trail. This closes the loop to your lollipop. Continue walking uphill toward the High Peaks back to the trailhead the way you came.

7.95 Arrive back at the trailhead.

33 Juniper Canyon Trail to Bear Gulch Caves

The hike up the canyon on the west side to a saddle rewards you with panoramic views, and the hike downhill to the east side is like being invited to look behind a strange and seductive, otherworldly volcanic curtain. The lollipop route takes you to the edge of a reservoir via an amazing subterranean climb threading under colossal boulder tunnels between rock faces and up sculpted rock staircases. This scenic hike through the talus caves challenges your limberness.

Start: From the wooden trailhead sign in the Chaparral Picnic Area and trailhead parking lot

Distance: 7.95-mile lollipop

Hiking time: 4.5 hours

Difficulty: Strenuous

Trail surface: Dirt, rock, and gravel

Trailhead elevation: 1,389 feet

Highest point: 2,478 feet

Best seasons: Spring for wildflowers, late fall and winter for cooler temperatures (summer and early fall can be very hot); cool in the cave

Maps: USGS North Chalone Peak; Pinnacles National Park map; Tom Harrison map of Pinnacles National Park

Nearest town: Soledad

Trail contact: Pinnacles National Park, 5000 CA 146, Paicines, CA 95043-9770; (831) 389-4485 or (831) 389-4427; www.nps.gov/pinn

Trail tips: There are trash and recycling receptacles, flush toilets, and a drinking fountain between the parking lot and the developed picnic area. Each picnic site has a table and grill. There are "self-pay" envelopes and maps by the fee box in the parking lot. Be aware that the uneven rock surfaces through the cave are very slippery when wet. Check the park website for the cave's seasonal schedule dependent on the bat migration. If you wear a cap with a brim, turn it backward so the brim does not obstruct your view of overhanging rocks.

Finding the trailhead: From US 101 at Soledad, take exit 302/CA 146 and drive 0.3 mile to the traffic signal. Follow the signs for West Pinnacles. Turn left onto Front Street and drive 0.3 mile to East Street. Turn right onto East Street and drive 0.2 mile to Metz Road/CA 146. Turn right onto Metz Road/CA 146, drive 2.5 miles to the Pinnacles National Park sign, and turn left. The road becomes narrower and winding. Drive 5.8 miles on CA 146 to the intersection of Stonewall Canyon Road (left) and CA 146 (right). Bear right and continue on CA 146 for 0.8 mile to the Pinnacles National Park entrance/gate. Drive 0.2 mile to the West Pinnacles Visitor Contact Station parking lot. Stop in the contact station to pay the park entrance fee and pick up a map and information. Take the time to view the park film and look at the various exhibits before driving 2 miles to the end of the road in the Chaparral Picnic Area and trailhead parking lot. (If the station is closed, maps and envelopes are at the self-pay fee box in the parking lot.) The trail begins at the wooden Trailhead sign at the head of the parking lot to the right of the information and map board. GPS: N36 29.50' / W121 12.56'.

Note: In winter to early spring, if Chalone Creek is running too high for a dry crossing, you can walk 250 feet to the right (south) and bypass the creek crossing to join up with the trail. There is also an alternate trailhead marked Balconies Trail at the far end of the large picnic area past the parking area. A junction for Juniper Canyon is on the right off the Balconies Trail just a few hundred yards up the trail. You can see that short alternate route above the parking lot.

The Hike

The hike begins in a canyon cooled by a creekbed lined with juniper shrubs and trees. You cross a typically dry creek at the trailhead and walk 150 feet to the first junction and the Condor Crags interpretive panel. Turn right at the interpretive sign and walk 250 feet to a seasonal creek; cross on the wooden footbridge.

The first 0.5 mile benefits from a shady canopy among valley oaks and some gray pines before the trail begins to climb up the exposed rocky flanks. The switchbacks quickly reveal expansive views of hilly California chaparral and Pinnacles wilderness. If you happen to hike following a winter or spring rain, the moss-covered boulders will look like they are draped in rich green velvet.

At 1.2 miles you come to a trail junction for the High Peaks via Tunnel Trail. Bear right to continue on the Juniper Canyon Trail. The trail narrows, tracing the foot of colossal stone knuckles, towers, and volcanic spirals sculpted by wind, water, and time. The views just get grander as you approach the "Continental Divide" of Pinnacles National Park at 1.8 miles. This is the saddle beneath Scout Peak where you can take a water break sitting on the bench straddling the east and west sides of Pinnacles National Park. You may get lucky and spot condors riding the thermals in the early afternoon.

Looking eastward the trail bears left just below the bench where the spur trail leads to a stone building with toilets. Walk down to the trail, bear left at the marker, and follow the trail downhill to the Bear Gulch area on the east side. Looking at the cluster of rock on your right is like peering into the giant molar of a prehistoric animal. Farther down on your right, the landscape changes to a steep stadium of stone knolls and pinnacles dotted with gray pine trees.

The trail traces the base of the stone palisades as you continue walking downhill. At 2.3 miles you walk through a short tunnel carved out of the volcanic rock. Take time to admire this one of many trail-building and sculpting marvels accomplished by the Civilian Conservation Corps (CCC) between 1933 and 1938. Just ahead the trail levels off, and the canyon on your left softens into more of a swale.

At 2.6 miles the trail comes to a wide saddle with views opening southward up the chaparral-covered slopes of the Gabilan Range toward North Chalone Peak and the fire tower. You can see the outline of the Salinas Mountains in the distance and the ridge of the San Lucia Range on the far western horizon.

Just past the lone anvil-shaped rock on your left is a climber access spur trail to another rock outcrop at 2.8 miles. The trail hugs left and sweeps back down along the canyon. This is one of many areas where the CCC terraced the volcanic terrain to construct the park's tapestry of trails and unique hiking routes.

At 3.3 miles you will come to a trail junction signed Rim Trail to Reservoir going uphill on your right. Continue walking downhill past a couple of climber access spurs and to the trail junction for the Moses Spring Trail. The High Peaks trail ends at this junction. Turn right and walk up the Moses Spring Trail and through a rock tunnel

Hiking up the stone stairway from the cave toward Bear Gulch Reservoir

entrance just before the trail junction signed Reservoir via Bear Gulch Area. Bear left at the junction and continue walking along the narrow passages between the sheer rock walls.

At 3.9 miles the fun begins on the amazing lower talus cave's intricate path leading up to the reservoir. Turn on your flashlight before entering the cave. Farther along the path your light will flash on a trail junction with a gate on your right (this small cave is closed periodically during the Townsend's big-eared bat breeding season). Look for a metal bridge ahead beneath a large boulder. Crouch under the boulder to walk across the metal bridge and climb twelve rock steps into the light on the other side of the boulder and out of the Lower Cave. Emerge at a trail junction for Bear Gulch Reservoir to the left, Bear Gulch Nature Center on the right, and a climber access spur. Bear left to the reservoir and pass two climber access trails on the right before the entrance to a cavernous tunnel. Step down into the cavern to navigate the short passage.

About 4.2 miles come to the last trail junction before the reservoir. Bear left and follow the arrow to the reservoir up the rock staircase. Emerging from the cave to

Juniper Canyon Trail to Bear Gulch Caves

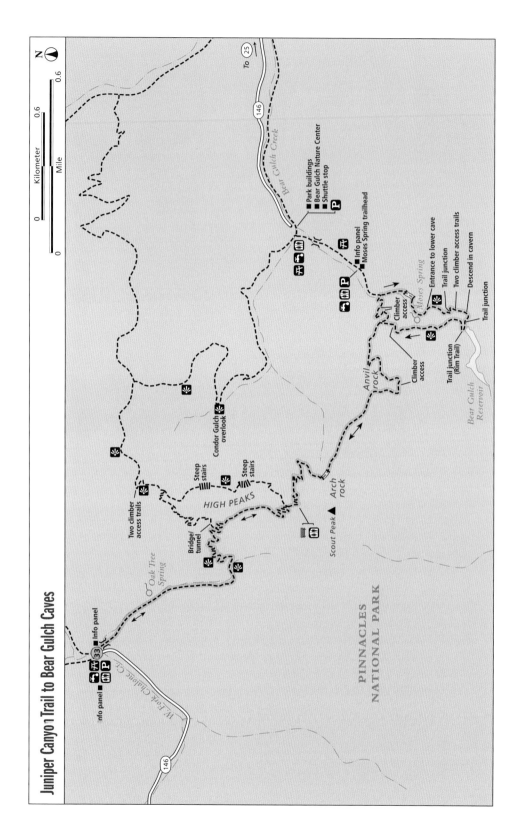

the head of the small reservoir cradled by crags and North Chalone Peak's chaparral slopes is like landing in another world. The narrow reservoir with the stone dam built by the CCC is home to the threatened red-legged frog. The shore of this very natural-looking reservoir makes an ideal picnic stop before continuing on the Rim Trail to your right.

The Rim Trail skirts the top of the cave and several impressive rock formations inviting climbers to test their skills. At 4.65 miles the Rim Trail drops down at a junction with the High Peaks Trail. This is the close of your lollipop. Turn left toward the High Peaks and go back to the trailhead the way you came.

Miles and Directions

0.0 Start at the wooden Trailhead sign in the Chaparral Picnic Area parking lot. Walk across the typically dry West Fork Chalone Creek and follow the fenced trail for 150 feet to the T-junction and the Condor Crags interpretive panel. Turn right, walk 250 feet to a seasonal creek, and cross on the wooden footbridge.

0.3 Come to unmarked Oak Tree Spring, which feeds the seasonal creek on the right.

0.7 The trail becomes more exposed, rewarding you with an embracing view of Juniper Canyon below.

0.9 The trail reveals expansive views northward as it begins a series of switchbacks.

1.2 Come to the junction with Tunnel Trail. Bear right and continue walking up Juniper Canyon trail.

1.8 Arrive at a bench and the saddle straddling the east and west sides of Pinnacles National Park just below Scout Peak. This is the perfect perch to take a water break and soak up the stunning views while hoping for condors to glide by. Continue on the trail below the bench on the east side toward the spur trail going to the toilets in the stone building. Bear left to Bear Gulch at the spur intersection and begin walking downhill.

2.3 Walk through a short but impressive stone tunnel.

2.6 The exposed trail offers expansive southward views toward North Chalone Peak and the fire tower.

2.8 Come to an anvil-shaped rock formation on your left with a spur trail to a climber access to another rock outcrop just ahead on your right.

3.3 Come to a trail junction signed Rim Trail to Reservoir on the right. Continue walking down the High Peaks Trail.

3.4 Walk past a climber access trail on the right. In 0.1 mile pass the climber access to the top of Tourist Trap.

3.6 Come to the trail junction for the Moses Spring Trail where the High Peaks Trail ends. Turn right onto the Moses Spring Trail.

3.75 Walk through an arched rock tunnel and immediately come to the trail junction signed Reservoir via Bear Gulch Caves going uphill. Bear left through the narrow rock passage.

3.9 Enter Lower Cave (turn on your flashlight).

4.05 Come to an unnamed trail junction with a gate on the right. (If the gate is open, you have the option of going through the Upper Cave and walking about 1,500 feet before merging with the Moses Spring Trail at mile 4.2 up to the reservoir.) If the gate is closed, continue walking straight across a metal bridge and crouch down so your head clears the bottom of the large boulder above the bridge. Walk up twelve rock steps on the other end of the metal bridge and come to a trail junction for Bear Gulch Reservoir, the Bear Gulch Nature Center, and a climber access. Bear left to the reservoir.

4.1 Pass two climber access trails on the right, then immediately step down into a cavernous boulder tunnel.

4.2 Come to a trail junction for the Bear Gulch Caves. (This is where you would merge into the Moses Spring Trail if you had walked through the Upper Cave.) Bear left and follow the arrow toward the reservoir and up the narrow rock staircase to the top of the cave.

4.25 Arrive at the reservoir and the trail junction for North Chalone Peak and the Rim Trail. Turn right onto Rim Trail.

4.65 Come to the trail junction for High Peaks Trail. This is the close of your lollipop. Turn left and walk up the High Peaks Trail back to the trailhead the way you came.

7.95 Arrive back at trailhead.

34 Juniper Canyon Trail to Bear Gulch Day Use Area via Bench Trail

This is a west to east traverse lollipop with good climbing, beginning in the shaded Juniper Canyon and switchbacking up the exposed western flank for a panoramic close-up of the peaks. The descent on the backside crosses rolling, oak-studded meadows before dropping down to the banks of seasonal Chalone Creek and up the scenic, shaded Bear Gulch back over the High Peaks saddle beneath Scout Peak for the last descent to the trailhead.

Start: From the wooden trailhead sign in the Chaparral Picnic Area and trailhead parking lot

Distance: 9.95-mile lollipop

Hiking time: 5 hours

Difficulty: Strenuous

Trail surface: Dirt and rock

Trailhead elevation: 1,389 feet

Highest point: 2,552 feet

Best seasons: Spring for wildflowers, late fall and winter for cooler temperatures (summer and early fall can be very hot)

Maps: USGS North Chalone Peak; Pinnacles National Park map; Tom Harrison map of Pinnacles National Park

Nearest town: Soledad

Trail contact: Pinnacles National Park, 5000 CA 146, Paicines, CA 95043-9770; (831) 389-4485 or (831) 389-4427; www.nps.gov/pinn

Trail tips: There are trash and recycling receptacles, flush toilets, and a drinking fountain between the parking lot and the developed picnic area. Each picnic site has a table and grill. There are "self-pay" envelopes and maps by the fee box in the parking lot. Restrooms, water, picnic tables, grills, trash, and recycling containers are in Bear Gulch Day Use Area. There are vault toilets at the base of Scout Peak but no water.

Finding the trailhead: From US 101 at Soledad, take exit 302/CA 146 and drive 0.3 mile to the traffic signal. Follow the signs for West Pinnacles. Turn left onto Front Street and drive 0.3 mile to East Street. Turn right onto East Street and drive 0.2 mile to Metz Road/CA 146. Turn right onto Metz Road/CA 146, drive 2.5 miles to the Pinnacles National Park sign, and turn left. The road becomes narrower and winding. Drive 5.8 miles on CA 146 to the intersection of Stonewall Canyon Road (left) and CA 146 (right). Bear right and continue on CA 146 for 0.8 mile to the Pinnacles National Park entrance/gate. Drive 0.2 mile to the West Pinnacles Visitor Contact Station parking lot. Pay the park entrance fee and pick up a map and information in the contact station. View the park film and see the various exhibits before driving 2 miles to the end of the road in the Chaparral Picnic Area and trailhead parking lot. (If the station is closed, maps and envelopes are at the self-pay fee box in the parking lot.) The trail begins at the wooden Trailhead sign at the head of the parking lot to the right of the information and map board. GPS: N36 29.50' / W121 12.56'.

Note: In winter to early spring, if Chalone Creek is running too high for a dry crossing, you can walk 250 feet to the right (south) and bypass the creek crossing to join up with the trail. There is also an alternate trailhead marked Balconies Trail at the far end of the large picnic area past the parking area. A junction for Juniper Canyon is on the right off the Balconies Trail just a few hundred yards up the trail. You can see that short alternate route above the parking lot.

The Hike

The hike begins in a canyon cooled by a creekbed lined with juniper shrubs and trees. You cross the typically dry West Chalone Creek at the trailhead and walk 150 feet to the first junction and the Condor Crags interpretive panel. Turn right at the interpretive panel and walk 250 feet to a seasonal creek; cross on the wooden footbridge.

The next 0.5 mile benefits from a shady canopy among valley oaks and some gray pines before the trail begins to climb up the exposed rocky flanks. The switchbacks quickly reveal expansive views of hilly California chaparral and Pinnacles wilderness. At 1.2 miles you come to a trail junction for the High Peaks via Tunnel Trail. Bear left on Tunnel Trail. Just ahead is a short arched rock tunnel, one of many engineering accomplishments made by the Civilian Conservation Corps (CCC) during the 1930s when they improved and constructed trails in the then Pinnacles National Monument. Walk through the tunnel (no flashlight needed) and across the narrow metal bridge over the ravine. On a clear day you can catch your first striking view of the Balconies Cliffs to the north.

Tunnel Trail ends just ahead at the T-junction for High Peaks Trail. Turn left onto High Peaks Trail toward the Bear Gulch area and Old Pinnacles Trail. The trail threads past rock towers like a portal to another world. Regardless of whether you are here on a sparkling sunny day bursting with views or on a misty winter day, there is a "power spot" quality to this geological portal straddling the east and west sides of the park.

Continue walking past two climber access trails on the left with expansive views across the canyon to the Balconies Cliffs. The trail comes to a junction with the unmarked Condor Gulch Trail going right. Continue walking straight along High Peaks Trail along the exposed saddle toward Bench Trail. At about 3.1 miles you come to a panoramic viewpoint northward and eastward where the trail veers left and begins a steady downhill in the chaparral canyon and over swales of oak-studded meadows and rolling hills before the long switchbacks begin to trace chaparral and gray pine–studded slopes.

At 4.4 miles High Peaks Trail ends at the junction for the unmarked Bench Trail above Chalone Creek. This is your loop back point. Turn right onto the Bench Trail. Just ahead you will walk under the park road overpass before coming to two boardwalk sections along the eroded side of the creekbank.

At 5.0 miles you will come to a T-junction with unmarked Bear Gulch Trail. Turn right toward Bear Gulch Day Use Area. You crisscross the creek on several footbridges as you walk up this pretty section of the gulch in the shade of buckeyes and cottonwoods past clumps of green ferns for about a mile.

The trail crosses the employee residence driveway at about 5.8 miles just before the last footbridges and the Bear Gulch Nature Center and day-use parking lot.

There are restrooms and a picnic table across the road from the nature center, along with water and trash and recycling containers. This is also the park headquarters area with administrative offices in the stone buildings next to the seasonally open nature center. Use the crosswalk from the parking lot to the restroom and single picnic table and turn left to continue walking on the unmarked trail. Follow the sign for the Picnic Area, Bear Gulch Caves, and High Peaks Trail over the footbridge and through the picnic area. The picnic area has several tables with grills and water. This trail ends at the Moses Spring trailhead. Follow the trail and sign to High Peaks.

At 6.35 miles you come to a junction where Moses Spring Trail goes uphill to the left and High Peaks Trail goes to the right. Bear right on High Peaks Trail past a couple of climber access trails and the junction for the Rim Trail. Stay on High Peaks Trail, which climbs for about 1 mile, passing a couple more climber access trails and an anvil-shaped rock before the trail views open southward to the North Chalone Peak fire tower.

At 7.65 miles the trail passes through an arched rock tunnel compliments of the 1930s CCC crew. From here the trail switchbacks up for about 0.5 mile before reaching the bench on the saddle straddling the East and West Pinnacles at the base

Hikers at junction of High Peaks and Condor Gulch Trails

Juniper Canyon Trail to Bear Gulch Day Use Area via Bench Trail

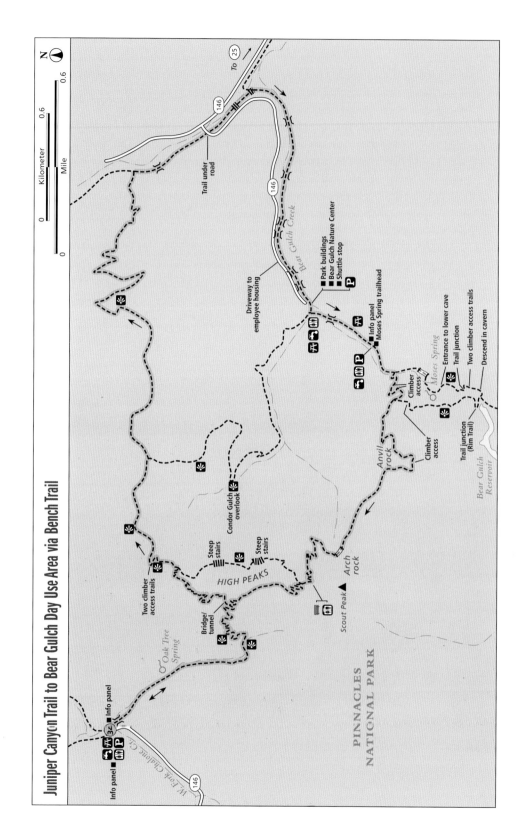

N

Kilometer 0 0.6 0.6
Mile 0 0.6

To 25

146

Trail under road

146

Bear Gulch Creek

Driveway to employee housing

Park buildings
Bear Gulch Nature Center
Shuttle stop

Info panel
Moses Spring trailhead

Moses Spring

Climber access

Entrance to lower cave
Trail junction
Two climber access trails
Descend in cavern

Anvil rock

Climber access

Trail junction
(Rim Trail)

Bear Gulch Reservoir

Condor Gulch overlook

Two climber access trails

Steep stairs

Steep stairs

HIGH PEAKS

Bridge/tunnel

Oak Tree Spring

Arch rock

Scout Peak

PINNACLES
NATIONAL PARK

Info panel

W. Fork Chalone Cr.

146

Info panel

of Scout Peak. There is a stone building housing two toilets to the left before the bench.

Enjoy the views and refuel with a snack before the last descent back to the trailhead.

The junction for High Peaks Trail and Juniper Canyon Trail is just past the bench. Bear left at the Chaparral Picnic Area via Juniper Canyon Trail and Juniper Canyon to Tunnel Trail signs and begin walking downhill.

You come to the trail junction for High Peaks via Tunnel Trail at 8.75 miles. This is the close of your lollipop. Bear left down Juniper Canyon Trail and continue back to the trailhead the way you came.

Miles and Directions

0.0 Start at the wooden Trailhead sign in the Chaparral Picnic Area parking lot. Walk across the typically dry West Fork Chalone Creek and follow the fenced trail for 150 feet to the T-junction and the Condor Crags interpretive panel. Turn right, walk 250 feet to a seasonal creek, and cross on the wooden footbridge.

0.3 Come to the unmarked Oak Tree Spring, which feeds the seasonal creek on the right.

0.7 The trail becomes more exposed, rewarding you with an embracing view of Juniper Canyon below.

0.9 The trail reveals expansive views northward as it begins a series of switchbacks.

1.2 Come to the junction with Tunnel Trail. Bear left to High Peaks via Tunnel Trail.

1.3 Walk through a tunnel and across the concrete footbridge over the ravine.

1.8 Come to a T-junction for High Peaks Trail and turn left onto High Peaks Trail. Tunnel Trail ends here. In 0.1 mile the trail crests and veers left downhill with two climber access trails on the left ahead. On a clear day the view across the canyon to the Balconies Cliffs is splendid.

2.4 Come to a trail junction for the unmarked Condor Gulch Trail to Bear Gulch Area on the right. Bear left and continue walking on High Peaks Trail to Bench Trail.

3.1 Come to a panoramic viewpoint. The trail veers left and downhill.

4.4 Come to the T-junction for the unmarked Bench Trail. High Peaks Trail ends here. This is your loop back point. Turn right, then shortly walk across Chalone Creek on the wooden footbridge.

4.7 Walk under the park road overpass. In 0.2 mile walk on two closely spaced boardwalks along an eroded section of Chalone Creek.

5.0 Come to the trail junction with unmarked Bear Gulch Trail. Turn right to Bear Gulch Day Use Area.

5.2 Walk across a footbridge over the creek. Cross three more footbridges in the next 0.5 mile.

5.8 Crosses the employee residence driveway, then walk across two more footbridges in quick succession. Park buildings are on the left.

6.0 Come to the Bear Gulch Nature Center parking lot and the end of Bear Gulch Trail. Walk across the road in the crosswalk and turn left.

6.05 Come to a sign for Bear Gulch Caves and High Peaks Trail.

6.1 Walk across the footbridge and enter the picnic area.

6.25 Come to the Moses Spring trailhead. Walk up the trail to High Peaks.

6.35 Come to the trail junction for High Peaks Trail and Moses Spring Trail. Bear right and walk uphill on High Peaks Trail. In 0.1 mile come to the climber access trail to the top of Tourist Trap on the right.

6.55 Come to a climber access on the left. Bear right and continue walking on High Peaks Trail.

6.65 Come to the trail junction signed Rim Trail to Reservoir on the left. Bear right and continue walking uphill on High Peaks Trail.

7.15 Come to a climber access on the left and an anvil-shaped rock ahead on the right. In 0.2 mile enjoy the viewpoint toward the south and North Chalone Peak fire tower.

7.65 Walk through the arched rock tunnel.

8.15 Come to the bench at the base of Scout Peak and the junction for High Peaks Trail to the right and Chaparral Picnic Area via Juniper Canyon and Tunnel Trail via Juniper Canyon to the left. Bear left downhill to Chaparral Picnic Area on Juniper Canyon Trail.

8.75 Come to the trail junction for Tunnel Trail on the right. This is the close of your lollipop. Bear left and continue walking down on Juniper Canyon Trail the way you came back to the trailhead.

9.95 Arrive back at the trailhead.

35 Juniper Canyon Trail to Chalone Peaks

If you are a hardy hiker and your goal is to reach the park's southernmost point and soak up views from the highest point, this hike is for you. The trail climbs out of a shaded canyon to a panoramic saddle before descending along the volcanic east flank past the reservoir, then climbs up exposed chaparral slopes to the fire tower on North Chalone Peak, before continuing down and up again to lower South Chalone Peak.

Start: From the wooden trailhead sign in the Chaparral Picnic Area and trailhead parking lot
Distance: 17.2 miles out and back
Hiking time: 8.5 hours
Difficulty: Strenuous
Trail surface: Dirt and rock
Trailhead elevation: 1,389 feet
Highest point: 3,304 feet
Best seasons: Spring for wildflowers, late fall and winter for cooler temperatures (summer and early fall can be very hot)
Maps: USGS North Chalone Peak; Pinnacles National Park map; Tom Harrison map of Pinnacles National Park
Nearest town: Soledad

Trail contact: Pinnacles National Park, 5000 CA 146, Paicines, CA 95043-9770; (831) 389-4485 or (831) 389-4427; www.nps.gov/pinn
Trail tips: There are trash and recycling receptacles, flush toilets, and a drinking fountain between the parking lot and the developed picnic area. Each picnic site has a table and grill. There are "self-pay" envelopes and maps by the fee box in the parking lot. Take advantage of the restrooms and drinking water at the trailhead. This is a long, dry hike with 2 vault toilets on the saddle beneath Scout Peak and 2 vault toilets on North Chalone Peak. There is no drinking water on this trail beyond the trailhead. Make sure you carry plenty of water.

Finding the trailhead: From US 101 at Soledad, take exit 302/CA 146 and drive 0.3 mile to the traffic signal. Follow the signs for West Pinnacles. Turn left onto Front Street and drive 0.3 mile to East Street. Turn right onto East Street and drive 0.2 mile to Metz Road/CA 146. Turn right onto Metz Road/CA 146, drive 2.5 miles to the Pinnacles National Park sign, and turn left. The road becomes narrower and winding. Drive 5.8 miles on CA 146 to the intersection of Stonewall Canyon Road (left) and CA 146 (right). Bear right and continue on CA 146 for 0.8 mile to the Pinnacles National Park entrance/gate. Drive 0.2 mile to the West Pinnacles Visitor Contact Station parking lot. Stop in the contact station to pay the park entrance fee and pick up a map and information. Take the time to view the park film and look at the various exhibits before driving 2 miles to the end of the road in the Chaparral Picnic Area and trailhead parking lot. (If the station is closed, maps and envelopes are at the self-pay fee box in the parking lot.) The trail begins at the wooden Trailhead sign at the head of the parking lot to the right of the information and map board. GPS: N36 29.50' / W121 12.56'.

Note: In winter to early spring, if Chalone Creek is running too high for a dry crossing, you can walk 250 feet to the right (south) and bypass the creek crossing to join up with the trail. There is also an alternate trailhead marked Balconies Trail at the far end of the large picnic area past the parking area. A junction for Juniper Canyon is on the right off the Balconies Trail just a few hundred yards up the trail. You can see that short alternate route above the parking lot.

The Hike

The hike begins in a canyon cooled by a creekbed lined with juniper shrubs and trees. You cross a typically dry creek at the trailhead and walk 150 feet to the first junction and the Condor Crags interpretive sign. Turn right at the interpretive sign and walk 250 feet to a seasonal creek; cross on the wooden footbridge.

The next 0.5 mile benefits from a shady canopy among valley oaks and some gray pines before the trail begins to climb up the exposed rocky flanks. The switchbacks quickly reveal expansive views of hilly California chaparral and Pinnacles wilderness. At 1.2 miles you come to a trail junction for the High Peaks via Tunnel Trail. Bear right to continue on the Juniper Canyon Trail. The trail narrows, tracing the foot of colossal stone knuckles, towers, and volcanic spirals sculpted by wind, water, and time. The views just get grander as you approach the "Continental Divide" of Pinnacles National Park at 1.8 miles. This is the saddle beneath Scout Peak, where you can sit on a bench straddling the east and west sides of Pinnacles National Park; it's a perfect perch for a picnic break. You may get lucky and spot condors riding the thermals in the early afternoon.

Looking eastward the trail bears left just below the bench where the spur trail leads to a stone building with toilets. Walk down to the trail, bear left at the marker, and follow the trail downhill to the Bear Gulch area on the east side. Looking at the cluster of rock on your right is like peering into the giant molar of a prehistoric animal. Farther down on your right, the landscape changes to a steep stadium of stone knolls and pinnacles dotted with gray pine trees.

The trail traces the base of the stone palisades as you continue walking downhill. At 2.3 miles you walk through a short tunnel carved out of the volcanic rock. Take time to admire this one of many trail-building and sculpting marvels accomplished by the Civilian Conservation Corps (CCC) between 1933 and 1938. Just ahead the trail levels off, and the canyon on your left softens into more of a swale.

At 2.6 miles the trail comes to a wide saddle with views opening southward up the chaparral-covered slopes of the Gabilan Range toward North Chalone Peak and the fire tower where your trail will soon climb. You can see the outline of the Salinas Mountains in the distance and the ridge of the San Lucia Range on the far western horizon.

Just past the lone anvil-shaped rock on your left is a climber access spur trail to another rock outcrop at 2.8 miles. The trail hugs left and sweeps back down along the canyon. This is one of many areas where the CCC terraced the volcanic terrain to construct the park's tapestry of trails and unique hiking routes.

At 3.3 miles you come to a trail junction signed Rim Trail to Reservoir on your right. Bear right uphill on the Rim Trail, then pass an unnamed climber access just ahead on your left. Rim Trail approaches the crest, where a splendid view opens above Bear Gulch. You begin a gradual downhill and pass through a rock corridor. The head of the stone dam built by the CCC in the 1930s comes into view with the reservoir behind it. At about 3.7 miles you arrive at the reservoir and a trail junction for North

Breaking for a view of the High Peaks from Chalone Peak Trail

Chalone Peak across the dam, the Bear Gulch area via Bear Gulch Caves, and Moses Spring Trail. Look to your right for the interpretive panel about the threatened red-legged frog whose habitat this is. Walk across the head of the dam along the concrete path and continue following the trail as it gradually climbs away from the reservoir. Notice how the water seems to snake along the narrow, undulating volcanic walls of the flooded canyon. In a low precipitation year, you can see the dark high water line against the rock walls.

The trail passes a couple of climber access trails before transitioning from volcanic terrain to exposed, dry chaparral hillsides. The only shade you can expect on your way up to North Chalone Peak and the fire tower is from the shadow of the tall chamise.

At 4.3 miles you get an unobstructed view of the High Peaks as you look back. In about half a mile, where the trail crests and levels for a short distance, the fire tower comes into view ahead; the High Peaks remain in view on your right.

At 6.2 miles you come to a wire fence. This is the pig fence built to protect the main park area from the rooting damage of nonnative pigs. There is a trail sign for North Chalone Peak 0.8 at the fence. Use the wooden pedestrian access stile to climb over the fence. The trail merges with a service road just ahead before you come to a gate and a pedestrian access over another wooden stile. You pass the trail junction and marker for South Chalone Peak 1.6 on your right before reaching the fire tower at 7.0 miles. This is the highlight of the hike if you are in it for the views.

Although the green fire tower is nonoperational, its location provides hikers with commanding 360-degree views reaching to Monterey Bay on the northern horizon and across to the coastal Santa Lucia Range to the west, with the San Andreas Fault rift zone east and vineyard and agricultural valleys running north and south.

There is an air quality monitoring station and interpretive sign at the peak along with two vault toilets in a CCC-built stone building on a volcanic perch just below the tower off a spur trail to the east. The fire tower is a great destination to end your hike on a high note. If you are focused on South Chalone Peak, however, North Chalone and the fire tower are a must for the views and a great spot for a water break and refueling snack.

Retrace your steps to the trail junction and sign for South Chalone Peak 1.6 (back at 6.8 miles), just short of the gate with the wooden stile. Turn left at the junction and walk along the narrow trail on the slope. The fire tower is above on your left, and the pig fence is on your right. At the foot of the mountain in the distance you can see the hint of CA 146 tracing the landscape behind a rust-roofed barn. The trail here is exposed, and the breeze fluttering through the occasional pine is the only sound to break the silence.

The trail bottoms out at 8.0 miles and then climbs up again to South Chalone Peak from the backside, veering away from the pig fence. The North Chalone Peak fire tower is visible on your left and behind you as you reach the chamise-covered ridge where the trail ends in a clearing at 8.8 miles. The end of the trail is actually 46 feet below the highest point for South Chalone Peak, which is inaccessible because of the dense chamise. The end of the trail will be anticlimactic if you are expecting grand views. The reward for your accomplishment is the knowledge that you have hiked to the southernmost point in the park—and a good snack. Thread your way through a few bushes to the volcanic outcrop in the clearing and sit down to savor your favorite treat before you head back to the trailhead the way you came.

Miles and Directions

0.0   Start at the wooden Trailhead sign in the Chaparral Picnic Area parking lot. Walk across the typically dry West Fork Chalone Creek and follow the fenced trail for 150 feet to the T-junction and the Condor Crags interpretive panel. Turn right, walk 250 feet to a seasonal creek, and cross on the wooden footbridge.

0.3   Come to unmarked Oak Tree Spring, which feeds the seasonal creek on the right.

0.7   The trail becomes more exposed, rewarding you with an embracing view of Juniper Canyon below.

0.9   The trail reveals expansive views northward as it begins a series of switchbacks.

1.2   Come to the junction with Tunnel Trail. Bear right and continue walking up Juniper Canyon Trail.

Juniper Canyon Trail to Chalone Peaks

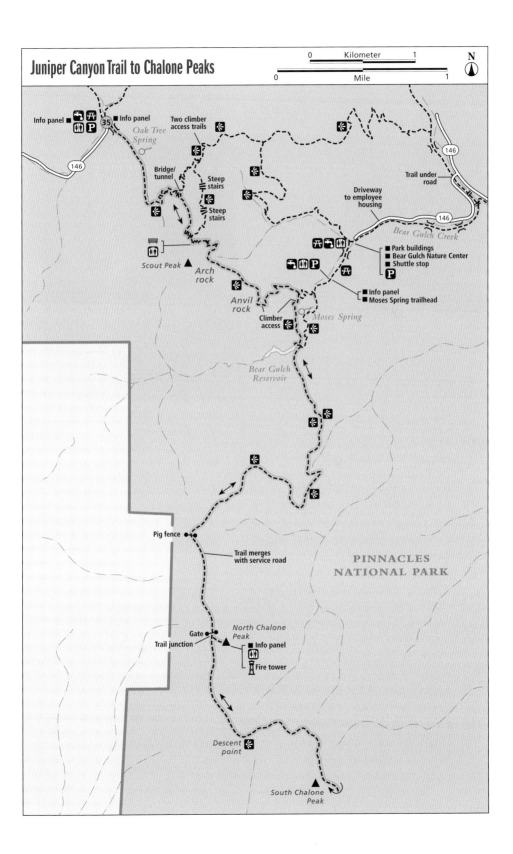

Info panel ■

Info panel ■

Oak Tree Spring

Two climber access trails

Bridge/ tunnel

Steep stairs

Steep stairs

Scout Peak ▲ *Arch rock*

Anvil rock

Climber access

Driveway to employee housing

Trail under road

Bear Gulch Creek

■ Park buildings
■ Bear Gulch Nature Center
■ Shuttle stop

■ Info panel
■ Moses Spring trailhead

Moses Spring

Bear Gulch Reservoir

Pig fence ●━●

Trail merges with service road

PINNACLES NATIONAL PARK

Gate ●━●
Trail junction

North Chalone Peak ▲
■ Info panel
🔭 Fire tower

Descent point

South Chalone Peak ▲

Kilometer

Mile

N

1.8 Arrive at a bench and the saddle straddling the east and west sides of Pinnacles National Park just below Scout Peak. This is the perfect perch to take a water break and soak up the stunning views while hoping for condors to glide by. Continue on the trail below the bench on the east side toward the spur trail going to the toilets in the stone building. Bear left to Bear Gulch at the spur intersection and begin walking downhill.

2.3 Walk through a short but impressive stone tunnel.

2.6 The exposed trail offers expansive southward views toward North Chalone Peak and the fire tower.

2.8 Come to an anvil-shaped rock formation on your left with a spur trail to a climber access to another rock outcrop just ahead on your right.

3.3 Come to a trail junction signed Rim Trail to Reservoir. Bear right uphill on the Rim Trail and immediately come to an unnamed climber access on the left.

3.5 Arrive at the crest and walk downhill to the reservoir. The bouldery head of the reservoir comes into view a few feet ahead.

3.7 Arrive at the reservoir and a trail junction signed North Chalone Peak, Moses Spring Trail, and Bear Gulch via Cave. Rim Trail ends. Walk across the dam on the concrete path to continue to North Chalone Peak. Shortly pass two climber access trails on the left.

4.3 Come to a viewpoint looking back at the High Peaks.

4.9 Come to a viewpoint looking toward the fire tower on North Chalone Peak. Another viewpoint is 0.6 mile farther.

6.2 Come to the pig fence and trail sign for North Chalone Peak 0.8. Climb over the fence on the wooden stile.

6.3 The trail merges with the gravel service road coming up from the left. Continue walking uphill on the service road.

6.8 Come to a gate and wooden stile for pedestrian access over the gate. The trail junction signed South Chalone Peak 1.6 is on the right. Continue up the service road to the fire tower on North Chalone Peak.

7.0 Arrive on North Chalone Peak at the fire tower. Soak up the views, use the vault toilet, and read the air quality interpretive sign. This makes a great destination if you are in it for the views. If your goal is to make it to South Chalone Peak to reach the southernmost point in the park, then hydrate and retrace your steps back to the junction for South Chalone Peak (at 6.8 miles) and turn left onto the narrow South Chalone Peak trail going downhill.

7.2 Arrive back at the trail junction for South Chalone Peak. Turn left.

8.0 Come to the bottom of the trail where it begins the climb upward, veering away from the pig fence.

8.8 Arrive at the end of the trail in a clearing surrounded by chamise. (GPS: N36 26.14'/ W121 10.96'. Elevation: 3,223 feet.) Sit on the volcanic outcrop in a clearing obscured by chamise bushes and catch your breath. Hydrate and enjoy a high-energy treat before retracing your steps back to the trailhead.

17.2 Arrive back at the trailhead.

36 Juniper Canyon Trail to South Wilderness

West Pinnacles has the North Wilderness and East Pinnacles has the South Wilderness. Fit hikers who want to sample the solitude of the South Wilderness on the eastern side will be treated to a strenuous but scenic uphill traverse over the imposing volcanic ridge known as the Pinnacles. This long full-day hike is punctuated by the lush Bear Gulch area on the descent to the banks of the seasonal Chalone Creek. Finally you enter the meadows and woodlands of the South Wilderness.

Start: From the wooden Trailhead sign in the Chaparral Picnic Area and trailhead parking lot
Distance: 16 miles out and back
Hiking time: 9 hours
Difficulty: Strenuous
Trail surface: Dirt, rock, gravel, and sand
Trailhead elevation: 1,389 feet
Highest point: 2,478 feet
Best seasons: Spring for wildflowers, late fall and winter for cooler temperatures (summer and early fall can be very hot)
Maps: USGS North Chalone Peak; Pinnacles National Park map; Tom Harrison map of Pinnacles National Park

Nearest town: Soledad
Trail contact: Pinnacles National Park, 5000 CA 146, Paicines, CA 95043-9770; (831) 389-4485 or (831) 389-4427; www.nps.gov/pinn
Trail tips: There are trash and recycling receptacles, flush toilets, and a drinking fountain between the parking lot and the developed picnic area. Each picnic site has a table and grill. There are "self-pay" envelopes and maps by the fee box in the parking lot. Last chance to refill your water on the way is at Peaks View Day Use Area.

Finding the trailhead: From US 101 at Soledad, take exit 302/CA 146 and drive 0.3 mile to the traffic signal. Follow the signs for West Pinnacles. Turn left onto Front Street and drive 0.3 mile to East Street. Turn right onto East Street and drive 0.2 mile to Metz Road/CA 146. Turn right onto Metz Road/CA 146, drive 2.5 miles to the Pinnacles National Park sign, and turn left. The road becomes narrower and winding. Drive 5.8 miles on CA 146 to the intersection of Stonewall Canyon Road (left) and CA 146 (right). Bear right and continue on CA 146 for 0.8 mile to the Pinnacles National Park entrance/gate. Drive 0.2 mile to the West Pinnacles Visitor Contact Station parking lot. Stop in the contact station to pay the park entrance fee and pick up a map and information. Take the time to view the park film and look at the various exhibits before driving 2 miles to the end of the road in the Chaparral Picnic Area and trailhead parking lot. (If the station is closed, maps and envelopes are at the self-pay fee box in the parking lot.) The trail begins at the wooden Trailhead sign at the head of the parking lot to the right of the information and map board. GPS: N36 29.50' / W121 12.56'.

Note: In winter to early spring, if Chalone Creek is running too high for a dry crossing, you can walk 250 feet to the right (south) and bypass the creek crossing to join up with the trail. There is also an alternate trailhead marked Balconies Trail at the far end of the large picnic area past the parking area. A junction for Juniper Canyon is on the right off the Balconies Trail just a few hundred yards up the trail. You can see that short alternate route above the parking lot.

The Hike

True to its name, the hike begins in a canyon cooled by a creekbed lined with juniper shrubs and trees. You cross a typically dry creek at the trailhead and walk 150 feet to the first junction and the Condor Crags interpretive panel. Turn right at the interpretive panel and walk 250 feet to a seasonal creek; cross on the wooden footbridge.

The next 0.5 mile benefits from a shady canopy among valley oaks and some gray pines before the trail begins to climb up the exposed rocky flanks. The switchbacks quickly reveal expansive views of hilly California chaparral and Pinnacles wilderness. At 1.2 miles you come to a trail junction for the High Peaks via Tunnel Trail. Bear right to continue on the Juniper Canyon Trail. The trail narrows, tracing the foot of colossal stone knuckles, towers, and volcanic spirals sculpted by wind, water, and time. The views just get grander as you approach the "Continental Divide" of Pinnacles National Park at 1.8 miles. This is the saddle beneath Scout Peak, where you can sit on a bench straddling the east and west sides of Pinnacles National Park; it's a perfect perch for a picnic break. You may get lucky and spot condors riding the thermals in the early afternoon.

Looking eastward the trail bears left just below the bench where the spur trail leads to a stone building with toilets. Walk down to the trail, bear left at the marker, and follow the trail downhill to the Bear Gulch area on the east side. Looking at the cluster of rock on your right is like peering into the giant molar of a prehistoric animal. Farther down on your right, the landscape changes to a steep stadium of stone knolls and pinnacles dotted with gray pine trees.

The trail traces the base of the stone palisades as you continue walking downhill. At 2.3 miles you walk through a short tunnel carved out of the volcanic rock. Take time to admire this one of many trail-building and sculpting marvels accomplished by the Civilian Conservation Corps (CCC) between 1933 and 1938. Just ahead the trail levels off, and the canyon on your left softens into more of a swale.

At 2.6 miles the trail comes to a wide saddle with views opening southward up the chaparral-covered slopes of the Gabilan Range toward North Chalone Peak and the fire tower. You can see the outline of the Salinas Mountains in the distance and the ridge of the San Lucia Range on the far western horizon.

Just past the lone anvil-shaped rock on your left is a spur trail for climber access to another rock outcrop at 2.8 miles. The trail hugs left and sweeps back down along the canyon. This is one of many areas where the CCC terraced the volcanic terrain to construct the park's tapestry of trails and unique hiking routes.

At 3.3 miles you come to a trail junction signed Rim Trail to Reservoir on your right. Bear left and continue walking down to the Bear Gulch area. Just ahead is a spur to the right for a climber access trail. Bear left toward Bear Gulch.

At 3.5 miles you come to the climber access to the top of Tourist Trap on your left. This is the last climber access trail on this hike. Watch for dangling rock climbers as switchbacks take you down the gulch.

A peaceful hike along the South Wilderness Trail

At 3.6 miles you come to a trail junction for the Moses Spring Trail to the reservoir caves to the right. This is the end of the High Peaks Trail, where it merges with Moses Spring Trail. Continue walking downhill on Moses Spring Trail to the Moses Spring trailhead at the paved road. There is a parking lot on your left and a restroom. Walk across the paved road and continue along the hiker trail through the developed picnic area (tables, grills, water, recycling and trash bins).

Bear left and walk across the wooden footbridge. At 3.9 miles you arrive at the Bear Gulch Nature Center on your right next to the parking lot. There is a restroom, a picnic table, and recycling and trash bins on your left.

Use the pedestrian crosswalk ahead by the bench to walk to the nature center. Enjoy browsing the exhibits if the nature center is open. Notice the row of small stone buildings. Some of these historic buildings were built by the CCC in the 1930s. There are a couple of picnic tables in the parking area by the nature center. Pick a spot for a rest and refueling break before continuing along the concrete path to the trailhead to Peak's View.

The next mile is an easy and enchanting downhill along Bear Gulch Creek across six wooden footbridges through a corridor of stunning rock formations, passing a 15-foot drop-off for the beloved waterfall effect after a rainfall. The canopy of sycamore, buckeye, and oak makes for a shady, cool journey as your eyes feast on a garden of ferns and clump grass–like sedges in the creekbed. The creekbed fans out at the bottom of the gulch where Bear Gulch Creek flows into Chalone Creek. Bear Gulch Trail ends at the trail junction ahead for Old Pinnacles Trail and the unmarked Bench Trail. Continue walking straight toward Peaks View Day Use Area and Pinnacles Visitor Center. Cross the two wooden footbridges across Chalone Creek and bear right at the trail sign toward Pinnacles Visitor Center. The trail parallels the road on the left and the creek on the right.

You pass Peaks View Day Use Area 0.3 mile ahead. There is a portable toilet, picnic tables, and water. Look back for a striking view of the park's High Peaks as you continue along the Bench Trail (Bench Trail is named for its location above the creekbed and not for the solitary bench).

At 5.65 miles the trail comes to a T-junction at a service/fire road and the trail marker for South Wilderness Trail to the right. Turn right toward South Wilderness Trail. Continue straight on the service/fire road and bear right on the narrower South Wilderness Trail where the service road forks left at the No Entry sign. The trail continues in the meadow interrupted by sycamore, pine, and oak woodland until it reaches the banks of seasonal Chalone Creek. This is the only tricky section of the trail, with an unmarked junction and a spur trail to the left. Bear right and cross the creek. The creek will stay on your left until you reach the pig fence and the "end of South Wilderness Trail" sign.

At about 6.8 miles, the trail narrows and skirts the bank on a steep hillside above the creek before meandering back into what feels like the creek's floodplain corralled between the chaparral-covered hills. At 8.0 miles you come to the end of the South Wilderness Trail at the pig fence. Soak up the solitude and go back the way you came.

Miles and Directions:

0.0 Start at the wooden Trailhead sign in the Chaparral Picnic Area parking lot. Walk across the typically dry West Fork Chalone Creek and follow the fenced trail for 150 feet to the T-junction and the Condor Crags interpretive panel. Turn right, walk 250 feet to a seasonal creek, and cross on the wooden footbridge.

0.3 Come to the unmarked Oak Tree Spring, which feeds the seasonal creek on the right.

0.7 The trail becomes more exposed, rewarding you with an embracing view of Juniper Canyon below.

0.9 The trail reveals expansive views northward as it begins a series of switchbacks.

1.2 Come to the junction with Tunnel Trail. Bear right and continue walking up Juniper Canyon trail.

1.8 Arrive at a bench and the saddle straddling the east and west sides of Pinnacles National Park just below Scout Peak. This is the perfect perch to take a water break and soak up the stunning views while hoping for condors to glide by. Continue on the trail below the bench on the east side toward the spur trail going to the toilets in the stone building. Bear left to Bear Gulch at the spur intersection and begin walking downhill.

2.3 Walk through a short but impressive stone tunnel.

Juniper Canyon Trail to South Wilderness

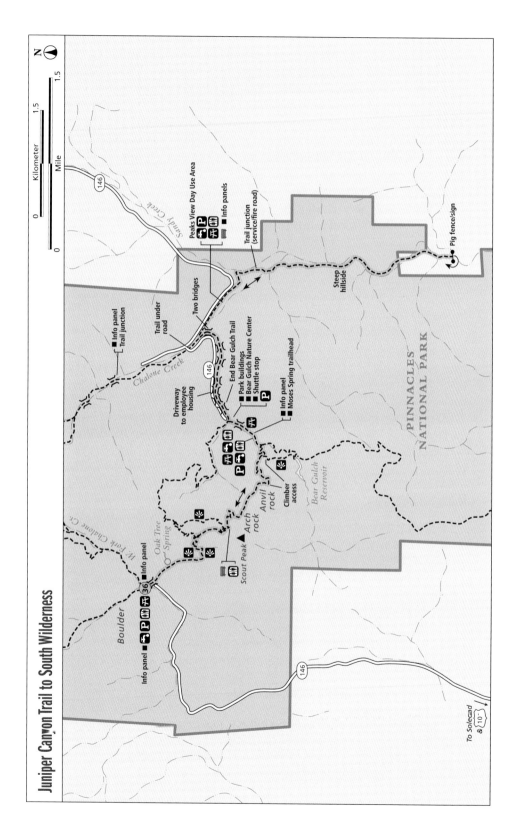

2.6 The exposed trail offers expansive southward views toward North Chalone Peak and the fire tower.

2.8 Come to an anvil-shaped rock formation on your left with a spur trail to a climber access to another rock outcrop just ahead on your right.

3.3 Come to a trail junction signed Rim Trail to Reservoir. Bear left and continue walking downhill to the Bear Gulch area. Shortly come to a climber access spur trail on your right. Bear left. In 0.1 mile come to another climber access to the top of Tourist Trap on the left.

3.6 Come to the trail junction for the Moses Spring Trail to the reservoir caves. High Peaks Trail ends and merges with Moses Spring Trail. Continue walking downhill.

3.7 Arrive at the Moses Spring trailhead, with a parking lot and restroom on the left and a paved road. Walk across the paved road and continue walking on the hiker trail through the picnic area, then bear left and walk across the wooden footbridge.

3.9 Arrive at the parking lot, restroom, and picnic table across from the Bear Gulch Nature Center and a parking lot across the road. Cross the road at the crosswalk and turn left. Walk along the concrete walkway to the Peaks View Day Use Area sign and begin walking on the unmarked Bear Gulch Trail.

4.05 Walk across seasonal Bear Gulch Creek on a wooden footbridge, quickly followed by another footbridge crossing. In 0.1 mile you walk across the driveway of the employee residence.

4.3 Walk across Bear Gulch Creek on a wooden footbridge. You will cross the creek three more times in the next 0.5 mile. The trail leaves the narrow, shaded gulch and the creekbed widens at the third crossing.

4.95 Bear Gulch Trail ends at the trail junction for the Bench Trail (unmarked) and the trail sign for Old Pinnacles Trail (left). Continue walking straight and follow the sign for Peaks View Day Use Area and Pinnacles Visitor Center across seasonal Chalone Creek on two wooden footbridges to the road and the trail sign.

5.0 Bear right on Bench Trail (unmarked) and follow the sign to Pinnacles Visitor Center. The trail parallels the road on the left and the creek on the right.

5.3 Come to Peaks View Day Use Area and continue on Bench Trail, still paralleling the road on the left.

5.65 Come to the T-junction and a service/fire road. Turn right onto the South Wilderness Trail.

5.8 Come to a fork in the road at the No Entry sign on the service/fire road on the left. Bear right on the South Wilderness Trail.

6.0 Come to an unmarked trail junction with a spur to the left. Bear right and cross the seasonal Chalone Creek. The creek will remain on your left to the end of the South Wilderness Trail.

6.8 The trail narrows and skirts the bank on a steep hillside above the creek.

8.0 Arrive at the end of the South Wilderness Trail at the pig fence. (GPS: N36 27.16'/ W121 09.23'. Elevation: 877 feet.) Have a snack and go back to the trailhead the way you came.

16.0 Arrive back at the trailhead.

37 Juniper Canyon Trail to Balconies Cave via Bench Trail

The contrasts of eco-zones on this hike demonstrate why relatively small Pinnacles National Park has such habitat diversity. You begin up the scenic, heart-pumping Juniper Canyon to the volcanic peaks and down the east side across oak-studded meadows, following the Bench Trail above the seasonal Chalone Creek, then finish through the talus Balconies Cave agility course.

Start: From the wooden Trailhead sign in the Chaparral Picnic Area and trailhead parking lot

Distance: 7.85-mile loop

Hiking time: 4.5 hours

Difficulty: Strenuous

Trail surface: Dirt and rock

Trailhead elevation: 1,389 feet

Highest point: 2,552

Best seasons: Spring for wildflowers, late fall and winter for cooler temperatures (summers and early fall can be very hot)

Maps: USGS North Chalone Peak; Pinnacles National Park map; Tom Harrison map of Pinnacles National Park

Nearest town: Soledad

Trail contact: Pinnacles National Park, 5000 CA 146, Paicines, CA 95043-9770; (831) 389-4485 or (831) 389-4427; www.nps.gov/pinn

Trail tips: There are trash and recycling receptacles, flush toilets, and a drinking fountain between the parking lot and the developed picnic area. Each picnic site has a table and grill. There are "self-pay" envelopes and maps by the fee box in the parking lot. In wet weather, check with the ranger station about cave conditions.

Finding the trailhead: From US 101 at Soledad, take exit 302/CA 146 and drive 0.3 mile to the traffic signal. Follow the signs for West Pinnacles. Turn left onto Front Street and drive 0.3 mile to East Street. Turn right onto East Street and drive 0.2 mile to Metz Road/CA 146. Turn right onto Metz Road/CA 146, drive 2.5 miles to the Pinnacles National Park sign, and turn left. The road becomes narrower and winding. Drive 5.8 miles on CA 146 to the intersection of Stonewall Canyon Road (left) and CA 146 (right). Bear right and continue on CA 146 for 0.8 mile to the Pinnacles National Park entrance/gate. Drive 0.2 mile to the West Pinnacles Visitor Contact Station parking lot. Stop in the contact station to pay the park entrance fee and pick up a map and information. Take the time to view the park film and look at the various exhibits before driving 2 miles to the end of the road in the Chaparral Picnic Area and trailhead parking lot. (If the station is closed, maps and envelopes are at the self-pay fee box in the parking lot.) The trail begins at the wooden Trailhead sign at the head of the parking lot to the right of the information and map board. GPS: N36 29.50' / W121 12.56'.

Note: In winter to early spring, if Chalone Creek is running too high for a dry crossing, you can walk 250 feet to the right (south) and bypass the creek crossing to join up with the trail. There is also an alternate trailhead marked Balconies Trail at the far end of the large picnic area past the parking area. A junction for Juniper Canyon is on the right off the Balconies Trail just a few hundred yards up the trail. You can see that short alternate route above the parking lot.

The Hike

The hike begins in a canyon cooled by a creekbed lined with juniper shrubs and trees. You cross a typically dry creek at the trailhead and walk 150 feet to the first junction and the Condor Crags interpretive panel. Turn right at the interpretive panel and walk 250 feet to a seasonal creek; cross on the wooden footbridge.

The next 0.5 mile benefits from a shady canopy among valley oaks and some gray pines before the trail begins to climb up the exposed rocky flanks. The switchbacks quickly reveal expansive views of hilly California chaparral and Pinnacles wilderness. At 1.2 miles you come to a trail junction for the High Peaks via Tunnel Trail. Bear left on the Tunnel Trail. Just ahead is a short arched rock tunnel, one of many engineering accomplishments made by the Civilian Conservation Corps during the 1930s when they improved and constructed trails in the then Pinnacles National Monument. Walk through the tunnel (no flashlight needed) and across the narrow metal bridge over the ravine. On a clear day you can catch your first striking view of the Balconies Cliffs to the north.

Tunnel Trail ends just ahead at the T-junction for High Peaks Trail. Turn left onto High Peaks Trail toward the Bear Gulch area and Old Pinnacles Trail. The trail threads past rock towers like a portal into another world. On drizzly, wet winter days, the veils of fog give this hike a mystical feel as the silhouettes of these sentinels appear and disappear through the wispy gray. Continue walking past two climber access trails on the left with expansive views across the canyon to the Balconies Cliffs. The trail comes to a junction with the unmarked Condor Gulch Trail going right. Continue walking straight along High Peaks Trail along the exposed saddle toward Bench Trail.

At about 3.1 miles you come to a panoramic viewpoint northward and eastward where the trail veers left and begins a steady downhill in the chaparral canyon and over swales of oak-studded meadows and rolling hills before the long switchbacks begin to trace chaparral and gray pine–studded slopes.

At 4.4 miles High Peaks Trail ends at the junction with the unmarked Bench Trail. Walk left, heading toward Balconies Cave and the Chaparral Picnic Area, above seasonal Chalone Creek. The creekbed is wide for the next 0.5 mile as you walk along the narrow "bench" above the creek.

At 4.9 miles Bench Trail ends at the junction with Old Pinnacles Trail and you cross the creek on a wooden footbridge. Continue walking straight. The Chalone Creek Restoration information panel is just ahead. At 5.2 miles you cross the Chalone Creek on another footbridge.

You come to the trail junction for the North Wilderness Trail on your right at about 5.4 miles. This is where seasonal Chalone Creek divides into North Fork Chalone Creek along the North Wilderness Trail and West Fork Chalone Creek. Continue walking on Old Pinnacles Trail toward Balconies Cave and Chaparral Picnic Area. You will walk across seasonal West Fork Chalone Creek seven times before coming to the trail junction for Balconies Cliffs Trail at 6.7 miles. Be aware that these

Crossing the seasonal West Fork Chalone Creek along Old Pinnacles Trail

seven crossings have no bridges and that the amount of water in this mostly dry seasonal creek always depends on the amount of winter rainfall. At the trail junction continue walking to the Chaparral Picnic Area via Balconies Cave. If you are not comfortable with dark tight spaces, you may wish to use the Balconies Cliffs Trail detour to the Chaparral Picnic Area. This trail goes uphill and drops back down near the Balconies Cave exit.

For the talus cave route, continue walking up the rock steps ahead and across a short metal bridge, following the trail to the gate at the entrance to the cave. The gates at either end of the cave's short, dark, and primitive path are closed when the cave is unsafe due to rain. Keep your flashlight on the faint white arrows on the rock walls to help you stay on the path up and down and back up to the exit. Shortly after exiting the cave (about 200 strides long), you pass the trail junction with the Balconies Cliffs Trail on your right. Walk across West Fork Chalone Creek on the wooden footbridge. You will walk across three more wooden footbridges before coming to the climber access for The Citadel and Elephant Rock on the left and one last footbridge before arriving at the trail fork at 7.7 miles and an information board. Continue walking straight to the Condor Crags information board. Turn right and walk 150 feet to the Chaparral Picnic Area parking lot and trailhead.

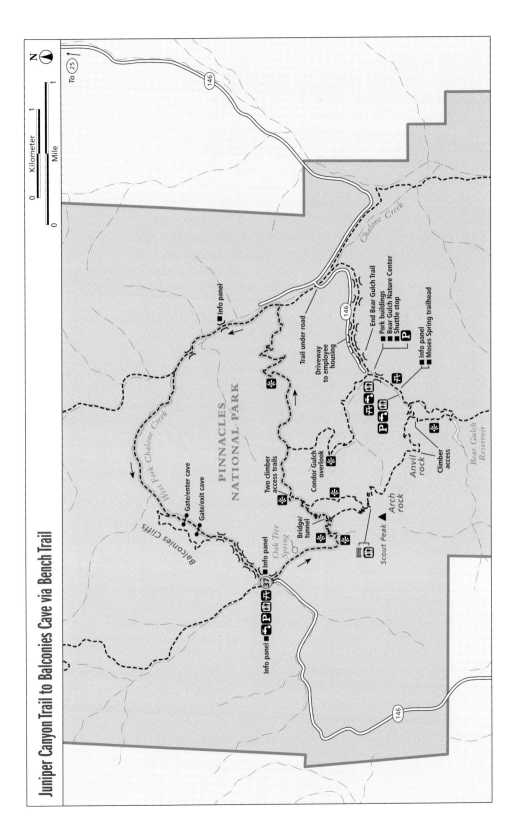

Juniper Canyon Trail to Balconies Cave via Bench Trail

PINNACLES NATIONAL PARK

Info panel
Oak Tree Spring
Info panel

Balconies Cliffs
West Fork Chalone Creek
Gate/enter cave
Gate/exit cave

Info panel

Two climber access trails
Condor Gulch overlook
Bridge/ tunnel
Scout Peak
Arch rock
Anvil rock
Climber access
Bear Gulch Reservoir

Trail under road

Driveway to employee housing

End Bear Gulch Trail
Park buildings
Bear Gulch Nature Center
Shuttle stop

Info panel
Moses Spring trailhead

Chalone Creek

To 25

0   Kilometer   1
0   Mile   1

N

Miles and Directions

0.0 Start at the wooden Trailhead sign in the Chaparral Picnic Area parking lot. Walk across the typically dry West Fork Chalone Creek and follow the fenced trail for 150 feet to the T-junction and the Condor Crags interpretive panel. Turn right and walk 250 feet to a seasonal creek and walk across the wooden footbridge.

0.3 Come to the unmarked Oak Tree Spring, which feeds the seasonal creek on the right.

0.7 The trail becomes more exposed rewarding you with an embracing view of Juniper Canyon below.

0.9 The trail reveals expansive views northward as it begins a series of switchbacks.

1.2 Come to the junction with Tunnel Trail. Bear left to High Peaks via Tunnel Trail.

1.3 Walk through a tunnel and across the concrete footbridge over the ravine.

1.8 Come to a trail junction for High Peaks Trail and turn left onto High Peaks Trail. Tunnel Trail ends here. In 0.1 mile the trail crests and veers left downhill with two climber access trails on the left ahead. On a clear day the view across the canyon to the Balconies Cliffs is splendid.

2.4 Come to a trail junction for the unmarked Condor Gulch Trail to Bear Gulch Area on the right. Bear left and continue walking on High Peaks Trail to Bench Trail.

3.1 Come to a panoramic viewpoint. The trail veers left and downhill.

4.4 Come to the T-junction for the unmarked Bench Trail. High Peaks Trail ends here. Turn left, heading toward Balconies Cave and Chaparral Picnic Area.

4.9 Walk across Chalone Creek on the wooden footbridge. Come to the trail junction with Old Pinnacles Trail to Balconies Cave. Bench Trail ends here; continue straight on Old Pinnacles Trail. The Chalone Creek Restoration information board is just ahead.

5.2 Walk across Chalone Creek on a wooden footbridge.

5.4 Come to the junction with North Wilderness Trail on your right. Continue walking on Old Pinnacles Trail.

5.7 Cross the seasonal West Fork Chalone Creek. You will cross the creek five more times in the next 0.5 mile.

6.7 Cross West Fork Chalone Creek and come to the trail junction for Chaparral Picnic Area via Balconies Cliffs on the right. Continue via the Balconies Cave route.

6.8 Walk up the rock steps and across the short metal footbridge toward the cave entrance.

6.9 Enter the cave at the metal gate. Exit the cave in 0.1 mile, then immediately walk across a seasonal creek.

7.1 Come to the trail junction with the Balconies Cliffs Trail on the right and walk across the wooden footbridge. You will cross West Fork Chalone Creek on wooden footbridges three more times in the next 0.4 mile.

7.5 Come to the climber access trail for The Citadel and Elephant Rock and walk across West Fork Chalone Creek on the wooden footbridge.

7.7 Come to an interpretive sign and a fork in the trail. Continue walking straight. Shortly come to the Condor Crags information board. Turn right.

7.85 Arrive back at the Chaparral Picnic Area parking lot and trailhead.

38 Juniper Canyon Trail to North Wilderness via Visitor Center

If you like the idea of experiencing as much of the park's biodiversity as is possible in a full day's hike and want to claim that you walked to the Pinnacles Visitor Center at the East Entrance from the west-side trailhead, then this challenging circuit is for you. If you stop in the West Pinnacles Visitor Contact Station at the West Entrance when you drive into the park and if the Bear Gulch Nature Center is open (seasonal hours) when you hike by on your way to the visitor center at the East Entrance, you just might be among the few who can say they have hit the park's three visitor centers in one day. This hike shows off the diversity of the park's habitats, from shaded gray pine and juniper canyons and towering volcanic palisades to oak meadows and wide seasonal creekbeds surrounded by steep California chaparral–covered hills. Although the Bear Gulch area is bustling with hikers on weekends, you can look forward to solitude on the last 7 miles back to the west side along the North Wilderness Trail.

Note: This is also a natural route for making an overnight hike, staying on the east side in Pinnacles Campground next to the visitor center. Reservations are recommended on weekends in the spring.

Start: From the wooden Trailhead sign in the Chaparral Picnic Area and trailhead parking lot

Distance: 17.2-mile lollipop

Hiking time: 8 hours

Difficulty: Strenuous due to length and two uphills

Trail surface: Dirt, sand, and small gravel

Trailhead elevation: 1,389 feet

Highest Point: 2,478 feet

Best seasons: Spring for wildflowers, late fall and winter for cooler temperatures (summer and early fall can be very hot)

Maps: USGS North Chalone Peak; Pinnacles National Park map; Tom Harrison map of Pinnacles National Park

Nearest town: Soledad

Trail contact: Pinnacles National Park, 5000 CA 146, Paicines, CA 95043-9770; (831) 389-4485 or (831) 389-4427; www.nps.gov/pinn

Trail tips: There are trash and recycling receptacles, flush toilets, and a drinking fountain between the parking lot and the developed picnic area. Each picnic site has a table and grill. There are "self-pay" envelopes and maps by the fee box in the parking lot. Take advantage of restrooms and water in the Bear Gulch Day Use Area and especially at the Pinnacles Visitor Center on the return. The camp store at the visitor center is your only chance to buy snacks. There is a vault toilet but no drinking water on the saddle at the base of Scout Peak before you drop down the east side on the way over and a portable toilet at Peaks View Day Use Area. There is no water along the North Wilderness Trail, and the last climb can leave you parched.

Finding the trailhead: From US 101 at Soledad, take exit 302/CA 146 and drive 0.3 mile to the traffic signal. Follow the signs for West Pinnacles. Turn left onto Front Street and drive 0.3

mile to East Street. Turn right onto East Street and drive 0.2 mile to Metz Road/CA 146. Turn right onto Metz Road/CA 146, drive 2.5 miles to the Pinnacles National Park sign, and turn left. The road becomes narrower and winding. Drive 5.8 miles on CA 146 to the intersection of Stonewall Canyon Road (left) and CA 146 (right). Bear right and continue on CA 146 for 0.8 mile to the Pinnacles National Park entrance/gate. Drive 0.2 mile to the West Pinnacles Visitor Contact Station parking lot. Stop in the contact station to pay the park entrance fee and pick up a map and information. Take the time to view the park film and look at the various exhibits before driving 2 miles to the end of the road in the Chaparral Picnic Area and trailhead parking lot. (If the station is closed, maps and envelopes are at the self-pay fee box in the parking lot.) The trail begins at the wooden Trailhead sign at the head of the parking lot to the right of the information and map board. GPS: N36 29.50' / W121 12.56'.

Note: In winter to early spring, if Chalone Creek is running too high for a dry crossing, you can walk 250 feet to the right (south) and bypass the creek crossing to join up with the trail. There is also an alternate trailhead marked Balconies Trail at the far end of the large picnic area past the parking area. A junction for Juniper Canyon is on the right off the Balconies Trail just a few hundred yards up the trail. You can see that short alternate route above the parking lot.

The Hike

The hike begins from a popular trailhead in a canyon cooled by a creekbed lined with juniper shrubs and trees. You cross a typically dry creek at the trailhead and walk 150 feet to the first junction and the Condor Crags interpretive panel. Turn right at the interpretive panel and walk 250 feet to a seasonal creek; cross on the wooden footbridge.

The next 0.5 mile benefits from a shady canopy among valley oaks and some gray pines before the trail begins to climb up the exposed rocky flanks. The switchbacks quickly reveal expansive views of hilly California chaparral and Pinnacles wilderness. At 1.2 miles you come to a trail junction for the High Peaks via Tunnel Trail. Bear right to continue on the Juniper Canyon Trail. The trail narrows, tracing the foot of colossal stone knuckles, towers, and volcanic spirals sculpted by wind, water, and time. The views just get grander as you approach the "Continental Divide" of Pinnacles National Park at 1.8 miles. This is the saddle beneath Scout Peak, where you can sit on a bench straddling the east and west sides of Pinnacles National Park; it's a perfect perch for a picnic break. You may get lucky and spot condors riding the thermals in the early afternoon.

Looking eastward the trail bears left just below the bench where the spur trail leads to a stone building with toilets. Walk down to the trail, bear left at the marker, and follow the trail downhill to the Bear Gulch area on the east side. Looking at the cluster of rock on your right is like peering into the giant molar of a prehistoric animal. Farther down on your right, the landscape changes to a steep stadium of stone knolls and pinnacles dotted with gray pine trees.

The trail traces the base of the stone palisades as you continue walking downhill. At 2.3 miles you walk through a short tunnel carved out of the volcanic rock. Take time to admire this one of many trail-building and sculpting marvels accomplished by the Civilian Conservation Corps (CCC) between 1933 and 1938. Just ahead the trail levels off, and the canyon on your left softens into more of a swale.

At 2.6 miles the trail comes to a wide saddle with views opening southward up the chaparral-covered slopes of the Gabilan Range toward North Chalone Peak and the fire tower. You can see the outline of the Salinas Mountains in the distance and the ridge of the San Lucia Range on the far western horizon.

Just past the lone anvil-shaped rock on your left is a spur trail for climber access to another rock outcrop at 2.8 miles. The trail hugs left and sweeps back down along the canyon. This is one of many areas where the CCC terraced the volcanic terrain to construct the park's tapestry of trails and unique hiking routes.

At 3.3 miles you come to a trail junction signed Rim Trail to Reservoir on your right. Bear left and continue walking down to the Bear Gulch area. Just ahead is a spur to the right for a climber access. Bear left toward Bear Gulch.

At 3.5 miles you come to the climber access to the top of Tourist Trap on your left. This is the last climber access trail on this hike. Watch for dangling rock climbers as switchbacks take you down the gulch.

At 3.6 miles you come to a trail junction for the Moses Spring Trail to the right. This is the end of the High Peaks Trail, where it merges with the Moses Spring Trail. Continue walking downhill on Moses Spring Trail for 0.2 mile to the Moses Spring trailhead at the paved road. There is a parking lot on your left and a restroom. Walk across the paved road and continue along the hiker trail through the developed picnic area (tables, grills, water, recycling and trash bins).

At 3.85 miles there is an overflow parking lot on your right across the road. Bear left and walk across the wooden footbridge. The Bear Gulch Nature Center is on your right next to the parking lot just ahead. There is a restroom, a picnic table, and recycling and trash bins on your left. This is a good spot to break for a snack before the next leg of your long journey.

Use the crosswalk ahead by the bench to walk to the Bear Gulch Nature Center. Take a moment to browse the exhibits if the nature center is open. Notice the row of small stone buildings. These were built by the CCC and are on the National Register of Historic Places. Turn left and follow the cement walkway to the trailhead for Peaks View. This is the beginning of unmarked Bear Gulch Trail. Follow the trail toward Peaks View Day Use Area. You will cross several footbridges across Bear Gulch Creek along the way down this lovely little gulch alive with cottonwoods, oaks, buckeyes, and ferns.

At 4.95 miles the trail becomes more exposed where the creekbed widens. Bear Gulch Trail ends at the trail junction ahead for Old Pinnacles Trail and the unmarked Bench Trail. Bear Gulch Creek flows into Chalone Creek. Continue walking straight toward Peaks View and Pinnacles Visitor Center. Cross the two wooden footbridges across Chalone Creek and bear right at the trail sign toward Pinnacles Visitor Center. The trail parallels the road on the left and the creek on the right.

You pass Peaks View Day Use Area 0.35 mile ahead. There is a portable toilet, picnic tables, and water. Look back for a striking view of the the park's High Peaks as you continue along the Bench Trail (Bench Trail is named for its location above the creekbed and not for the solitary bench).

At 5.65 miles the trail comes to a T-junction at a service/fire road and the trail marker for South Wilderness Trail to the right. Walk left toward Pinnacles Visitor Center on the unmarked Bench Trail along the service/fire road in this oak meadow for about 300 feet, then turn right at the trail sign and arrow to continue along the Bench Trail. If you get to the gate at the paved road, you have gone too far. Just ahead on the trail is an interpretive panel about the air quality monitoring stations in the park. Look across the road to see one of these monitoring stations on the hillside.

Bench Trail skirts along Sandy Creek on your right as it flows toward Chalone Creek behind you. Farther up the Bench Trail you come to a fence with a gate and a sign reminding you to keep the gate closed. This is part of the park's pig fence, designed to keep the nonnative, habitat-disrupting wild boars out of the core of the park. There is an interpretive panel about the pigs on the other side of the gate. Make sure the gate latches closed behind you. Bench Trail merges into the campground's paved road just ahead at the southwest end of the campground. Walk along the paved road past campsites and the campground restrooms, which have flush toilets and sinks. The paved-road section of the Bench Trail ends less than half a mile ahead at the two ADA-accessible telescope pad and bench. The telescopes point toward the Chaparral Ridge where condors are frequently soaring.

The Pinnacles Visitor Center is just ahead across the road at the campground entrance. This is your turnaround point. Although this is the park's main entrance and visitor center, it does not boast the freshness and jazziness of the new West Pinnacles Visitor Contact Station at the West Entrance. The park shares this older building with the camp store and campground registration counter. The park shuttle runs from the visitor center parking area to Bear Gulch Day Use Area, which makes this area especially busy on weekends.

Take advantage of the store supplies, which are your only opportunity for a cold drink or a candy bar sugar boost for the last 10 miles of your journey.

Retrace your route from the Bench trailhead and walk about 2 miles back to the trail junction for Bench Trail toward Old Pinnacles Trail at 8.65 miles. Turn right toward Old Pinnacles Trail on Bench Trail, which is unmarked. Chalone Creek in now on your right.

You cross two boardwalks along the eroded edge of the seasonal Chalone Creek and walk under the park road overpass within the first 0.5 mile. At 9.25 miles you come to the trail junction for the High Peaks on your left. Continue walking straight on Bench Trail until the trail junction for Old Pinnacles Trail across a wooden footbridge. Bear left on Old Pinnacles Trail toward North Wilderness Trail. The Chalone Creek Restoration information panel is just ahead on your left. Continue along the trail with rock walls and chaparral hills on the left across the creekbed. Just as

A lizard basks in the sun on a rock cairn in the North Wilderness.

you begin to think the trail is heading into a box canyon, it veers left and you cross a wooden footbridge. At 10.25 miles you come to a trail junction for the North Wilderness Trail. Turn right onto the North Wilderness Trail. In the spring you may have the privilege of seeing nature's workshop with the wide variety of bees busy pollinating wildflowers along the trail. You will be lacing across the north and south banks of the seasonal North Fork Chalone Creek for the next 4 miles, sometimes walking in the typically dry creekbed. The vegetation varies from mostly chaparral-covered hillsides, but Willow Spring, between 10.45 and 10.75 miles, feeds a willowy riparian oasis.

A couple of miles up the creek, the trail veers away from the main channel and enters a pine and oak woodland that turns into a burgeoning meadow after a nourishing wet winter. The trail is primitive, especially in the creekbed, but it is well worn, with cairns visibly stacked at possible tricky locations.

At 13.85 miles the trail crosses back to the north bank toward a rock outcrop, and after a few more zigzags in the creekbed, you come to the final crossing of North Fork Chalone Creek. Pick up the trail on the other side and begin your climb to the ridge for the final stretch back to the west side at the north end of the volcanic pinnacles. Expect the gradual climb to be interrupted by short, steep sections.

Juniper Canyon Trail to North Wilderness via Visitor Center

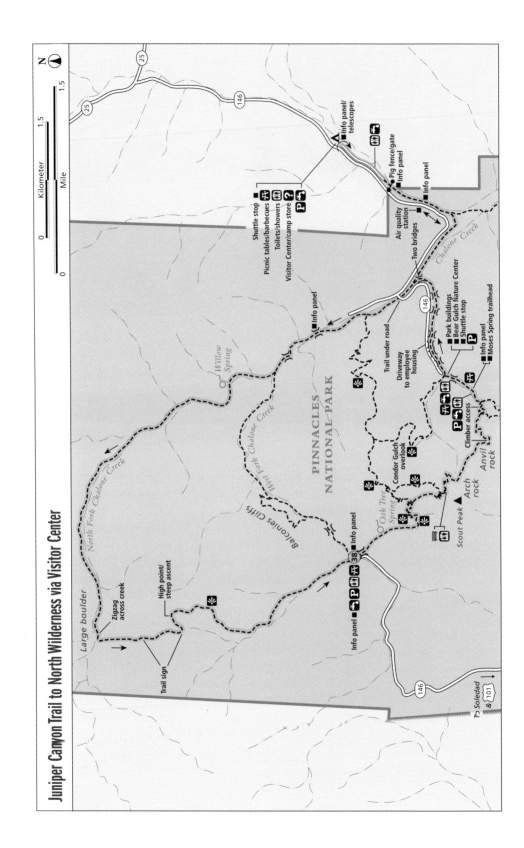

PINNACLES NATIONAL PARK

At 14.65 miles the trail marker for the North Wilderness Trail reassures hikers that they are on the correct trail. Another mile of hoof and huff and the trail emerges closer to the ridge at another marker for the North Wilderness Trail, which directs you to a sharp left. Shortly after the turn the views open southward to the High Peaks and the North Chalone Peak fire tower just short of the ridgeline's summit-uplifting viewpoint.

At 15.55 miles you come to another stunning viewpoint. Walk about 50 feet left off the trail in the chamise clearing and imagine a moonrise over the pinnacles. The pinnacles and the fire tower on North Chalone Peak stay in view all the way down to the trailhead, only occasionally disappearing behind a curtain of tall chamise. Some vantage points in the late afternoon light make it feel like you could reach out and touch the High Peaks. Savor this last 0.5 mile of leveling terrain where the breeze tickling the pines on the nearby ridges is the only background sound as you approach the Chaparral Picnic Area. The North Wilderness Trail ends in the Chaparral Picnic Area at 17.05 miles. Walk across the picnic area past the restrooms and water fountain to the parking lot and the trailhead at the west end to complete your 17.2-mile excursion.

Miles and Directions

0.0   Start at the wooden Trailhead sign in the Chaparral Picnic Area parking lot. Walk across the typically dry West Fork Chalone Creek and follow the fenced trail for 150 feet to the T-junction and the Condor Crags interpretive panel. Turn right, walk 250 feet to a seasonal creek, and cross on the wooden footbridge.

0.3   Come to the unmarked Oak Tree Spring, which feeds the seasonal creek on the right.

0.7   The trail becomes more exposed, rewarding you with an embracing view of Juniper Canyon below.

0.9   The trail reveals expansive views northward as it begins a series of switchbacks.

1.2   Come to the junction with Tunnel Trail. Bear right and continue walking up Juniper Canyon Trail.

1.8   Arrive at a bench and the saddle straddling the east and west sides of Pinnacles National Park just below Scout Peak. This is the perfect perch to take a water break and soak up the stunning views while hoping for condors to glide by. Continue on the trail below the bench on the east side toward the spur trail going to the toilets in the stone building. Bear left to Bear Gulch at the spur intersection and begin walking downhill.

2.3   Walk through a short but impressive stone tunnel.

2.6   The exposed trail offers expansive southward views toward North Chalone Peak and the fire tower.

2.8   Come to an anvil-shaped rock formation on your left with a spur trail to a climber access to another rock outcrop just ahead on your right.

3.3   Come to a trail junction signed Rim Trail to Reservoir. Bear left and continue walking downhill to the Bear Gulch area. Shortly come to a climber access spur trail on your right. Bear left. In 0.1 mile come to another climber access to the top of Tourist Trap on the left.

3.6 Come to the trail junction for the Moses Spring Trail to the reservoir caves. High Peaks Trail ends and merges with Moses Spring Trail. Continue walking downhill.

3.7 Arrive at the Moses Spring Trail trailhead, with a parking lot and restroom on the left and a paved road. Walk across the paved road and continue walking on the hiker trail through the picnic area, then bear left and walk across the wooden footbridge.

3.9 Arrive at the parking lot, restroom and picnic table across from the Bear Gulch Nature Center and a parking lot across the road. Cross the road at the crosswalk and turn left. Walk along the concrete walkway to the Peaks View Day Use Area and begin walking on the unmarked Bear Gulch Trail.

4.05 Walk across seasonal Bear Gulch Creek on the wooden footbridge, quickly followed by another footbridge crossing. In 0.1 mile you walk across the driveway of the employee residence.

4.3 Walk across Bear Gulch Creek on a wooden footbridge. You will cross the creek three more times in the next 0.5 mile. The trail leaves the narrow, shaded gulch and the creekbed widens at the third crossing.

4.95 Bear Gulch Trail ends at the trail junction for the Bench Trail (unmarked) and the trail sign for Old Pinnacles Trail (left). Continue walking straight and follow the sign for Peaks View Day Use Area and Pinnacles Visitor Center across seasonal Chalone Creek on two wooden footbridges to the road and the trail sign.

5.0 Come to a trail junction and bear right on Bench Trail (unmarked); follow the sign to Pinnacles Visitor Center. The trail parallels the road on the left and the creek on the right.

5.3 Come to Peaks View Day Use Area and continue on Bench Trail, still paralleling the road on the left.

5.65 Come to the T-junction and a fire road. South Wilderness Trail is on the right. Walk left on the fire road toward the Pinnacles Visitor Center. Shortly come to a trail sign on your right with an arrow. Turn right onto the unmarked Bench Trail.

5.9 Come to an interpretive sign about the park's air quality monitoring stations.

6.2 Come to a fence and a gate. Walk through the pedestrian gate and latch it. The Pig Fence information panel is on the other side of the gate and fence. In 0.1 mile arrive at the southwest end of the campground and a paved road. Walk along the paved road section of Bench Trail and shortly come to the campground restroom building on the right.

6.75 Come to the end of the paved road section of Bench Trail and the ADA telescope and bench pad. The visitor center is across the road and to the left of the park shuttle stop. This is the turnaround point for your circuit. Go back on Bench Trail the way you came to the junction where Bear Gulch Trail ended at Bench Trail at the other end and the sign for Old Pinnacles Trail.

8.65 Come to the trail junction across the double footbridge and turn right toward Old Pinnacles Trail on Bench Trail (unmarked). Immediately walk over two closely spaced boardwalks along an eroded section of Chalone Creek.

8.95 Walk under the park road overpass, then shortly come to a wooden footbridge across the seasonal creek.

9.25 Come to the trail junction for the High Peaks Trail on the left. Continue walking straight on Bench Trail (unmarked).

9.75 Come to the end of Bench Trail at the junction with Old Pinnacles Trail and cross the seasonal Chalone Creek on the wooden footbridge. Bear left on Old Pinnacles Trail to North Wilderness Trail. The Chalone Creek Restoration information board is just ahead.

10.05 Walk across Chalone Creek on a wooden footbridge. In 0.2 mile come to the trail junction for the North Wilderness Trail. Turn right onto North Wilderness Trail and prepare to lace the banks of seasonal North Fork Chalone Creek. Keep an eye out for the cairns.

10.45 Cross the outflow of Willow Spring, then shortly cross the trickling Willow Spring.

13.85 Cross the seasonal creek to the north bank and walk past a large rock outcrop on the right. In 0.2 mile zigzag across North Fork Chalone Creek (look ahead for cairns). In 0.1 mile come to the final crossing of North Fork Chalone Creek and begin climb up the swale to the ridge.

14.65 Come to a trail marker confirming you are on the North Wilderness Trail. In 0.3 mile come to a trail maker for the North Wilderness Trail. Turn left.

15.15 Come to a viewpoint at the summit of the ridgeline. The High Peaks and the North Chalone Peak fire tower are to the south. To the east you see the white, scalloped face of the mountain left behind a landslide.

15.55 Come to another viewpoint and walk 50 feet left off the trail in the chamise clearing for a stunning view of the High Peaks. Begin your descent off the ridge.

16.85 Walk across a seasonal creek.

17.05 Come to the end of North Wilderness Trail at the Chaparral Picnic Area.

17.2 Arrive back at the trailhead.

39 Balconies Trail to Machete Ridge

This less–than–2–mile route is an easy introductory hike to the chaparral- and rock-dominated Pinnacles realm. The trail is mostly flat, crossing a few seasonal creeks in the open before entering a shadier canyon to the base of Machete Ridge and a climber access trail junction. This hike is a good option for families with young children who cannot get a morning start for longer hikes in the spring, summer, and early fall when temperatures can rise quickly from warm to hot by midday.

Start: From the wooden Trailhead sign in the Chaparral Picnic Area and trailhead parking lot

Distance: 1.4 miles out and back

Hiking time: 1 hour

Difficulty: Easy

Trail surface: Dirt and rock

Trailhead elevation: 1,389 feet

Highest point: 1,404 feet

Best seasons: Spring for wildflowers; late fall and winter for cooler temperatures (summer and early fall can be very hot)

Maps: USGS North Chalone Peak; Pinnacles National Park map; Tom Harrison map of Pinnacles National Park

Nearest town: Soledad

Trail contact: Pinnacles National Park, 5000 CA 146, Paicines, CA 95043-9770; (831) 389-4485 or (831) 389-4427; www.nps.gov/pinn

Trail tips: There are trash and recycling receptacles, flush toilets, and a drinking fountain between the parking lot and the developed picnic area. Each picnic site has a table and grill. There are "self-pay" envelopes and maps by the fee box in the parking lot. The "marked" Balconies trailhead is at the far end of the large picnic area past the parking area. Unless you plan to picnic prior to hiking, it is more convenient and logical to start the hike from the wooden Trailhead sign at the head of the parking lot to the right of the information and map board. The trail from the parking lot and the "marked" Balconies Trail merge 0.2 mile ahead.

Finding the trailhead: From US 101 at Soledad, take exit 302/CA 146 and drive 0.3 mile to the traffic signal. Follow the signs for West Pinnacles. Turn left onto Front Street and drive 0.3 mile to East Street. Turn right onto East Street and drive 0.2 mile to Metz Road/CA 146. Turn right onto Metz Road/CA 146, drive 2.5 miles to the Pinnacles National Park sign, and turn left. The road becomes narrower and winding. Drive 5.8 miles on CA 146 to the intersection of Stonewall Canyon Road (left) and CA 146 (right). Bear right and continue on CA 146 for 0.8 mile to the Pinnacles National Park entrance/gate. Drive 0.2 mile to the West Pinnacles Visitor Contact Station parking lot. Stop in the contact station to pay the park entrance fee and pick up a map and information. Take the time to view the park film and look at the various exhibits before driving 2 miles to the end of the road in the Chaparral Picnic Area and trailhead parking lot. (If the station is closed, maps and envelopes are at the self-pay fee box in the parking lot.) The trail begins at the wooden Trailhead sign at the head of the parking lot to the right of the information and map board. GPS: N36 29.50' / W121 12.56'.

Note: In winter to early spring, if Chalone Creek is running too high for a dry feet crossing, you can walk 250 feet to the right (south) and bypass the creek crossing to join up with the trail. There is also an alternate trailhead marked Balconies Trail beyond the parking lot, past the restrooms about midway in the large picnic area.

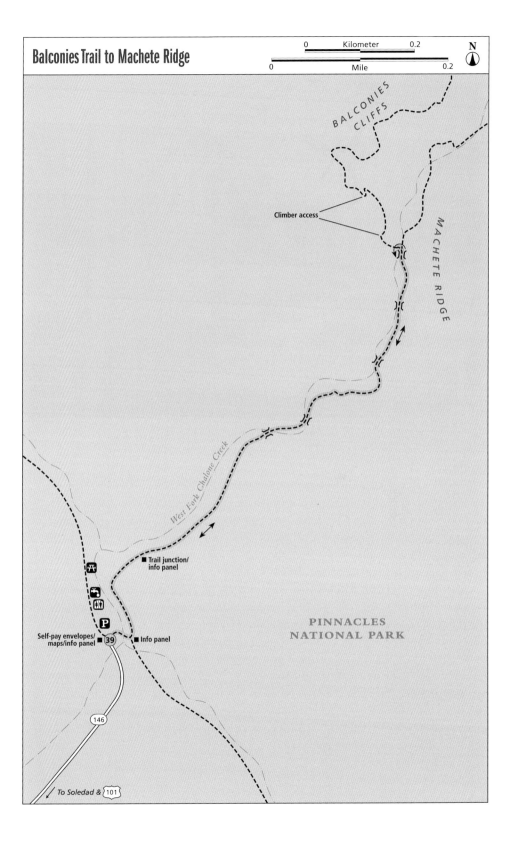

Balconies Trail to Machete Ridge

BALCONIES CLIFFS

Climber access

MACHETE RIDGE

West Fork Chalone Creek

Trail junction/
info panel

PINNACLES
NATIONAL PARK

Self-pay envelopes/
maps/info panel

39

Info panel

146

To Soledad & 101

0   Kilometer   0.2

0   Mile   0.2

N

Approaching Machete Ridge on Balconies Trail

The Hike

Take the time to read the interpretive panels about California condors and the connection between Pinnacles National Park and the condor rehabilitation program as you start up the trail. You pass a small picnic area with a couple of tables on your left and a sign reminding hikers that Pets, Bicycles and Wilderness Camping are Prohibited, then come to another information board and map ahead.

This hike is less than 2 miles long, and the trail's gentle, mostly level grade wending around the imposing stone sentinels makes it ideal for introducing young children to hiking or as a multigenerational family outing. There are five seasonal creek crossings with wooden footbridges to keep the kids hopping along. But the gargantuan boulder jam forming a stone archway just past the footbridge at 0.45 mile is what gives this short hike its adventurous flavor.

At 0.7 mile you reach the trail junction for the Balconies Cliffs Trail and the Balconies Cave just below Machete Ridge. This is your turnaround point and a good place to take a water or snack break sitting on a rock while scanning for dangling rock climbers on the rock walls above.

Miles and Directions

0.0 Start at the wooden trailhead sign to the right of the information board in the Chaparral Picnic Area parking lot. Walk across the "usually" dry West Fork Chalone Creek and along the split rail fence corridor 150 feet to the unmarked trail junction and the Condor Crags interpretive panel. Turn left, walking north for Balconies Trail. The fence is on your left.

0.1 Come to a trail junction where the Chaparral Picnic Area trail merges from the left. Bear right and continue toward the sign for Balconies Cave 0.6 and Old Pinnacles Trailhead 3.3. Come to a map board and interpretive panel. In 0.2 mile cross West Fork Chalone Creek on a footbridge.

0.35 Come to West Fork Chalone Creek and walk across the footbridge to a trail junction and a sign on the right for the climber access trail to Elephant Rock and The Citadel. Bear left and walk under the gargantuan boulder arch.

0.5 Cross two more footbridges in quick succession over West Fork Chalone Creek.

0.7 Come to West Fork Chalone Creek and walk across the footbridge to the trail junction for the Balconies Cliffs Trail and Balconies Cave. Machete Ridge and the climber access trail to the ridge are on your right. This is your destination. (GPS: N36 29.87'/ W121 12.19'. Elevation: 1,291 feet.) Pick a rock for your water and snack break as you scan Machete Ridge for rock climbers. Walk back to the trailhead the way you came.

1.4 Arrive back at the trailhead.

40 Balconies Trail to Balconies Cliffs via Balconies Cave

If you could do only one hike in Pinnacles National Park, this would be the one—as long as you are not anxious about small dark spaces and do not have issues with high places. This hike offers a close-up view of Pinnacles National Park from the bottom to the top. The trail begins in exposed chaparral before entering a cool canyon and portal to the boulder-tumble tunnel passage known as Balconies Cave. You will need a flashlight in the talus "cave." You emerge at the junction for the climb up the lofty panoramic trail at the base of the Balconies Cliffs, where raptors roost, before dropping back down to the canyon floor.

Start: From the wooden Trailhead sign in the Chaparral Picnic Area and trailhead parking lot
Distance: 2.6-mile lollipop
Hiking time: 1.5 hours
Difficulty: Strenuous due to Balconies Cave crawl and Balconies Cliffs uphill
Trail surface: Dirt and rock
Trailhead elevation: 1,389 feet
Highest point: 1,465 feet
Best seasons: Spring for wildflowers, late fall and winter for cooler temperatures (summer and early fall can be very hot)
Maps: USGS North Chalone Peak; Pinnacles National Park map; Tom Harrison map of Pinnacles National Park

Nearest town: Soledad
Trail contact: Pinnacles National Park, 5000 CA 146, Paicines, CA 95043-9770; (831) 389-4485 or (831) 389-4427; www.nps.gov/pinn
Trail tips: There are trash and recycling receptacles, restroom with flush toilets, and a drinking fountain between the parking lot and the developed picnic area. Each picnic site has a table and grill. Check with the ranger at the visitor contact station to confirm that the Balconies Cave is open, as it may be closed due to flooding after a winter or spring rainstorm. The cave section can be slippery in wet weather, and a flashlight is necessary.

Finding the trailhead: From US 101 at Soledad, take exit 302/CA 146 and drive 0.3 mile to the traffic signal. Follow the signs for West Pinnacles. Turn left onto Front Street and drive 0.3 mile to East Street. Turn right onto East Street and drive 0.2 mile to Metz Road/CA 146. Turn right onto Metz Road/CA 146, drive 2.5 miles to the Pinnacles National Park sign, and turn left. The road becomes narrower and winding. Drive 5.8 miles on CA 146 to the intersection of Stonewall Canyon Road (left) and CA 146 (right). Bear right and continue on CA 146 for 0.8 mile to the Pinnacles National Park entrance/gate. Drive 0.2 mile to the West Pinnacles Visitor Contact Station parking lot. Stop in the contact station to pay the park entrance fee and pick up a map and information. Take the time to view the park film and look at the various exhibits before driving 2 miles to the end of the road in the Chaparral Picnic Area and trailhead parking lot. (If the station is closed, maps and envelopes are at the self-pay fee box in the parking lot.) The trail begins at the wooden Trailhead sign at the head of the parking lot to the right of the information and map board. GPS: N36 29.50' / W121 12.56'.

Note: In winter to early spring, if Chalone Creek is running too high for a dry feet crossing, you can walk 250 feet to the right (south) and bypass the creek crossing to join up with the trail. There is also an alternate trailhead marked Balconies Trail beyond the parking lot, past the restrooms about midway in the large picnic area.

Threading through the narrow passageways of the Balconies Cave

The "marked" Balconies trailhead is at the far end of the picnic area across from the parking area, but you start the hike from the information board in the parking lot to the right of the wooden Trailhead sign. The "marked" Balconies Trail merges into this trail from the Chaparral Picnic Area 0.2 mile ahead. Take the time to read the interpretive panels about California condors and the connection between Pinnacles National Park and the condor rehabilitation program as you start up the trail.

Walk up the fenced trail corridor past a small picnic area with tables on your left and a sign reminding hikers that Pets, Bicycles and Wilderness Camping are Prohibited, before coming to another information panel and map about 150 feet up the trail. Turn left with the fence line on your left to the Balconies Trail.

At 0.1 mile the marked Balconies Trail from the Chaparral Picnic Area trail merges from the left. You come to another trail interpretive panel. Turn right onto the trail. You cross several seasonal creeks through chaparral shrubland of buckwheat interrupted by gray pines and some juniper. The trail continues toward the canyon walls with climber access trails to Elephant Rock and The Citadel towering above on the right and the Flume rock formation on your left.

You enter the canyon about half a mile ahead and cross seasonal West Fork Chalone Creek a few more times before coming to the trail junction for the Balconies Cliffs Trail straight ahead and the Balconies Cave Trail to the right. This is the junction where you will close your lollipop on the way down from the Balconies Cliffs Trail. Turn right to the cave entrance and a metal gate. There is a gate at both ends of the talus cave. The gates are closed and locked when conditions are too hazardous due to wet weather or flooding, as West Fork Chalone Creek runs through this cave.

The Balconies Cave is one of the highlights on this hike. The talus "cave" is more of a tunnel formed by a rockslide that stacked rock and gigantic boulders while wedging some of them against the rock walls. The cave passage is only about 0.1 mile in distance but seems longer the first time because of the dark, maze-like path and slow groping required on the way down the steep, uneven rocks before resurfacing. The route is a slow scooch, crouch, and squeeze adventure. Scan your flashlight beam on the faint white-painted arrows directing you in a couple of places.

If you are using a GPS, be aware that it will probably run wild trying to locate you while you are in the cave, and your readings will be off when you exit.

You exit the cave at 0.9 mile and come to a trail junction and sign for Balconies Cliffs Trail at 1.1 mile. Bear left uphill on Balconies Cliffs Trail. The narrow, exposed trail overlooks the canyon floor as it switchbacks up to the base of the massive Balconies Cliffs. The surrounding cliff walls make good habitat for bats, golden eagles, and condors.

As the trail levels off, you get a bird's-eye view of the Balconies Cave. Notice the spur trails for climber access and keep your eye out for dangling silhouettes on the

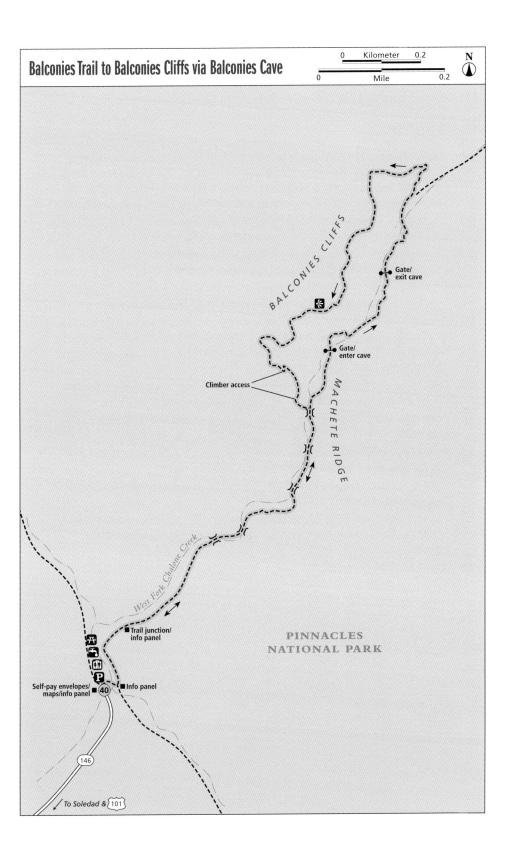

Balconies Trail to Balconies Cliffs via Balconies Cave

N

0   Kilometer   0.2

0   Mile   0.2

BALCONIES CLIFFS

Gate/
exit cave

Gate/
enter cave

Climber access

MACHETE RIDGE

West Fork Chalone Creek

PINNACLES
NATIONAL PARK

Trail junction/
info panel

Self-pay envelopes/
maps/info panel

Info panel

40

146

To Soledad & 101

rock faces, especially in the morning. The trail gradually descends back to the canyon floor, and at 1.9 miles you come to the trail junction. Walk across the creek on the footbridge and turn right to close your lollipop and go back to the trailhead.

Miles and Directions

0.0 Start at the wooden Trailhead sign to the right of the information board in the Chaparral Picnic Area parking lot. Walk across the "usually" dry West Fork Chalone Creek and along the split rail fence corridor 150 feet to the unmarked trail junction and the Condor Crags interpretive panel. Turn left, walking north for Balconies Trail. The fence is on your left.

0.1 The trail from Chaparral Picnic Area merges from the left at an interpretive panel. Turn right. In 0.2 mile cross seasonal West Fork Chalone Creek on a footbridge.

0.35 Come to West Fork Chalone Creek and walk across the footbridge to the trail junction and a sign on the right for the climber access trail to Elephant Rock and The Citadel. Bear left and walk under the gargantuan boulder arch.

0.5 Cross two more footbridges in quick succession over West Fork Chalone Creek.

0.7 Come to West Fork Chalone Creek and the footbridge and trail junction for Balconies Cliffs Trail. This is the junction where you will close the lollipop when you come down the Balconies Cliffs Trail. Walk across the footbridge and turn right to Balconies Cave. Immediately walk across the creek.

0.8 Come to the entrance of Balconies Cave. Turn on your flashlight to continue into the cave. You exit Balconies Cave in 0.1 mile.

1.1 Come to the trail junction for Balconies Cliffs Trail. Bear left and walk uphill on Balconies Cliffs Trail.

1.6 Come to a viewpoint overlooking Balconies Cave. Pick your favorite view for a chance to take a snack and water break beneath the massive Balconies Cliffs.

1.7 Come to a climber access trail on the right, then shortly pass another climber access on the right for Tilting Terrace.

1.9 Come to the trail junction for Balconies Cave. Walk across the West Fork Chalone Creek footbridge. This junction is where you close your lollipop. Turn right to return to the trailhead.

2.6 Arrive back at the trailhead.

41 Balconies Trail to Old Pinnacles Trailhead

This mostly flat trail follows a shady canyon through a narrow, formidable tumble of gargantuan boulder tunnels forming the Balconies Cave on the way to the West Fork Chalone Creek floodplain and Old Pinnacles trailhead. The 0.1–mile talus "cave" section requires a flashlight and is very challenging with some crawl spaces and hand-over-hand climbs. This spectacular "cave" route to the Old Pinnacles trailhead from the west to the east side of the park is not recommended for anyone with claustrophobia issues or for corpulent individuals.

Start: From the wooden Trailhead sign in the Chaparral Picnic Area and trailhead parking lot
Distance: 6.2 miles out and back
Hiking time: 3.5 hours
Difficulty: Moderate due to the length; challenging cave section
Trail surface: Dirt, sand, gravel, and rock
Trailhead elevation: 1,389 feet
Highest point: 1,404 feet
Best seasons: Spring for wildflowers, late fall and winter for cooler temperatures (summer and early fall can be very hot)
Maps: USGS North Chalone Peak and Bickmore Canyon; Pinnacles National Park map; Tom Harrison map of Pinnacles National Park
Nearest town: Soledad

Trail contact: Pinnacles National Park, 5000 CA 146, Paicines, CA 95043-9770; (831) 389-4485 or (831) 389-4427; www.nps.gov/pinn
Trail tips: There are trash and recycling receptacles, flush toilets, and a drinking fountain between the parking lot and the developed picnic area. Each picnic site has a table and grill. There are "self-pay" envelopes and maps by the fee box in the parking lot. Check with the ranger at the visitor contact station to confirm that the Balconies Cave is open, as it may be closed due to flooding after a winter or spring rainstorm. The cave section can be slippery in wet weather, and a flashlight is necessary.

Finding the trailhead: From US 101 at Soledad, take exit 302/CA 146 and drive 0.3 mile to the traffic signal. Follow the signs for West Pinnacles. Turn left onto Front Street and drive 0.3 mile to East Street. Turn right onto East Street and drive 0.2 mile to Metz Road/CA 146. Turn right onto Metz Road/CA 146, drive 2.5 miles to the Pinnacles National Park sign, and turn left. The road becomes narrower and winding. Drive 5.8 miles on CA 146 to the intersection of Stonewall Canyon Road (left) and CA 146 (right). Bear right and continue on CA 146 for 0.8 mile to the Pinnacles National Park entrance/gate. Drive 0.2 mile to the West Pinnacles Visitor Contact Station parking lot. Stop in the contact station to pay the park entrance fee and pick up a map and information. Take the time to view the park film and look at the various exhibits before driving 2 miles to the end of the road in the Chaparral Picnic Area and trailhead parking lot. (If the station is closed, maps and envelopes are at the self-pay fee box in the parking lot.) The trail begins at the wooden Trailhead sign at the head of the parking lot to the right of the information and map board. GPS: N36 29.50' / W121 12.56'.

Note: In winter to early spring, if Chalone Creek is running too high for a dry feet crossing, you can walk 250 feet to the right (south) and bypass the creek crossing to join up with the trail. There is also an alternate trailhead marked Balconies Trail beyond the parking lot, past the restrooms about midway in the large picnic area.

The Hike

The trail follows a fenced corridor for about 150 feet to two interpretive panels. One describes the Condor Crags ridge of the Pinnacles where condors roost and nest, and the other describes the two main hiking trailheads (Balconies and Juniper Canyon) originating on the west side of Pinnacles National Park.

Prior to becoming a national park, the area had been designated a national monument (in 1908) and was known to locals as East Pinnacles and West Pinnacles. West Pinnacles was accessed from the town of Soledad off US 101 and East Pinnacles was accessed from the town of Hollister off CA 146. Even today there is no vehicular road traversing the park and connecting the east and west sides, but hiking trails make it possible to experience both sides on short to longer day hikes.

To follow this route, turn left to the Balconies Trail with the fence on your left. At 0.1 mile the trail from the Chaparral Picnic Area merges from the left. There is another interpretive panel and trail signs for Balconies Cave 0.6 and Old Pinnacles Trailhead 3.3. Turn right toward the Old Pinnacles trailhead. The trail heads toward a canyon with Machete Ridge on your right and the Flume rock formation on your left. The landscape is mostly buckwheat shrub and some pine trees at the head of the canyon.

You will cross five seasonal creeks and pass several climber access trails before the trail narrows into the canyon at 0.7 mile and comes to the trail junction with the Balconies Cliffs Trail. Turn right and continue walking in the canyon to the Balconies

Hiking past bush lupine along Old Pinnacles Trail with the Balconies Cliffs in the distance

Balconies Trail to Old Pinnacles Trailhead

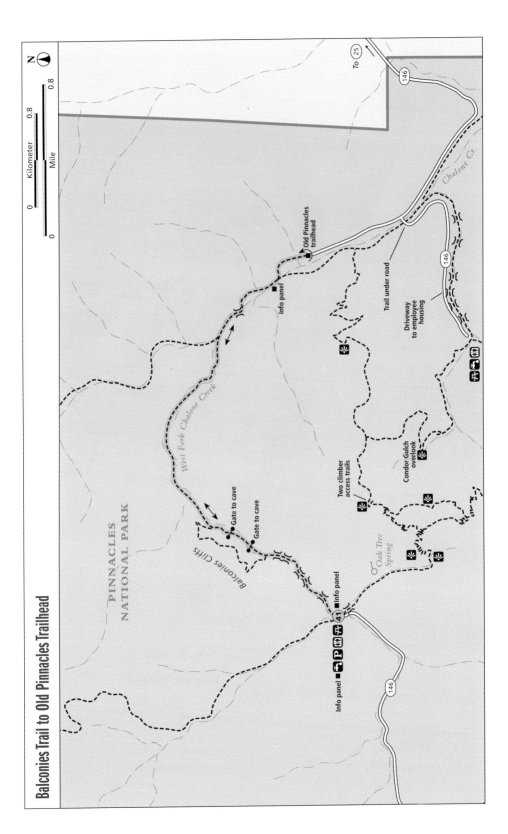

N

0   Kilometer   0.8

0   Mile   0.8

PINNACLES NATIONAL PARK

Balconies Cliffs

West Fork Chalone Creek

Gate to cave

Gate to cave

Oak Tree Spring

Info panel

Two climber access trails

Condor Gulch overlook

Driveway to employee housing

Trail under road

Old Pinnacles trailhead

Info panel

Chalone Cr.

146

146

146

To 25

Info panel

41

Cave. At 0.8 mile you come to the entrance of the Balconies Cave and an open gate. (The cave is sometimes closed due to flooding during wetter winters, as West Fork Chalone Creek runs through the cave). You need your flashlight to light your path through the talus cave.

The path through the "cave," which is actually a stack of wedged giant boulders that created tunnels, requires some crawling, sideways slithering, and hand-over-hand up and down. The colossal maze is nothing short of awesome. You exit back in the canyon and continue on the trail to a junction where the Balconies Cliffs Trail merges from the left. Bear right at the sign for Pinnacles Campground 3.7 and Pinnacles Visitor Center 4.1. Although it is not marked as such, you are now on the Old Pinnacles Trail. The trail crosses West Fork Chalone Creek several times until you come to the junction with the North Wilderness Trail. Continue walking straight toward the Old Pinnacles trailhead. Chalone Creek is on your left.

At 2.9 miles you come to the interpretive sign for the Chalone Creek Restoration project. Come to the Bench Trail junction and turn left to Old Pinnacles trailhead. Arrive at the Old Pinnacles trailhead parking lot, where there is a portable toilet but no drinking water. Go back to the trailhead the way you came.

Miles and Directions

0.0 Start at the wooden Trailhead sign to the right of the information board in the Chaparral Picnic Area parking lot. Walk across the "usually" dry West Fork Chalone Creek and along the split rail fence corridor 150 feet to the unmarked trail junction and the Condor Crags interpretive panel. Turn left, walking north for Balconies Trail. The fence is on your left.

0.1 Come to a trail junction where the Chaparral Picnic Area trail merges from the left. Bear right and continue toward the sign for Balconies Cave 0.6 and Old Pinnacles Trailhead 3.3. Come to a map board and interpretive panel. In 0.2 mile cross seasonal West Fork Chalone Creek on a footbridge.

0.35 Come to West Fork Chalone Creek and walk across the footbridge to the trail junction and a sign on the right for the climber access trail to Elephant Rock and The Citadel. Bear left and walk under the gargantuan boulder arch.

0.5 Cross two more footbridges in quick succession over West Fork Chalone Creek.

0.7 Come to West Fork Chalone Creek and walk across the footbridge to the trail junction for Balconies Cliffs Trail and Balconies Cave. Machete Ridge and a climber access trail are on your right. Turn right to Balconies Cave and immediately walk across the creek.

0.8 Come to the entrance of Balconies Cave. Turn on your flashlight to continue into the cave. You exit Balconies Cave in 0.1 mile.

1.1 Come to the trail junction for Balconies Cliffs Trail. Bear right on Old Pinnacles Trail (trail is not signed as such at junction).

1.4 Walk across West Fork Chalone Creek. You will cross the creek five more times in the next 0.7 mile.

2.4 Come to the junction with the North Wilderness Trail. Continue walking straight toward the Old Pinnacles trailhead. Chalone Creek is on your left. In 0.2 mile walk across Chalone Creek on a footbridge.

2.9 Come to the junction for Bench Trail and an interpretive sign about the Chalone Creek Restoration project. Turn left to the Old Pinnacles trailhead.

3.1 Arrive at the Old Pinnacles trailhead parking lot. (GPS: N36 29.70'/ W121 10.38'. Elevation: 1,059 feet.) Take a snack break. There is a portable toilet but no drinking water. Go back the way you came.

6.2 Arrive back at the trailhead.

42 North Wilderness Trail to Twin Knolls

This is a lovely hike away from the weekend crowds. Hikers get a taste of the Pinnacles wilderness area, crossing a meadow and walking through rolling chaparral with two knoll viewpoints looking back at the west face of the Pinnacles and the North Chalone Peak fire tower.

Start: From the Chaparral Picnic Area
Distance: 3.0 miles out and back
Hiking time: 1.5 hours
Difficulty: Moderate
Trail surface: Dirt
Trailhead elevation: 1,386 feet
Highest point: 2,099 feet
Best seasons: Spring for wildflowers, late fall and winter for cooler temperatures
Maps: USGS North Chalone Peak and Bickmore Canyon; Pinnacles National Park map; Tom Harrison map of Pinnacles National Park
Nearest town: Soledad

Trail contact: Pinnacles National Park, 5000 CA 146, Paicines, CA 95043-9770; (831) 389-4485 or (831) 389-4427; www.nps.gov/pinn
Trail tips: There are trash and recycling receptacles, flush toilets, and a drinking fountain between the parking lot and the developed picnic area. Each picnic site has a table and grill. There are "self-pay" envelopes and maps by the fee box in the parking lot. Plan on having a picnic snack in the Chaparral Picnic Area when you return from the knolls.

Finding the trailhead: From US 101 at Soledad, take exit 302/CA 146 and drive 0.3 mile to the traffic signal. Follow the signs for West Pinnacles. Turn left onto Front Street and drive 0.3 mile to East Street. Turn right onto East Street and drive 0.2 mile to Metz Road/CA 146. Turn right onto Metz Road/CA 146, drive 2.5 miles to the Pinnacles National Park sign, and turn left. The road becomes narrower and winding. Drive 5.8 miles on CA 146 to the intersection of Stonewall Canyon Road (left) and CA 146 (right). Bear right and continue on CA 146 for 0.8 mile to the Pinnacles National Park entrance/gate. Drive 0.2 mile to the West Pinnacles Visitor Contact Station parking lot. Stop in the contact station to pay the park entrance fee and pick up a map and information. Take the time to view the park film and look at the various exhibits before driving 2 miles to the end of the road in the Chaparral Picnic Area and trailhead parking lot. (If the station is closed, maps and envelopes are at the self-pay fee box in the parking lot.) Walk about 500 feet from the parking lot past the restrooms to the North Wilderness trailhead at the north end of the picnic area. GPS: N36 29.62' / W121 12.61'.

The Hike

This hike is a nice contrast to caves, tunnels, and steep trails into volcanic high peaks where you are hiking in the postcard. The trailhead at the far end of the Chaparral Picnic Area takes you away from the weekend fray and opens the portal to a more serene scene across a meadow rewarded with a colorful spring bloom of wildflowers following a wet winter and plum-colored buckwheat bushes in the drier months. The narrow dirt trail laces the edge of a seasonal creek on the right and remains level for

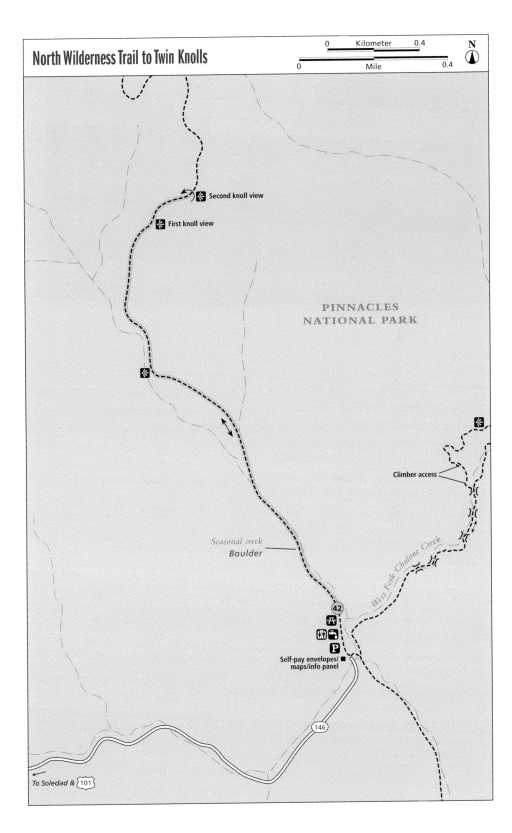

North Wilderness Trail to Twin Knolls

Second knoll view

First knoll view

PINNACLES
NATIONAL PARK

Climber access

Seasonal creek
Boulder

West Fork Chalone Creek

42

Self-pay envelopes/
maps/info panel

146

To Soledad & 101

0   Kilometer   0.4

0   Mile   0.4

N

North Wilderness Trail headed toward the twin knolls

the first 0.5 mile before heading into the chaparral country, where it begins to roll in the chamise-lined swales until it crests on a ridge above a ravine on the left, briefly revealing views of North Chalone Peak and the fire tower to the south.

The undulating climb gets a little steeper after the first mile as it approaches the first view knoll at 1.4 miles. Continue up to the second knoll just 0.1 mile farther for the most dramatic postcard-perfect view of the Pinnacles' west face. Walk about 50 feet to the right off the trail to a clearing and soak up the 360-degree views of the gray pine- and juniper-dotted chaparral hills and Pinnacles National Park's volcanic centerpiece. Look eastward from left to right and identify the Balconies Cliffs, The Citadel, High Peaks, and Juniper Canyon. North Chalone Peak and the fire tower stand apart farther south in the background.

Go back to the trailhead the way you came and delight in the fresh perspective and panorama as you approach the Chaparral Picnic Area and trailhead.

Miles and Directions

0.0   Start at the North Wilderness Trailhead at the far end of the Chaparral Picnic Area.

0.2   Walk across a seasonal creek at the boulder.

0.9   The trail crests, and views open briefly southward to North Chalone Peak and the fire tower. The trail undulates up and down a little more steeply.

1.4   Come to a knoll viewpoint of the West Pinnacles volcanic palisades and peaks and the North Chalone Peak fire tower.

1.5   Come to the second and higher knoll viewpoint and a spur trail to the right. Walk 50 feet on the spur trail for a 360-degree view. (GPS: N36 30.55'/ W121 13.04'. Elevation 2,098 feet.) Go back to the trailhead the way you came.

3.0   Arrive back at the trailhead.

43 North Wilderness Trail to Balconies Cliffs via Old Pinnacles Trail

This is not one of Pinnacles National Park's most panoramic hikes. Except for a couple of very scenic viewpoints before dropping down into the swales of the undulating chaparral ridges, the trail follows the wide creekbed of the seasonal North Fork Chalone Creek for about 8 of the nearly 10 miles. The changes in elevation are minimal and gradual except for the 0.5 mile climb up the Balconies Cliffs Trail. This hike is a perfect option for hikers seeking a quiet, less traveled route. This route through the park's less known wilderness area formerly known as Pinnacles Wilderness and recently renamed (and as yet unsigned) Hain Wilderness is an example of the variety of habitats within the park. This loop hike lets you experience a more primitive wilderness beauty and the stark contrast between the creekbed woodlands and the dramatic geology along the Balconies Cliffs Trail.

Start: From the Chaparral Picnic Area
Distance: 9.6-mile loop
Hiking time: 5 hours
Difficulty: Moderate
Trail surface: Dirt and rock
Trailhead elevation: 1,386 feet
Highest point: 2,117 feet
Best seasons: Spring for wildflowers, late fall and winter for cooler temperatures
Maps: USGS North Chalone Peak and Bickmore Canyon; Pinnacles National Park map; Tom Harrison map of Pinnacles National Park
Nearest town: Soledad

Trail contact: Pinnacles National Park, 5000 CA 146, Paicines, CA 95043-9770; (831) 389-4485 or (831) 389-4427; www.nps.gov/pinn
Trail tips: There are trash and recycling receptacles, flush toilets, and a drinking fountain between the parking lot and the developed picnic area. Each picnic site has a table and grill. There are "self-pay" envelopes and maps by the fee box in the parking lot. Keep on the lookout for the many rock cairns guiding you along the more primitive North Wilderness Trail where it crisscrosses North Chalone Creek along about 4 of the 10 miles.

Finding the trailhead: From US 101 at Soledad, take exit 302/CA 146 and drive 0.3 mile to the traffic signal. Follow the signs for West Pinnacles. Turn left onto Front Street and drive 0.3 mile to East Street. Turn right onto East Street and drive 0.2 mile to Metz Road/CA 146. Turn right onto Metz Road/CA 146, drive 2.5 miles to the Pinnacles National Park sign, and turn left. The road becomes narrower and winding. Drive 5.8 miles on CA 146 to the intersection of Stonewall Canyon Road (left) and CA 146 (right). Bear right and continue on CA 146 for 0.8 mile to the Pinnacles National Park entrance/gate. Drive 0.2 mile to the West Pinnacles Visitor Contact Station parking lot. Stop in the contact station to pay the park entrance fee and pick up a map and information. Take the time to view the park film and look at the various exhibits before driving 2 miles to the end of the road in the Chaparral Picnic Area and trailhead parking lot. (If the station is closed, maps and envelopes are at the self-pay fee box in the parking lot.) Walk about 500 feet from the parking lot past the restrooms to the North Wilderness trailhead at the north end of the picnic area. GPS: N36 29.62' / W121 12.61'.

The Hike

As the name of the trail indicates, you will be hiking in the wilderness area of Pinnacles National Park. Prior to the area's status being changed from national monument to national park, the 16,000-acre wilderness was called Pinnacles Wilderness. When the monument became a park in 2013, the Pinnacles Wilderness was renamed the Hain Wilderness after Schuyler Hain, a homesteader who arrived in the area in 1891. Mr. Hain was one of the first to recognize the uniqueness of the Pinnacles area and advocate its preservation. As of the publication of this book, there were no wilderness signs at the trailhead or anywhere along the trail to indicate the boundaries of the wilderness or identify it by its new name.

The narrow dirt trail begins at the north end of the monolithic volcanic palisades in a spring-splashed wildflower and winter-dotted buckwheat meadow with a seasonal creek on the right. The trail remains level for the first 0.5 mile heading into chaparral country interrupted by gray pine and juniper trees. The trail rises gently into a chamise-bordered swale and crests to a ridge above a ravine on your left. The view opens briefly southward toward North Chalone Peak and the fire tower.

Between 1.4 and 1.5 miles, the exposed trail surprises you with westward panoramic views of the volcanic palisades' distinctive features. On the second of two knolls, from left to right you can see the Balconies Cliffs, The Citadel, High Peaks, and Juniper Canyon. North Chalone Peak and the fire tower stand apart in the background.

At almost 2.0 miles the trail begins to descend in a southwest direction. The trail elbows to the right at 2.1 at a trail marker for the North Wilderness Trail. Turn right and continue walking downhill into a gully paralleling a seasonal creek.

At 2.9 miles you come to your first crossing of the seasonal North Fork Chalone Creek. Look across the creek for the first of many stacks of cairns to guide you, as the trail often zigzags along the creekbed. This is a good spot for a hydration and snack break. Walk 0.3 mile and come to a rock outcrop on the left. Follow the trail as it traces the base of this unusual rock with cavernous gouges and cavities. The creekbed morphs from canyon to valley to floodplain for the next 3 miles until the trail crosses an unexpected trickle known as Willow Spring. In the dry season this hint of moisture gives a glimpse of how California blackberry vines and willows can thrive at the head of the pine woodland. In the spring you may have the privilege of seeing nature's workshop with the wide variety of bees busy pollinating wildflowers along the trail.

At 6.8 miles you come to a T intersection where the North Wilderness Trail ends at Old Pinnacles Trail. The sign at the junction points left for Old Pinnacles trailhead and right for Balconies Cave. Turn right to Balconies Cave.

At 7.1 miles you cross West Fork Chalone Creek and enter a shaded corridor hemmed in by oaks, pines, and rock outcrops. You will cross the seasonal West Fork Chalone Creek six more times. At 7.7 miles you get your first open view of the

Poppies waiting for the warmth of day on the North Wilderness Trail

impressive Balconies Cliffs. At 8.1 miles you cross West Fork Chalone Creek just before the trail junction signed Chaparral Picnic Area via Balconies Cliffs 1.4, and Chaparral Picnic Area via Balconies Cave 1.0. You have a choice here, and a tradeoff. The talus cave route is shorter in distance but not necessarily in time; it is challenging and requires a flashlight and some fancy focused footwork with squeezing and crouching, but can be fun if you are not uncomfortable in tight spaces. On a weekend day expect a slow, single-file parade of hikers.

The Balconies Cliffs route is a 0.8-mile scenic huff and puff. This hike describes the Cliffs route that traces the base of the Balconies Cliffs where raptors nest. Turn right to Balconies Cliffs and walk uphill. The views open up to Machete Ridge and the Balconies Cave Trail below at 8.9 miles. The trail sweeps around and begins to drop back down just past the Tilting Terrace climber access spur on your right.

At 8.9 miles you reach the trail junction for Balconies Cave on the left (this is the exit to the cave if you chose the Balconies Cave option over the Balconies Cliffs back at the 8.1-mile trail junction). Continue walking straight and cross the wooden footbridge across West Fork Chalone Creek toward the Chaparral Picnic Area.

You have four more seasonal creek crossings over wooden footbridges before you reach a fork in the trail and an interpretive sign at 9.5 miles. Bear right at the fork; the

North Wilderness Trail to Balconies Cliffs via Old Pinnacles Trail

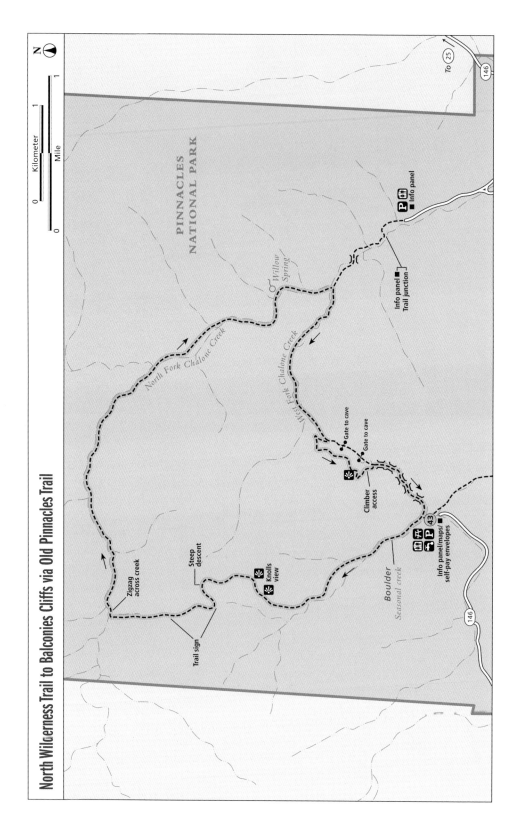

fence is on your left. Cross one last wooden footbridge and arrive at the Chaparral Picnic Area where the North Wilderness Trail and Balconies Trail begin. The North Wilderness trailhead where you began your hike is just a few feet ahead to the right. This picnic area is an ideal place to reward yourself with treats, water, and a front-row seat to the Pinnacles view before walking back to the parking lot at the west end of the picnic area.

Miles and Directions

0.0 Start at the North Wilderness trailhead at the far end of the Chaparral Picnic Area.

0.2 Walk across a seasonal creek at the boulder.

0.9 The trail crests, and views open briefly southward to North Chalone Peak and the fire tower.

1.4 Come to a viewpoint of the West Pinnacles volcanic palisades and peaks and the North Chalone Peak fire tower.

1.5 Come to a second knoll and spur trail to the right. Walk 50 feet on the spur trail for the 360-degree view.

1.9   The trail descends and changes direction toward the southwest. The Pinnacles are on your left. In 0.2 mile come to a trail marker and turn right to continue walking on the North Wilderness Trail at the elbow.

2.9   Reach the seasonal North Fork Chalone Creek. Walk across the creek to the stack of cairns. The trail becomes more primitive. In 0.1 mile crossNorth Fork Chalone Creek again at an almost 90-degree angle east to cairns across the creek and toward a rock outcrop.

3.2   Come to the rock outcrop on your left. The trail continues to zigzag along the creekbed with stacks of cairns guiding you along a well-defined but more primitive stretch.

6.3   Come to a faint trickle in the dry season. This trickle is known as Willow Spring. Walk across the trickle. In 0.3 mile come to the outflow trickle of Willow Spring and thread through the willows in the pine woodland.

6.8   Cross North Fork Chalone Creek and come to a trail junction for Old Pinnacles Trail with a sign for the Old Pinnacles trailhead to the left. Turn right to Balconies Cave.

7.1   Come to seasonal West Fork Chalone Creek. Walk across the creek. You will cross the creek five more times in the next 0.7 mile. Note the first open view of Balconies Cliffs at the fourth crossing.

8.1   Walk across West Fork Chalone Creek and come to the trail junction signed Chaparral Picnic Area via Balconies Cliffs 1.4, to the right, and Chaparral Picnic Area via Balconies Cave 1.0, to the left. Turn right and walk uphill to Balconies Cliffs.

8.6   Come to a viewpoint across Machete Ridge and the Balconies Cave Trail below, then pass a climber access on the right, followed by the Tilting Terrace climber access on your right. Bear left and walk downhill.

8.9   Come to the trail junction for Balconies Cave to the left. Continue walking straight across the wooden footbridge toward the Chaparral Picnic Area. Cross two more wooden footbridges in quick succession.

9.25 Walk across West Fork Chalone Creek on another wooden footbridge. Elephant and The Citadel climber access trails are on your left. Immediately cross the creek again.

9.5   Come to a fork in the trail and an interpretive sign. Bear right on the trail. The fence is on your left and the last footbridge on the trail is just ahead.

9.6   Arrive at the Chaparral Picnic Area. The North Wilderness trailhead where you began is on the right. Enjoy the picnic area and soak up the West Pinnacles views.

West Pinnacles Regional Information and Recreation

Soledad

Soledad, Spanish for "solitude," was named for the nearby Soledad Mission, founded in 1791 as the thirteenth of the twenty-one missions in the California mission system along the historic Camino Real (King's Highway). This low-key, at first glance undistinguished, small agricultural community was rated the eleventh-safest city in California in a 2013 Safe Cities report. It's at the south end of the Salinas Valley, also known as the "Salad Bowl of the World," and in the heart of prime grape growing territory with famous wineries such as Chalone, Hahn, and Ventana.

Soledad's commercial area has two faces. One is a generic commercial strip off US 101 with a few motels, a CVS pharmacy, Shop 'n Save supermarket, Starbucks, and a few mostly fast food restaurants. The other is the one-block, village-like heart of town with small local businesses and restaurants. For more information visit seemonterey.com.

Lodging

Inn at the Pinnacles, 32025 Stonewall Canyon Rd., Soledad, CA 93960; (831) 678-2400; innatthepinnacles.com. Closest lodging to the West Entrance of Pinnacles National Park and a true treat of a B&B. The top-of-the-hill, hacienda-style house with vineyard setting has warm innkeepers, a wine and cheese hour, hot breakfast, and luxurious rooms appointed with individual gas barbecue grills, small refrigerators, and basics to enjoy an on-property dinner.

Soledad Motel 8, 1013 Front St., Soledad, CA 93960; (831) 678-3814; soledadmotel8.com.

Valley Harvest Inn, 1155 Front St., Soledad, CA 93960; (831) 678-3833; Valleyharvestinn.com. Complimentary continental breakfast, outdoor pool, pet friendly.

Dining

La Fuente, 101 Oak St., Soledad, CA, 93960; (831) 678-3130. Fresh Mexican food with cozy ambience popular with locals and visitors.

La Plaza Bakery and Cafe, 901 Front St., Soledad, CA 93960; (831) 678-1452; laplazabakery.com. Mexican pastries and killer macaroons.

Windmill Restaurant, 1167 Front St., Soledad, CA, 93960; (831) 678-1775; soledadwindmillrestaurant.com. Conveniently located, good coffee shop next to the Harvest Inn and steps from Motel 8 with daily specials and freshly baked desserts.

King City

King City, named after its founder Charles King, first sprouted as a shipping point for wheat and cattle in the late 1880s before becoming the gateway to distribute and export some of the country's best produce. Irrigation and rails put King City on the map. King City is a jumping-off point for Pinnacles National Park closest to the West Entrance but is also the closest portal via US 101 for visitors who wish to drive to the East Entrance from the west side of the park. There are more services in King City than Soledad, including motels and restaurants. For more information visit kingcity.com.

Lodging

Best Western King City, 1190 Broadway, King City, CA 93930; (831) 385-6733.
Carriage House Inn B&B, 416 Lynn St., King City, CA, 93930; (831) 385-5714. Two guest rooms.
Keefer's Inn, 615 Canal St., King City, CA 93930; (831) 385-4843.

Dining

City Cafe, 223 Broadway St., King City, CA 93930; (831) 386-0917; citycafeking city.com. This is the Carriage House innkeeper's favorite Chinese food restaurant.
El Lugarcito, 128 Broadway, King City, CA 93930; (831) 385-4521. Mexican specialties.
The Grill, 200 Broadway, #34, King City, CA, 93930; (831) 386-9066.

Camping

San Lorenzo County Park, 1160 Broadway, King City, CA 93930; (888) 588-CAMP (2267) or (831) 755-4899.

Recreation

South County near King City has two reservoirs for hiking, camping, and boating—**Lake San Antonio** for hiking, fishing, camping, and boating; and **Lake Nacimiento** for fishing and boating (www.co.monterey.ca.us/parks/).

Monterey Peninsula Highlights

Whether base camp is the east or west side of Pinnacles National Park, visitors to the park have the added pleasure of discovering the Monterey Peninsula's cornucopia of outdoors recreation, activities, and events less than 1.5 hours from the park. The peninsula is gifted with stunning landscapes for hiking, biking, kayaking, and horseback riding, not to mention the dizzying lineup of world-renowned art, food and wine festivals, iconic musical concerts, bustling farmers' markets, and ethnic celebrations. A fertile region known for garlic, artichokes, olives, greens, strawberries, and wine grapes among other crops, along with the Pacific Ocean's bounty, inspires foodies and attracts some pretty tasty food fests.

The "peninsula" encompasses six distinct communities (Monterey, Carmel, Pacific Grove, Pebble Beach, Carmel Valley, and Big Sur) brimming with history, culture, and scenery. They highlight Central California as a unique gem in the state's crown. The region is a natural paradise crammed with national, state, county, and regional preserves, parklands, and beaches. Salinas, though not technically *on* the peninsula,

Half moon over Pinnacles

is a major portal to the Monterey Peninsula off US 101 and home to the National Steinbeck Museum in the heart of its historic downtown.

Soak up Monterey's Spanish colonial heritage in the waterfront state historic park. Savor fresh seafood on the old fisherman's wharf before a whale-watching cruise or a bike ride along the coastal recreational path to Steinbeck's Cannery Row and the Monterey Aquarium showcasing the marine sanctuary's wonders.

Be charmed by Pacific Grove's Victorian architecture and hometown feel. Pebble Beach's Seventeen-Mile Drive enclave of exclusive resorts and golf course estates are as eye-popping as the rocky coastline and its cypress sentinels.

Although Carmel-by-the-Sea is anyone's vision of a picturesque exclusive seaside village, it's the local canines romping off-leash on the mile-long white sand beach at the bottom of Ocean Avenue that enchants dog lovers the most.

Scenic CA 1 lures visitors south along Big Sur's untamed, humbling coastline in the shadow of the Santa Lucia Range and the foot of the Los Padres National Forest and Ventana Wilderness with state parks, campgrounds, cabins, inns, and a couple of discreet, ecologically sensitive, five-star retreats tucked in the dramatic ruggedness.

Looking eastward up the mouth of the Carmel River, it's majestic oaks in the valley sunshine, authentic cowboy character, Garland Ranch Regional Park's network of trails, and the rural village's cluster of wine-tasting rooms and courtyard restaurants. The choices for lodging and dining range from clean roadside motels and fresh fast food and pub food to quaint inns and upscale resorts with farm-to-table outdoor cafes or fine dining.

Lodging

Monterey

Monterey Hotel (406 Alvarado St., Monterey 93940, 831-375-3184; monterey hotel.com) and **The Portola Hotel** (2 Portola Plaza, Monterey, CA 93940; 831-649-4511; portolahotel.com) are both properties that sit in the heart of historic downtown Monterey.

Carmel

Carmel is all about cute and quaint.

Carmel Valley Ranch Resort, 1 Old Ranch Rd., Carmel, CA 93923; (831) 625-9500; carmelvalleyranch.com. The family-friendly resort conveniently sits between Carmel Valley Village's oak-studded hamlet and Carmel-by-the-Sea, the crème de la crème of seaside tourist towns. Step out the door and you're in Garland Ranch Regional Park to hike the day away with or without your pooch.

Cypress Inn, Lincoln St., Carmel, CA 93923, (831) 624-3871; cypress-inn.com. Mediterranean charm in the heart of Carmel-by-the-Sea. The lobby bar area is canine central with local and guest pooches in the evening, in keeping with owner Doris Day's pet-loving reputation.

La Playa Hotel, Camino Real St., Carmel, CA 93923; (831) 293-6100; laplayahotel. com. Historic Spanish-style hotel.

Quail Lodge Resort, 8205 Valley Greens Dr., Carmel, CA 93923; (888) 828-8787; Quaillodge.com. Located in a rural setting just 1.5 miles from the Carmel action and the beach, the resort is dog friendly too.

Pacific Grove

Asilomar Grounds and Conference Center at Asilomar State Beach, 800 Asilomar Ave., Pacific Grove, CA 93950; (888) 635-5310; visitasilomar.com. Exquisite Arts and Crafts–period architecture by Julia Morgan sits on 108 acres of beachfront land. The state park system's best-kept secret has lodging and dining.

Pebble Beach

Live it up in the lap of oceanfront golf links luxury in one of the **Pebble Beach Resorts** (pebblebeach.com).

Big Sur

The isolated majestic stretch of Central California coastline along CA 1 offers lodging from camping and cabins to luxury retreats. Visit bigsurcalifornia.org.

Camping

Veteran's Memorial Park campground (831-646-3865; www.monterey.org/en-us/departments/montereyrecreation.aspx) overlooking Monterey Bay is quiet, clean, and conveniently located within 2 miles of walking distance to the Monterey State Historic Park and waterfront attractions.

Peninsula Dining

The Big Sur Bakery and Restaurant (47540 CA 1, Big Sur, CA 93920; 831-667-0520; bigsurbakery.com) is a must-stop.

California Pizza Kitchen, 1100 Del Monte Center, Monterey, CA 93940; (831) 375-4975. Best chain restaurant for innovative Italian dishes, thin-crust pizza, and salads.

Dametra Cafe, Lincoln and Ocean Avenue, Carmel, CA 93923; (831) 622-7766; dametracafe.com. Mediterranean cuisine served in a vibrant atmosphere with warm hospitality. The combination plate hits all the palate high notes.

Lucky's Roadside, 1901 Fremont St., Seaside, CA 93955; (831) 899-5825; luckys roadside.com. Seaside is not the trendiest location for a new restaurant, but owner Bill Lee's natural sense of hospitality and his golden touch with design and menus are winning combinations. Bill had me at "come on in" when I first stood outside the restaurant perusing the menu. The fried chicken is a winner.

The Market Restaurant, 2329 Fremont St., Seaside, CA 93955; (831) 373-2200. Yet another welcome addition to Seaside's less robust roster of good restaurants. A bright, intimate interior pairs with a delicious fresh menu with Mediterranean flair and friendly service; you can't go wrong with the grilled chicken Greek salad. Truffle lovers should try the truffle lamb burger.

Nepenthe (48510 CA 1, Big Sur, CA 93920; 831-667-2345; nepenthebigsur.com) remains the classic destination for a meal in Big Sur, featuring one of the most transporting and ethereal ocean views.

Sea Harvest Fish Market and Restaurant, 100 Crossroads Blvd., Carmel, CA 93923; (831) 626-3626. Fresh, perfectly prepared seafood dishes in a casual setting.

Recreation and Events

Asilomar State Beach and Conference Grounds, visitasilomar.com.

Ford Ord National Monument, www.blm.gov/ca/st/en/fo/hollister/fort_ord. html.

Los Padres National Forest, www.fs.usda.gov/lpnf.

Monterey County Calendar of Events, seemonterey.com/events.

Monterey County Parks Events Calendar, www.co.monterey.ca.us/parks/events.html.

Monterey Peninsula Regional Park District, www.mprpd.org.

Point Lobos State Preserve, pointlobos.org.

Appendix A: Resources

- Activities and information for national public lands, www.recreation.gov
- California Coastal Trail, www.californiacoastaltrail.info; updates on progress connecting California's 1,200-mile-long coastal network of trails
- California Welcome Center, 1213 N. Davis Rd., Salinas, CA 93907; (831) 757-8687 or (831) 759-8687; www.visitcalifornia.com (click on Welcome Centers and Salinas on the map)
- Friends of Pinnacles, www.pinnacles.org; a nonprofit rock climbing organization; Bruce Hildenbrand, president
- Los Padres Forest Watch, www.lpfw.org; a nonprofit promoting wilderness protection. Check out the news about a new wilderness bill recently introduced to connect the North and South Los Padres National Forest on the 421-mile-long Condor National Recreation Trail through the Central Coast Heritage Protection Act.
- Monterey County Visitor Information, www.seemonterey.com
- Pinnacles National Park, www.nps.gov/pinn
- Pinnacles Partnerships, www.pinnaclespartnership.org; services in the area
- San Benito County Visitor Information, www.sanbenitocounty.com
- State of San Juan Bautista Chamber of Commerce, www.sjbchamber.com

◀ *Bush poppy along Juniper Canyon Trail*

Appendix B: Recommended Reads and Reels

Reads

A Climber's Guide to Pinnacles National Monument by Brad Young (2007).
Of Mice and Men by John Steinbeck (1937). Set in Soledad.
The Pinnacles Story by Ross J. Miser (1961).

Reels

The Wild One (1953), starring Marlon Brando, was inspired by events on a 1947 Fourth of July weekend in Hollister.
Bell tower scenes in *Vertigo* (1958), directed by Alfred Hitchcock and starring James Stewart, were shot at the Mission San Juan Bautista.
Scenes from *The Candidate* (1972), starring Robert Redford, were filmed in King City.

Hike Index

About the Authors

Linda B. Mullally and **David S. Mullally** are a husband-and-wife team who share their passion for travel and the outdoors through her writing and his photography. He is an attorney/photographer and she is a travel columnist/author. They have been inspiring readers to experience the world's natural and cultural treasures on bike and on foot for over thirty years. They share their adventures in her *Monterey Herald* travel column "Away We Go" and her outdoor recreation blog at Falcon.com. *Hiking Pinnacles National Park* is their sixth book. Visit the authors at LindaBMullally.com.

The authors at their base camp in Pinnacles Campground

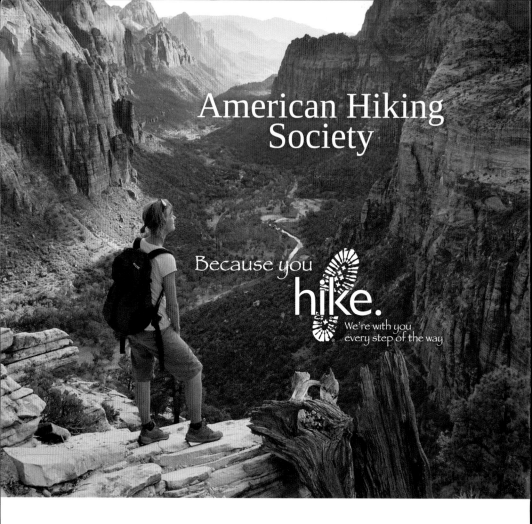